ADVANCED
ENGLISH
WRITING:
THINKING
AND
STRATEGIES

杨桂红 韩丽 著

高级英语写作突破

思维和策略

VANCED ENGLISH WRITING: THINKING AND STRATEGIES

U0367241

清华大学出版社

内 容 简 介

本书内容紧扣高级英语写作任务，将英语写作的基本要素与高分要素结合起来，侧重补充了写作者欠缺的逻辑和修辞方面的知识，以切实提高读者的英语写作水平。

本书的目标读者为大学生以及所有想提高英语写作技能及水平的学习者。

图书在版编目（CIP）数据

高级英语写作突破：思维和策略 / 杨桂红，韩丽著 . —北京：清华大学出版社，2016 （2022.8重印）

ISBN 978-7-302-42717-9

Ⅰ. ①高… Ⅱ. ①杨… ②韩… Ⅲ. ①英语－写作 Ⅳ. ①H315

中国版本图书馆 CIP 数据核字（2016）第 020006 号

责任编辑：刘 艳
封面设计：平 原
责任校对：王凤芝
责任印制：丛怀宇

出版发行：清华大学出版社
　　　　　网　　址：http://www.tup.com.cn, http://www.wqbook.com
　　　　　地　　址：北京清华大学学研大厦 A 座　　邮　编：100084
　　　　　社 总 机：010-83470000　　　　　　　邮　购：010-62786544
　　　　　投稿与读者服务：010-62776969, c-service@tup.tsinghua.edu.cn
　　　　　质量反馈：010-62772015, zhiliang@tup.tsinghua.edu.cn
印　装　者：涿州市京南印刷厂
经　　销：全国新华书店
开　　本：148mm×210mm　　印　张：11.5　　字　数：266 千字
版　　次：2016 年 9 月第 1 版　　　　　　　印　次：2022 年 8 月第 7 次印刷
定　　价：48.00 元

产品编号：065201-01

在英语教学实践中，我们经常遇到这种情况：有些学生口头表达能力、听力水平，甚至翻译水平都不错，词汇量也很大，但其写作水平却不理想。这是为什么呢？主要是因为他们还不了解一篇高水平的作文包含哪些要素，也不知道采用什么方法可以快速掌握这些要素。

一篇作文是否属于高水平的作文要从基础技能、修辞技能和思维能力三个方面来判断。其中，思维能力是指一个人可以符合逻辑地进行论证并公正客观地评价事物的能力，它涉及逻辑思维能力、辩证思维能力和批判性思维能力三个方面。

有些学生写作时总是存在这样或那样的不足。如果我们可以对症下药，就能在尽可能短的时间内帮助他们提高写作水平。问题在于如何让学生快速掌握这些写作要素。我们的建议是阅读各种体裁的文章，学生一旦知道自己需要掌握哪些要素，就会在阅读时有意识地进行模仿并加以吸收。这是最直接的途径，可以让他们少走很多弯路。

"写作即阅读"，这句话说得一点也不错，因为我们阅读的文章就是他人的作品，它们就是最好的范文。阅读可以帮助学生掌握高水平作文的必备要素，并积累更多的写作素材。笔者认为，学生写作进步速度慢的主要原因就是脱离了阅读，他们为了写作而写作，结果往往是事倍功半，加强阅读与写作之间的联系则会达到事半功倍的效果。

为进一步提高学生的写作水平，笔者在书中首先讲述高水平作文的必备要素，其次阐述这些要素在阅读材料中的使用情况，最后分析具体的作文，看哪些因素会导致作文得分不高，哪些要素有助于写出高分作文。

市面上并不缺少英语写作方面的书籍，然而，让学生从整体要素着手来提高英语写作水平的书至今少有。因此，笔者把多年来在这方面所做的研究及取得的一些成果与大家分享，以便大家能在相对较短的时间内让自己的英语写作水平上一个台阶。

多年以来，笔者通过这种方法培养了一大批写作高手，受到多方面的关注和好评。事实上，在教学中补充学生欠缺的写作要素以及他们在思维方面欠缺的知识是非常受学生欢迎的，也是非常有必要的。本书把高水平英语作文的要素呈现给大家，这些要素对于英语写作和日常问题的分析和思考都是必不可少的。笔者相信，这本书会给大家带来一种新的体验。学生可以感受到，要深入学习英语，或者要想更好地运用语言，就必须具备良好的思维能力。如果他们能够通过正确的方法切实提高自己的写作水平，那将是一件非常美好的事！

由于市面上针对作文语法和结构方面问题的书籍比较多，我们就将侧重点放在逻辑和修辞两方面，并通过诸多实例来帮助学生学会直接从各种体裁的文章中学习和掌握高分写作要素。本书直接引用学生作品作为例子。为使学生更清楚地认识到写作中易犯的错误，笔者保留了作品的原貌，未对这些原作中的错误进行修正。

在此，笔者把本书献给每一位学习者，并向敦促我早日出版此书的学生表示最诚挚的感谢！

杨桂红

2016 年 1 月于江西理工大学

目　录
CONTENTS

第1章
英语写作及其评分标准

与英语写作相关的问题

（一）为什么英语作文难写？

英语学习者总是希望可以写出好的作文来。然而，很多人认为作文很难写，甚至难以下笔，因为他们不了解高级作文的含义。高级写作要求我们在语法、思维和修辞层面都具备相当的能力。也就是说，高级写作不仅需要良好的语法知识和适量的词汇，而且还需要良好的思维能力，即综合分析的能力。前者大多可以通过反复的机械练习来掌握，后者则需要具有良好的思维能力和运用修辞的能力。因此，写作成了语言技能学习过程中难度最大、耗时最长的一项技能。

从语言技能角度来看，没有语法和词汇功底，学习者就难以下笔进行写作；从思维角度来看，没有良好的逻辑思维，学习者也很难写出高级作文。

如此说来，写作学习似乎成了难以企及的艰巨任务，但这不等于说学习者不能快速有效地提高英语写作水平。如果可以提高英语基础技能和思维能力，他们就能在一定时间内提高自己的英语写作水平。

（二）为什么自评和实际得分差异较大？

2012年，一名大三学生第二次参加了TEM-4考试（英语专业四级考试）。TEM-4考试是由国家组织的大型英语水平考试。这位学生觉得自己考得不错，估计作文可以得15分（满分20分），可是她的实际成绩才49分，其中作文才8分。

该生自身评估和实际得分之间的差异如此之大，促使我仔细地询问了她的写作情况。问过之后，我甚至觉得批改试卷的老师很仁慈。

那一年的考试题目是关于端午节的，题目要求如下：

> The Dragon Boat Festival is one of the important national festivals in China. Write on your ANSWER SHEET a composition of about 200 words on the following topic:
>
> The Dragon Boat Festival

该生告诉我她先写外国有很多重要的节日，中国亦然，比如端午节。我因此排除了她的分数是判错了的可能性，问题出在她不知道评分标准。

TEM-8考试（英语专业八级考试）作文、研究生入学考试作文、雅思作文或者其他出国留学考试的作文等都属于高级写作任务，因为它们的写作要求基本相同，都要求写作者深入分析问题，表达自己的深刻见解，字数要求都很多。它们的评分标准都包括两大部分：一部分是结构；另一部分是思维。前者占30%，后者占70%，这和高考语文作文的评分标准差不多。作文写得好，并非字写得好、句子正确就行的，还要看文章内容的深度和广度、文章的结构、逻辑关系和遣词造句等。

评估写作同评估其他语言技能一样，必须先清楚评估标准，而且这个评估标准必须是当前公认的，是公正客观、不受个人情感影响的。

有些英语写作，比如CET-4（大学英语四级考试）作文，从考试大纲的要求来看，它的评分标准稍微低一些。只要格式规范、语句通顺即可，对于思想的深度要求不高，因为它们的考查重点是语言的基本技能，如语法和词汇。

上文提到的例子中，既然题目是要写端午节，写作者就应该直接说"端午节是中国的重要节日之一"；而那位学生先说国外有很多重要的节日，有偏题的嫌疑，得分会因此降低。

CET-6（大学英语六级考试）作文字数要求更多一些，思想也深刻一些。至于雅思、托福等考试的作文，则无思想不能为之。TEM-8（英语专业八级考试）作文亦然，它向来被看成是高级英语写作，通常要求400词左右，无论是结构上还是思想深度上都要求比较高。字数的多少通常是衡量文章思想深刻与否的一个标准。现在，大部分英语专业的学生在参加研究生入学考试时，作文都要求写800词以上，有的学校作文要求写1000词以上，如果不表达深刻的思想，如何能够写出这么多字数的作文呢？

思想的深刻与否取决于我们的思维能力，即对一个问题或现象能够透彻分析、合理论证的能力。通常我们强调"批判性思维"（critical thinking）能力，即公正客观地评价一个事物好坏的能力。当然，一个能够公正客观评价事物好坏的人必须具备良好的逻辑知识、哲学知识和专业知识，以及通识知识（general knowledge）。

值得一提的是，"批判性思维"的英语缩写CT同时也是creative thinking，也就是"创造性思维"的缩写。我们必须了解的是，如果一个人没有批判性思维能力，那么，他具备创造性思维的可能性也很小。这就是20世纪50年代批判性思维在美国兴起的原因。

因此，评估作文的时候必须考虑文章思想的深刻性，这样就不会导致自评和实际得分之间的过大差异。

二

与英语作文评分相关的问题

（一）为什么作文以故事开头不可取？

曾经有位学生跟我谈起他写的一篇题为 "Do Talented Students Need Good Quality?" 的作文。他说他是以一个故事开头的，说的是一个学生因个人品质问题遭遇失败，以此来衬托好品质的重要性。

我想提醒大家，如果作文要求写阐释文（exposition），采用故事开头是不妥的，因为阐释文是说理的文体，所有说理的文体都要通过具体的证据来支持观点。论据通常还要按照主次逐条进行排列，没有叙事的空间。

故事或者小说都属于叙事文体（narration），不适合出现在阐释文体的作文当中，而像TEM-8、托福、雅思等考试的作文通常都要求写阐释文，因为阐释文写作更易看出一个学生是否具有良好的思维。

所谓阐释就是解释，阐释文就是需要通过事例来证明现象是否存在或某个观点是否合理的解释性文章。

在写题为 "What's Your Attitude Towards Monitors on Campus?" 的作文时，有学生这样开头：

> The first day when I came back to the campus, I was surprised because when I was walking on the grass, I found some monitors on the trees which made me think of something unpleasant happened

to me during the Spring Festival. During the holiday, I was shot by a monitor in the area and I was caught. Therefore, I am against to set up monitors on campus.

虽然该作文的开篇读来还算流畅,但还是存在一些问题。

首先,文章的标识词用得不妥。连接词because一般用在正文分析当中,也就是第二部分,而therefore是用来下结论的标识词,一般用在结尾。另外,过多叙事也不适合用于阐释文的写作中。

阐释文通常要先提出问题,然后分析其对错或好坏。为此,我们可以把上面一段开头调整如下:

The first day when I came back to the campus, I was surprised to find some monitors on the trees which made me think of its legality. Is it good or bad for us to have so many monitors in the campus? What are they for? And is it legal? My attitude towards it is whether or not to set up monitors depends on the situation of the college, including resources, discipline and security.

TEM-8或者CET-6等考试作文的第一部分内容通常包括两个方面:一是提出问题或给出现象;二是表明观点。这是这些英语考试写作题的规范,必须如此,没有其他选择。

在整体结构上,一篇300词左右的作文,第一段一般是3~5句话,不能写太多。另外,在提出问题或给出现象时,通常转述题目大意即可,即便要引用,也只能引用其中的一两句话,不能全部照抄。

比如"Do Talented Students Need Good Quality?"这个题目,开头可以是这样的:

Everyone needs good qualities no matter who he is and where he is from. Whether talented students need good quality causes great attention in colleges. Some people argue that talented students are like rare resource. We should not expect things to be perfect. Others hold that anyone should have good qualities no matter who he is. I accept the later view.

因此，我们审题时要先思考并明确题目的体裁。明确了体裁，我们才知道采用什么表达方式，如果是阐释文体，就不能用讲故事的方式开头。

下面几个题目，大家可以自己思考一下，写作时自己应该如何开头：

- Is It Wise to Make Friends on the Net?
- Importance of Women in Education
- Importance of Being Honest
- Results of Cheating in Exams
- Learn to Give

（二）作文评估不宜以自己的写作水平为衡量标准

清楚作文的评估标准才能正确评价作文的优劣。标准的特点之一是公正客观，不受个人因素影响。

我们以2012年TEM-8真题为例，其题目要求如下：

A recent survey made by Professor Baron of 2,000 college students asked about their attitudes towards phone calls and text-messaging (also known as short message service) and found the students' main goal was to pass along information in as little time, with as little small talk, as possible. "What they like most about their mobile devices is that they can reach other people," says Naomi Baron, a professor of linguistics at American University in

Washington, D.C., who conducted the survey. "What they like least is that other people can reach them." How far do you agree with Professor Baron?

我们先来审题。Baron教授对2000名大学生做了一项调查，内容是关于手机和短信问题的，结果发现学生使用手机的主要目的是尽快把信息传递出去。他们最喜欢的是可以用手机找到他人，最不喜欢的是他人也可以找到自己，问考生的看法。作文考查我们对问题的看法，属于阐释文体。

下面是网上的"参考答案"，我们一起来分析一下。

Along with the advance of science and technology, electronic products, such as computers, MP3, and cell phones and so on. Among them, cell phone exerts a big influence on our daily life. It has dramatically changed our way of communication and socializing. As to the virtues and defects about cell phone, people's opinions are widely varied.

Recently, a professor named Baron conducted a survey among 2,000 college students and consulted their attitudes toward cell phone. Conclusion was reached that the biggest advantage of cell phone is that it can connect the users with other people through short message, which is very convenient compared with traditional letter writing and also very cheap with the telephone call taking into consideration. As every coin has two sides, the very virtue of the cell phone is also the biggest disadvantage, which makes other people can easily find them with a call, even a message. Cell phones are gradually intruding upon the private space of people.

For the most part, I agree with professor Baron's conclusion. Let me first illustrate its virtues. It indeed saves much time and efforts when we want to find a helping hand. It also shortens the distance between people, no matter how far two people are, they can easily get in touch with each other through a call and tell each other about what funny or sad things they come upon. The most obvious advantage of short message is that it makes people familiar and intimate. Sometimes, people feel awkward to say something to others through face to face communication or making a phone call, the short message come as a rescue, all the discomfort will be diminished for the messages covering the emotional effect. Messages are very popular and prevailing when a festival or delightful event comes. People can pass their blessing and wish with decent to others, even they are just nodding acquaintances.

For its defects, it is really annoying. Scam messages and harassing calls have gained access to us. We have to take time and energy to tackle these problems. And whenever we want to have a break or do some interesting things, we would be interrupted by phone calls or messages. Therefore, some people put forward their solutions that we could turn off the phone when we deem it is necessary or change the situation model of the phone to unreachable. These solutions really bring consolation to us, but they are very hard to apply. Suppose you are working for a company and yearning for promotion and increase in wages, you hardly dare to do those things in fear a loss of big opportunity. Even if you are just an ordinary full-time housewife, you are also incapable of doing that, simply because you have a large family to take care. Thus a new term was coined recently—cell phone syndrome, which refers to people who cannot live without cell phones. Some people even suffer from it that they have to force themselves to get away from cell phones.

Though a lot of complaints about cell phone have emerged, its advantages, from my point of view, far outweigh its disadvantages. Just as a saying goes that there is no perfect man on earth, so does cell phones. Thanks to cell phones, we are launched into a more efficient information changing age. Every respect of our life is greatly benefited from it and it will certainly bring us to a brighter future.

从结构的角度来看，这篇作文的字数较多，框架也比较清晰。除了几处语法错误以外，其他语句都比较书面化和准确，而且选词非常好，句式很美，前后也比较连贯。不过作者没有给作文拟题这一点不妥，因为作文总是根据题目来评估是否跑题或偏题的，在没有给出题目的情况下，考生都必须自己拟题。这个问题我们后面还会提到。

而从思维的角度来看，该作文问题就比较多。

第一，开篇谈科技发展、手机革命及其优缺点，这显然绕得比较远。最符合英式思维习惯的是直接说Baron教授做了一项调查，调查对象是谁，调查内容是什么，调查结果怎样，然后表明自己是否认可被调查人的观点。

第二，题目问的是作者是否同意调查结果，也就是被调查学生的态度，至于这个调查是谁做的并不重要；而作者在第二段先写Baron教授做调查，并得出了"与传统信函方式相比，手机用户可以通过短信迅速便捷地与他人联系"这一结论，扯得很远，给人硬凑字数的感觉，从而使得文章不紧凑。作者继而声称"凡事有好坏两个方面"，仿佛话题是关于手机的优缺点对比的，这说明作者在对题目的理解上出现了一些偏差。

第三，从第三段一直到结尾，作者对手机的优缺点展开了分析。这不仅偏题，可以说还有些跑题，因为题目不是叫我们写手机的优缺点，而是侧重分析被调查者的观点。此文作者撇开被调查者的观点不提，一味谈手机的优缺点，是侧重点发生了偏移，这是偏题的一个表现，这些问题我们在后面都会具体讨论，这里仅简单提及。

一篇偏题或跑题的作文几乎没有得高分的可能性。当我们让学生对这篇作文进行评分的时候，大部分学生给的是70分左右，因为他们觉得此文结构比较规范，用词也比较高级，就是有些偏题。但少数几个给的分数很高，其中一个学生的评语这样写道：我知道这篇作文写得并不是那么好，但我觉得比我的作文写得好，所以我给他90分。

标准是公正客观的，不以我们的主观意志为转移。如果一篇作文写得比自己的好就是好，那我们就无法确定怎样的作文是真正的好作文，以及好到怎样的程度。因此，我们不仅要了解作文的评分标准，而且要知道，标准是公正客观的。

网络上的信息很多，可以说是鱼龙混杂。如果我们具有辨别能力，就可以识别良莠，从而取其精华、去其糟粕。

（三）作文评分涉及哪些方面？

作文评分通常从三个层面来考虑，分别是结构层面、逻辑层面和修辞层面。

1. 结构层面

作文结构原本是指段落的数量、内容及段落的规范问题，鉴于大家讨论作文问题时通常是从结构、逻辑和修辞三大层面进行分析的，因此，习惯上，一些格式和语法问题，包括标点符号、大小写、句式等，也归入结构的范畴。这些内容，我们将在第2章详细分析。

作文结构通常是有规定的，不可以随便改动。比如，作者应在第一部分提出相关问题或表明自己的立场或观点；又比如，therefore，so等标识词是用来引出结论的，不要轻易用在第一部分。

语法是写作的基础，写作时必须保证这一基础的准确性，这就好像盖房子，没有材料不行，破旧或变质的材料也不行。通常，高分作文不允许出现五个以上的语法错误。

2. 逻辑层面

从逻辑层面来说，写作者首先要检查自己的思维是否符合逻辑规则，有没有犯逻辑错误；其次要检查句与句之间是否具有逻辑关系，关系是否密切；还要检查文章的条理是否清晰，主次是否分明。

逻辑之父亚里士多德指出："在某个特殊领域里有知识的人，其职责就是避免在自己的知识范围内进行荒谬的论证，并能够向进行错误论证的人指出其错误所在。"（谷振诣，2007）

学习者得不到逻辑方面的培养是我们教育中存在的一个重要问题。逻辑方面的问题不是一两天可以纠正的，我们会在第3章提到一些逻辑知识，但要了解更多的逻辑知识，建议大家购买一两本这方面的书，自己去学习。

3. 修辞层面

修辞的范围很广，不仅包括词的用法，还包括句子和段落的先后以及整体布局等。但是，我们在这里说的修辞通常是指修辞手法，也就是为了某一目的刻意选择某个词句，以便让文字看起来更美、听起来更悦耳的语言运用方式，比如比喻、拟人、排比等。

我们将在第4章对修辞展开说明，尤其是修辞手法的使用，比如排比、押韵、拟人、比喻（明喻、暗喻、提喻、借代）等。有些手法在阐释文体的写作过程中经常使用，比如排比；而有的手法基本不使用，比如夸张和讽刺。实际上，科学论证性文体一般都不使用夸张和讽刺。

布局是指在文章中表达什么内容，以什么方式表达，以什么顺序表达。这也是修辞范畴的问题。事实上，修辞的范围如此之广，说"一切尽在修辞"也并不为过。

简而言之，修辞就是选词，因此，我们在学习过程中要注意积累词的用法。这样，写作时我们才能有词可选，而不是脑子空白，千篇一律。

归根结底，写作要回归到三大层面上来，即结构层面、逻辑层面和修辞层面。只有在各个层面上进行改进，学生才能从整体上提高写作水平。

（四）自评涉及哪些学习要点？

对于学生而言，要进行自评，必须把自评的方法具体化，否则有些人很难把握。教学的要点之一是让学生学会自评的方法，并且方法是具体的，越通俗易懂越好，因此，我们从学习方法的角度来强调作文的评估问题。

许多学生采用背诵的方式来提高写作技能，但是他们背得很辛苦，效果却不好。

我们当然不是反对背诵，反而还大力支持。但是，机械记忆有两个特点：一个是枯燥乏味，很难坚持；另一个是影响灵活运用，致使创造性思维始终难以实现。事实上，写作中有许多东西不需要机械记忆，只要掌握一定的技巧即可。

特别喜欢背诵的学习者可以试着调整自己的学习方法，看看效果是不是会更好一些。在实际练习过程中，有了正确的方法，大部分学习者都能取得明显的进步。因此，我们把学习写作的两种方法列表如下，目的不仅是引起大家的重视，更是让大家养成正确思考的习惯。正确的写作学习方法可以让学习者的写作水平迅速提高，而不当的方法只会让他们的写作水平停滞不前。

表1-1　两种写作学习方法对比

错误的学习方法	正确的学习方法
喜欢背诵作文范文。	清楚作文结构和高分要素，无须过多背诵范文。
很少动手写作文。	每个月会写几篇作文。
从不问问题，不会写也经常写。	向老师请教，搞清楚自己的作文存在哪些问题并有针对性地进行改进。
不仔细审题或者不知道审题。	总是先认真审题。
写作好像随手做翻译。	列出框架，思考清楚后再进行语言转换。
不懂英式思维习惯，写出的内容不像英语作文。	按照英式思维习惯来写，做到行文流畅。
无语体意识，简单句较多，作文字数不够。	善于用书面语，字数符合要求。
喜欢从自己出发看问题，主观因素较多。	习惯公正地看待问题，客观性更强。
从来不注意概念。	特别关注概念。
不会找事物之间的相关性。	习惯找事物之间的相关性。
习惯采用三段式。	根据作文的字数要求来确定段落数量。
没有逻辑关系的意识。	特别注意句子之间的逻辑关系。
不会从阅读材料中吸收写作要素。	注意模仿和吸收阅读材料里的写作要素。

第2章

英语写作的基础要素

整体要素

（一）语法的重要性

语法是写作的基础，其重要性不言而喻，语法基础不好则写不出高级作文来。遗憾的是，很多人的语法基础并不好。比如在翻译"蓝蓝的天，蓝蓝的海"时，有人居然写出"Blue sky, blue sea."这样的句子，这显然是不了解英汉语言之间的差异。

汉语重意合而轻语法，话没有讲完之前可以一直使用逗号；而英语表达意思的过程必须遵守语法规则，句子必须完整，不能有成分残缺。因此，在进行汉译英时，学习者必须严格按照语法规则来完成任务。至于标点符号，在英语中，一个完整的句子应该用句号，而不是逗号。

英语要求句子完整，这就意味着一个句子至少要有主语和谓语。这样，我们就可以把上面提到的句子翻译成：The sky is blue. The sea is blue. 这才符合英语的表达习惯，这才是英语中的规范句子。

事实上，写作过程中随想随写的问题很普遍。有的人甚至直接按照汉语的思维方式来写英语作文，结果一点也不符合英语的思维习惯。我们可以用汉语来思考，但是必须用英语习惯来表达。确保语法正确是书面表达的第一要务，在句子正确的同时，也兼顾了英语的其他方面。

我们看下面一个例子，这是一篇散文开头的两个小段以及几个不同版本的译文。

幸福有时会同我们开一个玩笑，乔装打扮而来。

　　机遇、友情、成功、团圆……，它们都酷似幸福，但它们并不等同于幸福。

译文 1

　　Sometimes, happiness <u>make</u> fun of us, <u>make up</u> themselves. Opportunity, friendship, success and reunion, <u>they</u> are all like happiness but actually they are not.

译文 2

　　Happiness makes fun of us. They make up themselves. Opportunity, friendship, success and reunion are all like happiness but actually they are not.

译文 3

　　Happiness sometimes makes fun of us, cloaked in opportunity, friendship, success or reunion, an image which makes us feel happy but not the same as happiness.

译文 4

　　Sometimes happiness will play a joke with us under the cloak of opportunity, friendship, success, reunion, etc., which are all similar to but not equal to happiness itself.

评析：译文1似乎是按照汉语来翻译的，画线部分语法不正确，表达也不地道。译文2不够书面化，而且理解上有偏差，缺乏汉英语言差异意识，不会整合句子，而是按照汉语原句的顺序来翻译的，因此，译文虽然语法正确，但表达不太地道。其实，仔细琢磨一下，机遇、友情、成功、团圆不正是幸福的装扮吗？翻译时为何要分开呢？完全可以整合在一起嘛！所以，译文3和译文4处理得更好。

事实上，译文4翻译成一个句子意思到位，句式优美。此外，译者的选词也很好，比如under the cloak，similar to，equal to等。然而，它的将来时态用得不是太好，用一般现在时可能更好。

2014年TEM-8真题写作中，一篇只得了8分的作文是这样开篇的：

> <u>In nowadays</u>, with the developing of economy and the widely using of Internet, work-from-home is not a dream. Some companies even try to use the work-from-home instead of working in the company. What I want to say is that work-from-home is not a proper way in the financial society.

虽说笔误或语法错误是在所难免的，有时稍不留意，动词可能就忘记加s了，或者过去式拼写错了。但是，in nowadays可以算是"亮瞎眼"的语法错误，很多学生看到这里都笑了。这个错误反映出该学生的语法基础非常薄弱，这也正是我们始终强调打好基础的原因。

英语短语不容易记，但是高级写作的考查点之一便是词汇量，如果词汇量不过关，就达不到要求，也不可能写出高水平的作文。以TEM-8考试为例，该考试要求考生掌握的词汇量由六千上升到八千，又上升到近几年的一万两千，可见词汇量在写作中的重要地位。Nowadays是常用副词，前面无须加介词，和here或there的用法相似。一般来说，大四的学生不应该犯这样低级的语法错误，但是有些人基本功仍然没有过关。

开篇就出现语法错误是一件非常糟糕的事情。我们在弥补思维能力不足的时候，切忌不能忽略基础技能，因为这二者都是写作得高分的重要因素。没有基础，则无法表达深刻的思想内容。

学生的水平参差不齐，对于语法基础不太好的学生，我们一方面建议他们课外补习，另一方面也会在课堂上对语法要点进行分析和讲解。

鉴于语法是写作的基础，而不少学生的语法基础还不扎实，我们把写作中需要特别注意的语法问题列表如下：

表2-1　写作时需要注意的语法问题列表

要　求	常见问题	例　子
句子不能缺少主语和谓语。	句子缺少动词。	• The Chinese dream is that to realize the great revival of Chinese nation.
不能用动词作主语。	用动词作主语。	• Take a taxi is hard. • Kneel doesn't mean gratefulness.
主谓一致。	第三人称单数时谓语动词不加 s。	• It never show that… • Someone find that…
时态一致。	现在时和过去时混用。	• It was cloudy that day. And the passers-by look gloomy.
熟悉一些固定搭配。	介词搭配有误。	• in nowadays • in the sight of…
集体名词是复数。	把集体名词看成是单数。	• The crowd shouts.
准确使用助动词。	助动词使用混乱。	• Do they beautiful? • It is not mean that…
分清楚谓语动词和非谓语动词。	缺少谓语动词。	• It means the ability and fortune or something looking lofty.
正确使用 There be 句型。	There be 句型中出现两个动词。	• There are more and more people play cell phones.
分清楚主动和被动。	现在分词和过去分词用法错误。	• When asking, they will say...
副词修饰形容词或动词。	不清楚副词的作用。	• definite wrong • general speaking • extraordinary important
不能用陈述句当问句。	忽略了问句的形式。	• Why it will be so?

（二）结构的重要性

在欣赏"2006年满分作文"时，有的学生很纠结，他们想知道为什么这篇作文有五段而不是三段。

这里所谓的"2006年满分作文"是指出现在网络上的一篇2006年的TEM-8考试作文。因为它写得极好，大家称它为满分作文。它是一篇布局巧妙、写得非常精彩的作文，我们在后面好几个章节中都会引用它。

我们奇怪的是学生为什么会认为一篇作文只能有三段，而不能有更多段落。后来发现，他们所谓的三段式作文基本上指的是一些字数要求较少的作文，比如CET-4的作文。

值得注意的是，许多学生都深信作文就只有三段，我认为这个问题有必要讨论一下。其实写作文时，我们通常是说作文应包含三个部分：开头、正文和结尾。

字数要求少的作文，即初级写作，比如初高中英语作文、大学英语1~4级作文等，写三段即可。字数要求少的作文，通常都不要求内容深刻，写得流畅即可，因此三段也就足够了。基础写作教材的编写者往往采用这种简单明了的方式，让学习者掌握基本格式。比如下文：

Noise Problems

We can hear unpleasant noise everyday everywhere around us, like loud harking in the street or market, music in some big shops, horn of vehicles, and the clanging and banging of building sites.

Noise refers to loud, unpleasant and unwanted sounds, which disturb people's life and are harmful to people's health. Studies show that people living in an environment of many noises can be easily irritated and upset. The continuity of this situation can make them suffer a lot both in physical and mental health. So, noise should be forbidden or be limited just like the speed limit of cars, both of which are dangerous to people's life. Recently, horning is banned in the main streets of cities, which is good for citizens. But what about the noise from shops and building sites, especially noise from building at night?

In my opinion, the noise must be banned too. And the sooner, the better. Some regulations should be made so that people who are disturbed by the noise can complain to a particular organization. And those who make the noise should be stopped immediately and be punished.

这就是典型的三段式作文，它之所以只有三段，是因为字数有限，不需要也几乎不可能有更多段落了。

然而，高级写作一般要求字数在400词左右，甚至更多。赣南师范大学2007年英国语言文学专业研究生入学考试的写作试卷要求1000词，当时的题目是"The Power of Language"。从2014年开始，又改为1200词。字数要求多的作文往往要求写作者更深刻地分析问题。

如果让一名初中生去写"The Power of Language"，有三段就足够了。比如下文：

The Power of Language

Languages are very important and they are very powerful. We cannot live well without them.

First, it is a tool of communication. We use it everyday in our life, work and study. Second, it is a tool of passing information. And third, it is a way of expressing our feelings.

So, language is a tool that we must use everyday. And we

must learn it well so that we can work and live better by using this magical tool.

如果字数要求增加到400词，写作者就可以交代其他许多内容，在这种情况下，第二部分写一段就不够，可能会有2~3小段，但整篇作文依然是三部分。通常，写作者在第一部分提出问题，在第二部分通过例子或证据分析问题，在第三部分进行结尾。请看下面的例文：

The Power of Language

We cannot imagine what our world will be if we human beings do not have language because language is so useful and powerful that we cannot be called the dominant of the earth without it. Language is the distinction of mankind. Language is used to express our feelings, emotions and thoughts, etc., in our work, study and life.

First, language makes man different from animals. With language, man can express their consciousness or awareness, a fundamental distinction between man and animals.

Second, with the power of language, man quickly stepped into a more civilized world, handing down more varied culture and greater intelligence and enlightenment.

In addition, language makes one person different from another. Some people are good at speaking. They use language to discuss problems, to argue with others and to persuade people to do or not to do something. Teachers use it to pass knowledge to students. Parents use it to cultivate their children. Fighters use it as weapons, like Socrates in ancient Greek, and Kong Ming, the ancient Chinese military master, etc.

Yet, language is just a carrier used to express thoughts. Man's thinking ability divides people into rational and irrational, wise and stupid, just and object and unjust and subject, persuasive and awkward. So, it is clear that the power of language depends on one's thinking ability. In other words, if we want to use it properly and rationally, we need to have good thinking ability. The relationship between language and thinking ability is close. We cannot part them. On the one hand, we use language to express our thoughts or ideas. On the other hand, we need good thinking to express reasonably and rationally.

Language has two forms: written and spoken. No matter which, it is the same important. We can find many examples to prove it. Take Shakespeare for example, who is regarded as the greatest writer in the world in using language. But he wrote more than spoke. Confucius in China is another example, who wrote and who lectured.

In modern society, people have more chance and right to express themselves both at home and in public. So, the ability to speak becomes more significant. As a famous saying goes that a good speaker is more than one million soldiers.

However, language must be employed properly because it is an art to have a good mastery of language. If maliciously used, bad results may occur. Looking back from the history, killing for a misuse of words happened in almost every part of the world. And failure of negotiation was recorded in many places. The words by Aesop enlighten us that the best thing in the world is our tongue and so is the worst.

In conclusion, language is powerful whose power makes us different from other animals and makes us progress rapidly. To become more civilized and successful, we should properly use the powerful tool.

这篇作文字数多，相对小段落就多，但它还是三大部分。第一段为第一部分，第二部分有7个小段，最后一段是结尾。在这里，我们仅强调段落的数量问题，暂时不对该作文的其他方面进行分析。

综上所述，作文不一定是三段，但通常是三部分。字数要求少的作文，一般有三段就足够了。字数要求多的作文，它们的第二部分往往会有几个小段。

（三）关于题目的若干问题

指导本科毕业论文的老师会发现，很多学生的论文提纲存在不少标题方面的问题，如题目过长、大小写不规范、用祈使句当题目或题目缺少动词，等等。这一点也不奇怪，因为很多学生没有写过论文，对于论文的基本规范一无所知。

论文的提纲一般包含三个级别的标题。无论哪一级别的标题都要求实词的首字母大写。英语作文也是一样。但事实却相反，很多学生都存在这方面的问题。因此，对于每一届学生，我们都会在大小写问题上做一个检测，看他们是否具有这方面的意识，并强调进入高年级以后，许多问题因为没有意识到，所以容易犯错。如果能够提高这方面的意识，就很容易改进。

大家一起看下面的例子，它们是关于考试作弊情景的自拟作文题目。

- my view on cheating in exams
- A common standard doesn't mean a correct standard
- What's the matter with you?
- School should be blamed

- He deserves the Punishment

上述五个题目都出现了大小写问题。第一个题目里面没有一个词的首字母大写，这是完全错误的。中间三个题目只有第一个单词的首字母大写，这也是不对的。最后一个题目中有两个单词的首字母大写了，动词的首字母却没有大写，也不对。

实词是指可以单独作某一句子成分的词，比如名词、代词、数词、动词、形容词、副词，它们在题目中一般都要求首字母大写。不能单独充当句子成分的词是虚词，如介词、冠词、连词、叹词，它们在题目中一般不需要首字母大写。

题目中的首字母大小写问题远比正文中多。为什么题目中经常出现这种问题呢？一个可能的原因是平时作文多是命题作文，自拟题目的情况很少，学生写作文时无须拟题，所以看不见问题，纠正也就无从说起。指导毕业论文的老师都深有体会，让人头疼的不是提纲的好坏问题，而是各级标题的大小写混乱不堪。

除了问号和感叹号之外，标题结尾一般无须加标点符号。

一般来说，作文都要求题目简短。像My Attitude Toward the Phenomenon of Students' Cheating in the Exams这样的题目就太长；而From Cheating in the Exam to See the Self-discipline这个题目不仅长，而且采用的是不定式短语，不是太好；How to Avoid Cheating in the Exam as a Junior Student这个题目去掉后面的as短语会比较好。

我们可以把上一页的五个作文题目分别修改为：

- My View on Cheating in Exams
- A Common Standard Doesn't Mean a Correct Standard
- What's the Matter with You?
- School Should Be Blamed
- He Deserves the Punishment

由此可见，写作时养成规范的习惯是非常重要的，我们把上面
说过的问题总结如下：

- 没有给出题目的作文，必须自拟题目；
- 题目不宜过长；
- 题目中实词的首字母必须大写；
- 题目中一般不用祈使句或不定式短语；
- 除了问号和感叹号，句尾不加标点符号。

（四）标点符号的问题

　　写作要养成良好的习惯，包括使用标点符号的习惯，但有的学
生写作习惯不好。比如，有的人喜欢写一个字点一个标点，有的人
特别喜欢一逗到底，还有的人写完一句话不紧接着使用标点符号，
而是空一格再用，这些都是不正确的做法。

　　我们先来看看下面的小段落：

　　　　Speaking of gratitude, I suppose our parents should be the
first persons to be thanked for, people always say that parents' love
is the most selfless in the world, but, how many of us are there to
remember to thank them?

　　当这位学生被问及为何一直使用逗号时，他说他觉得意思还没
有说完。意思确实没说完，但是英语的标点符号使用规范和汉语不
同。汉语是根据意思来断句的，一般来说，只要是表达同一内容，
就可以一直打逗号，只在结尾打上句号；而英语是按照语法来断句
的，一个句子结束了就应该打句号。

　　逗号在英语中用得比较少，通常是替代顿号（英语中无书名号
和顿号）表示并列关系。另外，还有一些附属成分和主句之间要用
逗号，比如时间状语、地点状语、状语从句、插入语、分词短语作

后置定语等。

高分作文首先意味着作文既规范又符合语法。我们把上面段落的标点问题修正如下：

> Speaking of gratitude, I suppose our parents should be the first persons to be thanked for. People always say that parents' love is the most selfless in the world. But, how many of us are there to remember to thank them?

（五）句式美的刻意追求

我们经常会读到一些英语美文，遗憾的是，很多学生读不出英语原文的美，因为他们不熟悉英语行文的特点。比如，讲授张汉熙《高级英语》中"The Middle Eastern Bazaar"（《中东集市》）一课时，我问学生下面这个句子美不美，美在哪里。

> You pass from the <u>heat</u> and <u>glare</u> of a big, open square into a <u>cool</u>, <u>dark</u> cavern which extends as far as the eye can see, <u>losing itself in the shadowy distance</u>.

大部分学生都保持沉默，因为他们不知道到底是美还是不美。有些比较大胆的学生回答说很美，可是，细问一下美在何处，他们又并不知道。有的学生则说是里面的形容词美。我们先来看看下面的句子美不美：

- This is a room.
- This is a big room.

显然，上面两个句子中，我们不会因为第二个句子添加了一个形容词big，就觉得它更美了。可见，句子的美不是从这里产生的。那么，它到底是从哪里体现的呢？

句子或者段落的美通常来自两个方面：一是修辞；二是结构。修辞可以狭义地理解成修辞手法，结构重点指句式。因此，前面提到的《中东集市》中的句子之所以美，是因为它使用了两组对比（我们在后文的常用修辞手法中会继续讨论），结构上使用了一个现在分词短语。

修辞是刻意的（for a particular purpose），句式通常也是刻意的，一切为了达到美的目的所使用的表达手法都属于修辞的范畴。我们先看看下面的情景：

Some people say that if we take away love, our earth will become a tomb. What do you think of this? Write a composition of about 400 words.

对于这个情景，我们给学生布置过一篇作文，题目自拟，但要求他们用定义法开篇（在第4章我们会讨论这种方法）。通常一些含义不清或者概念外延不清的题目采用定义法开篇比较好。

我们举三个例子进行对比。

例1

Love is a feeling between people which accompanies us all our life. Love is a feeling that we cannot lack. It is a feeling that will make our life more meaningful.

这个例子把love定义为人与人之间的感情，并强调其伴随我们一生，不可或缺，它使得我们的生活更有意义。例句在定义上解释无误，句式一般。其美主要是来自修辞上的排比，而不是句式。

例2

The world is full of love. We need love. We cannot live without it. Love is a strong feeling between human beings. We can also find it in other animals, such as foxes, dogs and cats, etc.

这个例子把love的外延扩大了一些，既指人与人之间的强烈感情，也指动物之间的感情。但其在句式美方面显得很一般。

例3

Love is a kind of emotion expressing our likeness, happiness, our care or concern about someone or something we treasure, we like, want and we need, not only between human beings, but also between man and other living things in the world, including animals, plants, our earth and our environment.

这个例子无论是在定义的把握上，还是在营造句式美方面都做得比较好。三个例子都把love解释成a feeling。但是，在概念的外延把握方面，例3比前两个更宽泛，它指万事万物之间的情感。通过并列，作者把笼统的情感具体化为"喜爱、喜欢、关爱"等。扩大概念的外延（当然不能是随意放大）最大的优点就是可以突出写作意义。

古今中外都有无数感人的爱情故事，如果我们侧重写人与人之间的爱，就很难写出什么新意；相反，很可能会流于表面或空洞。这个话题谁都可以写，但又难成好文，因为这里要写的是一篇阐释文，不能采用叙事手法，这样就无法写出精彩的故事来。那么，在这种情况下，如果我们写被大部分人忽略的爱，也就是人和其他生命体之间的爱，岂不是更有意义？

例3就是从这个角度入手的，难道破坏环境不是今天的普遍现象吗？难道我们的大地母亲不是最需要我们关心和爱护的吗？这样，写作意义就更大了。

在句式方面，现在分词短语使用频率较高。概念的外延最好用现在分词来表示，当然也可以使用其他方法，下文会进一步说明。了解了这种特点之后，想要把句式弄得漂亮一点以增加文章的形式美就不是什么难事了。

在基础写作课程教学过程中，我们布置过一个小练习，要求学生用一句话来描述自己第一天踏进学校大门时的心情。大部分学生是这样写的：

I stood in front of the big gate of the campus, and I looked worried.

当我指出这样写意思准确但句式不够美时，有学生把它修改成：

I stood in front of the big gate of the campus, feeling worried and waiting for someone to take me in.

相比之下，这句比上一句要好一些。

我给学生提供了另一种表达，不过强调这种表达在文学作品中用得比较多。文学作品创作时有一条规则叫Just show. Don't tell.（显示即可，无须直言。）

I stood in front of the big gate of the campus, looking around.

句式美通常表现在以下几个方面：

1. 分词短语

例 1

The oratorial storm that Clarence Darrow and Dudley Field Malone blew up in the little court in Dayton swept like a fresh wind through the schools and legislative offices of the United States, bringing in its wake a new climate of intellectual and academic freedom that has grown with the passing years.

参考译文：

克莱伦斯·达罗和杜德利·菲尔德·马龙在小小的戴顿法庭掀起的这场辩论风暴，犹如一股劲风，吹遍美国的各大校园和立法机构，随之而来的是日渐增长的思想自由和学术自由的新气象。

评析：这是《震惊世界的审判》（The Trial That Rocked the World）的结尾。整段就一句话，主句是比喻，它生动地体现了这次庭审的壮观景象。分词短语是辩论带来的结果，它使得语言更加书面化、更加优美。

例2

Two of my pupils testified, grinning shyly at me that I had taught them evolution, but added that they had not been contaminated by the experience.

参考译文：

我的两个学生朝我害羞地咧咧嘴，证实我确实教他们进化论，但补充说他们并未因此而被污染。

评析：这也是《震惊世界的审判》里的句子，分词短语使得语言不仅生动形象，而且更加书面化、更加优美。

例3

Where there should have been gentle blue-green waves lapping against the side of the ship, there was nothing but hot dry sand.

参考译文：

在这里，原来是一片碧波荡漾、海浪轻拍船体的美景，如今除了干燥酷热的沙子，一无所有。

评析：这是《沙漠之舟》（Ships in the Desert）里的句子，描述了曾经的美景，句子之所以让人感觉美，分词短语起到了关键作用。

例 4

Industry meant coal, and later oil, and we began to burn lots of it—bringing rising levels of carbon dioxide (CO_2), with its ability to trap more heat in the atmosphere and slowly warm the earth.

参考译文：

工业意味着煤，继而是石油，然后我们大量燃烧它们，这会增加二氧化碳的含量，二氧化碳具有吸收大气中更多热量的特点，从而慢慢使地球变暖。

评析：这是《沙漠之舟》里面的一个片段，它用现在分词短语和带with的介词短语来表示伴随，使得句子读起来特别美。

例 5

Meanwhile, in the nearby town of Muynak the people were still canning fish—brought not from the Aral Sea but shipped by rail through Siberia from the Pacific Ocean, more than a thousand miles away.

参考译文：

此时，在穆娜科附近的城镇，人们依然在做鱼罐头，可是这些鱼不是来自咸海，而是从千里之外的西伯利亚途经太平洋运送过来的。

评析：这也是《沙漠之舟》里面的内容，过去分词短语和现在分词短语用法一致，但是过去分词短语的使用频率相对较低。越是别人不敢使用的东西，你能正确使用，你的作文就更有价值。

例 6

This done, I entered one of the low-ceilinged rooms of the little floating house, treading cautiously on the soft matting and experiencing a twinge of embarrassment at the prospect of meeting the mayor of Hiroshima in my socks.

参考译文：

我脱掉鞋子后，进到一间顶棚很低的船屋，小心翼翼地踩在榻榻米上面，想到要穿着袜子去见市长，内心很纠结。

评析：独立结构也是过去分词的用法，它通常用在书面语中，这样主句前后分别是过去分词和现在分词短语，作者非常刻意地使用这些结构来营造句式美。

例 7

Everyone bowed, including the Westerners.

参考译文：

包括西方人在内的所有人一起鞠躬。

评析：这个句子虽短，添加一个分词短语非但不显得累赘，还格外协调。

例 8

I was just about to make my little bow of assent, when the meaning of these last words sank in, jolting me out of my sad reverie.

参考译文：

我正准备略微勾下身子，表示赞同，这时，最后几个字让我明白过来，使我从悲伤的遐想中惊醒。

评析：例6到例8都是《广岛——日本"最快乐"的城市》（Hiroshima—the "Liveliest" City in Japan）里的句子。作者多次在主句后面用了现在分词短语，以此来体现他当时的复杂心情。在英语写作的过程中，分词短语是使用非常频繁的句式，也是让结构非常优美的句式。

例9

Moving with surprising speed, the fat man walked around the suite, opening doors and inspecting the space behind them.

评析：这是《讹诈》（Blackmail）里面的一个句子。该句突出一个谓语动词walk，前后都是非谓语动词。

这就是汉语的"线"形与英语的"凸"字形之间的差别。汉语习惯于多个动词连用，而英语往往只突出一个重点动词，用它当作谓语，把其他动词都处理成非谓语形式。

2. 插入语

例1

Leading counsel for the prosecution was William Jennings Bryan, the silver-tongued orator, three times Democratic nominee for President of the United States, and leader of the fundamentalist movement that had brought about my trial.

参考译文：

控方主辩律师是能说会道的演讲家威廉·詹宁斯·布莱恩，他曾三次被民主党提名为美国总统候选人，是原教旨主义运动的领袖人物。正是原教旨主义运动把我卷入了这次审判。

评析：这是《震惊世界的审判》里的句子，对于指控自己的负责人布莱恩先生，作者使用了三个插入语排比，一是突出他的成就，二是交代自己曾经多么崇拜他。插入语的好处在于整合意思，使句子主次分明，结构灵活。遗憾的是，很多学生不敢或者不习惯使用插入语。

例2

A few weeks before I had been an unknown school-teacher in Dayton, a little town in the mountains of Tennessee.

参考译文：

几周之前，我还是田纳西乡间一个叫戴顿小镇的默默无闻的中学教师。

评析：这也是《震惊世界的审判》里的句子，人名、地名后面经常使用插入语，用来解释或说明。遗憾的是，这么简单地道的好方法，居然很少有学生运用在写作中。所以，我们强调要提高学生的高分作文意识。

例3

Howard Morgan, a bright lad of 14, testified that I had taught that man was a mammal like cows, horses, dogs and cats.

参考译文：

霍华德·摩根，一个聪明的十四岁的少年，证实我教的是人和牛、马、狗、猫一样，都是哺乳动物。

评析：这也是《震惊世界的审判》里面的句子。作者在人名后使用了插入语，简单明了。从简洁性来看，插入语的效果比定语从句更好。只要是人名、地名等，我们都可以考虑使用插入语。

例 4

Seldom has a city gained such world renown, and I am proud and happy to welcome you to Hiroshima, <u>a town known throughout the world for its—oysters.</u>

参考译文：

很少有城市获得这样的世界级称誉，我因此十分骄傲且高兴地欢迎大家光临广岛，一个以牡蛎闻名于世的小城镇。

评析：这是《广岛——日本"最快乐"的城市》里的句子，市长说到广岛这一地点的时候，在后面加了一个说明，即"一个以牡蛎闻名于世的小城镇"，起到了很好的修辞作用，它令来访者一颗充满内疚的心得到了放松和解脱。

例 5

朋友是暂时的，家庭是永久的。①<u>在好些人的行为里我发现了这个信条</u>。这个信条在我实在是不可理解的。对于我，要是没有朋友，我现在会变成怎样可怜的东西，连我自己都不知道。朋友给了我家庭所不能给的东西。②<u>他们的友爱，他们的帮助，他们的鼓励，几次把我从深渊的边沿救回来。他们对我表示了无限的慷慨</u>。

参考译文：

Friends are transient whereas family are lasting—<u>that is the tenet, as I know, guiding the behaviour in many people.</u> To me, that is utterly inconceivable. Without friends, I would have been reduced to I don't know what a miserable creature.

Friends give me things which are beyond my family to give me. Thanks to their fraternal love, assistance and encouragement, I have time and again been saved from falling into an abyss while on its verge. <u>They have been enormously generous towards me.</u>（张培基译）

评析：原文选自巴金先生的散文《朋友》，被散文翻译大家张培基先生翻译并收录在读者甚众的《英译中国现代散文选》中。张培基的翻译对原文理解到位，选词准确。

我们都知道，汉语和英语区别很大，中文主要强调表达情感和意境，逻辑关系和句法是次要的。而英语则不然，它始终讲究逻辑和语法，以增加句子之间的黏合度，使得各段落连贯得更加通畅、自然。从这一点上我们就会发现，画线部分①如果使用插入语，读起来感觉会更好。笔者当然不是来"挑剔"名家的翻译的，而是给学习者提供另一种选择，毕竟翻译本身就是理解基础之上的不同选择。画线部分①有如下两种选择：

选择 1

Friends are transient whereas family are lasting, <u>a tenet guiding the behaviour of many people</u>.

选择 2

Friends are transient whereas family are lasting, <u>a tenet found in many people's life</u>.

画线部分②如果整合在一起，读起来也会更好，因为"无限慷慨"就是指友爱、帮助和鼓励。画线部分②有如下两种选择：

选择 1

They have been generous in giving me so much friendship, assistance and encouragement that I was saved several times from falling into an abyss in my life.

选择 2

Thanks to their great generosity in friendship, assistance and encouragement, I have been saved several times from the verge of the abyss.

3. 倒装

例 1

And when they go, <u>so does a huge slice of the few traditional industries worth keeping</u>.

参考译文：

如果它们倒闭了，少数值得保留的传统工业中的大部分也会随之倒闭。

评析：这是《大不列颠望洋兴叹》（Britannia Rues the Waves）的结尾，倒装不仅起到了强调的作用，还可以协调句子各部分之间的关系。

例 2

<u>Hanging over the patient was a big ball made of bits of brightly colored paper</u>, folded into the shape of tiny birds.

参考译文：

一个大球吊在病人头顶上，它是用鲜艳彩纸做成的，这些彩纸被折叠成一只只小小的幸运鸟。

评析：这是《广岛——日本"最快乐"的城市》里的句子，倒装在这里主要起协调作用，而非强调，但是它让句式变得很美观，包括最后的过去分词短语的使用。

例 3

Scattered among notations about the weather and the tedious mining-camp meals lies an entry noting a story he had heard that day—an entry that would determine his course forever: "Coleman with his jumping frog—bet stranger $50—stranger had no frog, and C. got him one—in the meantime stranger filled C's frog full of shot and he couldn't jump. The stranger's frog won."

参考译文：

笔记本里面记满了天气和矿区单调的饭菜信息，其中有一则他那天听来的小故事——这则故事决定了他未来的事业。科尔曼和他的跳蛙——与陌生人赌 50 美金——陌生人没有青蛙，科尔曼去给他找了一只——此时，陌生人往科尔曼的青蛙肚子里塞满了铅弹，它跳不起来了。陌生人的蛙赢了。

评析：这是《马克·吐温——美国的镜子》（Mark Twain— Mirror of America）里面的句子，倒装在这里的作用和例2一样，主要是协调句子。从某种程度上说，倒装是平淡之中的一种点缀，好比一片绿色中的几朵小红花，会让人觉着赏心悦目。

4. 介词短语前置

例 1

At the very bottom of the earth, high in the Trans-Antarctic Mountains, with the sun glaring at midnight through a hole in the sky, I stood in the unbelievable coldness and talked with a scientist in the late fall of 1988 about the tunnel he was digging through time.

参考译文：

在地球的底端，南极山脉之上，半夜时分，太阳透过一个缝隙，依然闪耀。此时是 1988 年的深秋，我站在寒冷的雪地上，与一位科学家谈论他历时已久挖掘的一条隧道。

评析：这是《沙漠之舟》里的句子。它的语言非常书面化，在多个状语的情况下，作者把介词短语放在前面，反而更加协调。

例 2

At the bottom of the world, two continents away from Washington, D. C., even a small reduction in one country's emissions had changed the amount of pollution found in the remotest end least accessible place on earth.

参考译文：

一个国家，哪怕减少一点点有害释放物体，污染量就会产生变化，并在离美国首都华盛顿两个大陆之隔的南极这个人迹罕至的地方表现出来。

评析：这也是《沙漠之舟》里的句子，结构同例 1 一模一样，语言既书面，又优美。通常，我们读上几段，就会发现作者的写作风格。一般来说，具有较高水平的写作者都有自己的写作风格。

5. 后置修饰语

例 1
引起争议的小说

参考译文：

a novel likely to cause controversy

评析：后置修饰语是翻译的选择之一，在追求句式灵活方面是很好的备选项。在上下文中，短语式后置修饰语通常比定语从句更简洁，而且比前置修饰语更符合目的语的用法习惯。

例2

值得考虑的问题

参考译文：

a problem <u>worth of considering</u>

评析：如果我们说a problem which is worth of considering，显然不如参考译文中的句子来得简洁地道。

例3

大家都很感兴趣的话题

参考译文：

a topic <u>of great interest to all</u>

评析：同样，我们可以说 a topic that is interesting to all，但参考译文中提供了一个更精简的选择。那些只习惯用定语从句或前置修饰语的人可以好好借鉴和学习一下。

例4

适应社会主义市场经济体制的中国特色的行政管理体制

参考译文：

an administrative management system <u>with Chinese characteristics catering to socialist market economy</u>

评析：这句翻译处理得非常好，有前置修饰语和后置修饰语，行文很流畅。如果我们按照汉语的习惯把所有的修饰语都放在前面，表达就不地道了。

例5

I was standing in the sun on the hot steel deck of a fishing ship capable of processing a fifty-ton catch on a good day. But it wasn't a good day.

参考译文：

烈日下，我站在一艘捕鱼船炙热的甲板上，以前，渔船在旺季一天可以捕捞五十吨鱼，可是现在不再有这种好日子了。

评析：这是《沙漠之舟》里的句子，值得我们模仿或借鉴。既然名词的限定成分可以放在前面也可以放在后面，那我们就要关注不同的表现形式，从而使句式更加灵活。后置修饰语有很多，最常用的是定语从句，但是定语从句太普通了，有时一段出现几个定语从句，句式就显得很呆板。这时可以使用一些其他的表现形式，比如例5用capable of processing a fifty-ton catch来替代that has the ability to process a fifty-ton catch或者which can process a fifty-ton catch。

例6

And when they go, so does a huge slice of the few traditional industries worth keeping.

评析：这是《大不列颠望洋兴叹》里的句子，像worth doing这类的短语式后置修饰语是英语写作过程中会不时使用的一种句式，我们应该加以吸收和消化。

例7

This century has witnessed dramatic changes in two key factors that define the physical reality of our relationship to the earth: a sudden and startling surge in human population, ① with the addition of one China's worth of people every ten years, and a sudden acceleration of the scientific and technological revolution, which has allowed an almost unimaginable magnification of our power to affect the world around us ② by burning, cutting, digging, moving, and transforming the physical matter that makes up the earth.

参考译文：

　　本世纪见证了两大因素的巨变，它们构成了我们与地球之间关系的物质现实：一个是人口的急剧增长，每十年增长的人数是一个中国的人口；另一个是科技革命的迅猛发展，通过焚烧、砍伐、挖掘、移动以及改变地球的物质结构，展现出我们影响地球的难以想象的力量。

评析：这也是《沙漠之舟》里的句子，画线部分①采用伴随状语来突出数量，这是除现在分词短语之外的另一种伴随的选择，非常简洁适用。画线部分②则是定语从句中的方式状语。这种处理方式，使得整个句子非常协调，句式非常优美。

例8

　　"Hiroshima, as you know, is a city familiar to everyone," continued the mayor.

参考译文：

　　"正如大家所知，广岛是家喻户晓的一座城市，"市长继续说。

评析：这是《广岛——日本"最快乐"的城市》里的句子。familiar to也是经常后置的形容词短语。一个人的文章可以写得比别人好，原因之一就是句式灵活，会用各种结构，比如形容词短语作后置定语、插入语等。

6. 抽象名词的使用

例 1

<u>The introduction was made.</u>

参考译文:

进行了介绍。

评析:这也是《广岛——日本"最快乐"的城市》中的句子,它是市长接见外国记者时的一个情景。作者为了弱化"介绍"这个动作,就采用了抽象名词。通常,-tion,-sion,-ness,-ty,-cy,-ce,-ment等结尾的单词都是抽象名词。适当使用抽象名词是一种非常地道的英语表达法,因为有些动作是不用强调的。

例 2

<u>The transformation of the way we relate to the earth</u> will of course involve new technologies, but the key changes will involve new ways of thinking about the relationship itself.

参考译文:

转变我们依赖地球的方式自然需要引入新科技,但是,关键的变化还是对相互之间关系的思维转变。

评析:这也是《沙漠之舟》里面的句子,其用法和例1一样,在不需要强调动作的情况下,作者使用了抽象名词。

总之,任何写作,包括英语阐释文写作,在文字方面要刻意创造美感。刻意在句式上做文章就可以增加美感。一旦我们有了这个意识,写作得高分的筹码就多了一个。

（六）语体意识的必要性

有的学生感觉自己写出来的内容好像日常会话，而说出来的内容又和别人说的不一样，这就涉及语体问题。语体的基本要求是不能随便混用，也就是说在书面语中，不能随便穿插口语体，因为口语体和书面语体的语法要求不同，句式也相差很大。

有些考试的作文要求里会交代必须使用书面语体，可是，有人都没有听过语体这个词。语体分为口语体和书面语体两种。口语体是指用来说话的语言形式（informal），词典上用infml.来表示；书面语体是用来书写的语言形式（formal），词典上用fml.来表示。

通常，口语体多使用日常用词（everyday use），句子比较短，较少使用从句，也很少使用被动语态，有的句子成分可以不完整，甚至不符合语法，比如，Sounds great! Fits fine! You are concentrate. See? Long time no see. Let's go play! 等等。而书面语体正好相反，词汇不都是常用词，句子比较长，较多使用从句，还经常用被动语态，宾语从句的that不省略，语法必须完整。

我们拿温斯顿·丘吉尔《关于希特勒攻打苏联的演讲》中的一个句子为例，它足以证明一位英国人说的"有时书面语和口语仿佛一个天，一个地"。

- I said that notice should be given that I would broadcast on BBC at nine that night.
- Tell the BBC. I will broadcast at nine tonight.

评析：两句话的意思基本相同。前一句是书面语体，语法完整，而且里面有两个从句，还有一个被动语态，而且that没有省略。后一句是典型的口语体，句子简短，使用祈使句和简单的日常用语，而且未使用从句。

我们用表格把两者的差异列表如下：

表2-3 口语体和书面语体的差异

	口语体（informal）	书面语体（formal）
词汇	日常单词，如 very strange。	级别较高的词，如 extraordinarily curious。
句子	短句。	长句，多用宾语从句、定语从句和状语从句等，而且 that 不省略。
语法	省略，破碎，语法不完整，如 Sounds great! Fits fine! You are concentrate. Long time no see.	常用被动语态，语法完整，如 That sounds great. It fits fine. You are to concentrate. I haven't seen you for a long time.

对于语体有了一定的认识以后，我们需要做的就是多加模仿，比如练习口语会话，说出的内容就不会像书面语。而练习写作则要刻意模仿自己平常阅读的文章，这样写出来的东西就不会过度口语化。书面语体里夹杂着口语是不恰当的做法，因此，我们对语体问题要有清楚的认识。

（七）思维习惯的培养

有的学生的作文语法上没有问题，但就是让人看不明白是什么意思。一些申请出国留学的文章里也存在类似的问题。有些国外的教授看了中国学生写的作文后直皱眉头，不明白他想表达什么意思。

这些文章让人看不懂的主要原因是不符合英语的表达习惯。有的学生随想随写，简单机械地按照母语的思维习惯把句子翻译成英语，结果让别人感觉不知所云。

思维问题涉及两个方面：一个是思维能力，它不分中西，是全人类共有的公正客观分析判断问题的能力；另一个是思维习惯，它有中西之分，是一个民族在其历史发展过程中逐渐形成的看问题及表达问题的方式。思维习惯属于文化范畴，在语言学习中非常重要。比如，我们见了外国人如果问"吃了吗？""上哪儿去呀？"他们就不能理解；我们只要说"Hello"或"Hi"等符合他们习惯的问候语即可。

写作方面有一个我们非知不可的表达方式，那就是总分结构（from overview to details或者from general to specific），这个结构符合西方的思维习惯。

总分结构就是指先概括地说，然后再具体展开说的一种表达方式。它有两个特点：第一，它是典型的英式思维，按照这个思维习惯，句子之间的逻辑关系就很明显；第二，它能很好地增加作文的字数，是担心作文字数不够的学生特别要学会的写作技巧，我们在第4章会详细介绍。

通常，总和分是不可或缺的，否则就会让以英语为母语的人感到奇怪。比如，有位学生写了一封信，其中有这样的句子：

The campus is beautiful. The teachers are nice. I study very hard here. I go to bed at ten when the light is off. Oh, it's time for me to go to the library. Good-bye, Mum.

这些句子看似没有语法上的问题，也似乎成功地传递了让母亲放心的信息，但作为书面语体的书信，这样写很不妥。

首先，它不符合英语的思维习惯，即概括之后再提供细节；其次，内容不连贯，句与句之间的衔接不自然；最后，结尾过于口语化，不属于书面语体。如果增补以下细节，会让人更好理解：

The campus is beautiful. It is very quiet because there are many trees and flowers along the sides of the streets. And the buildings are tall and straight. The teachers are nice. They are kind, always with smiles on their faces. And they are ready to answer whatever questions we have. In such an atmosphere, I can concentrate on my study and I study hard.

结尾可以改成这样：

I can find something new here everyday, Mum. I will talk to you more next time.

Yours,

Lily

综上所述，英语写作不是按照中式思维简单地把句子翻译成英语，写作时必须符合英语的思维习惯，否则，写出来的东西就算没有语法错误，也可能让以英语为母语的人看不懂。

先总后分是英语中最常用的表达方式。学习写作时一定要知道这一基本规律，它能使我们的行文更加流畅。

（八）写作的前提条件

写作的前提是阅读，可以说，没有阅读，就无法写出高分作文。阅读的作用具体表现在两方面：

首先是精读方面，也就是从阅读篇章中吸收和消化我们需要的高分要素，这样我们可以更快地提高写作水平。有些人虽然语言基础不错，但写作水平始终无法提高，很可能是他们不知道哪些是高分要素，更不会从阅读中吸收。

其次是泛读方面，也就是通过大量阅读来获得各方面的知识和信息，它们在具体问题分析的过程中是提供强有力的证据的保障。

高水平的写作者无不读书甚多，因为好文章无法凭空编造出来，大都是建立在前人写作基础上的创新。在论证方面，引用已知的事实或前人所言来充当论据，加大论证的说服力，这也需要通过阅读来积累。

高级英语写作更是如此。通过阅读，学习者可以掌握英语作文的结构，学习规范的表达方式；然后通过模仿来掌握一系列写作技巧，包括如何选词、怎样营造句式美、有哪些增加美感的修辞手法、需要怎样引经据典，以及如何布局等。

这些要素我们都可以从阅读中学到，在这里，我们举一些例子，和大家分享一下阅读对于写作的好处，尤其是那些不知道看哪些书的学生。

需要看哪些书通常是一些考研学生纠结的问题。有学生问，"老师，我报考的学校参考书里只列了张汉熙的《高级英语》，我要怎么看呢？看什么？"

列《高级英语》并非告诉考生要考里面的某个具体内容，而是看考生的水平是否能达到与课本内文章同等的水平。迄今为止，我还不曾见过任何一个学校考过里面的任何一篇文章。但是，我们讨论的所有高级作文的要素都可以从中找到。因此，我们所举的例子，大部分都来自张汉熙先生的《高级英语》。

说到这本书，让我想起锤子手机创始人罗永浩在网上说过的一句话，"从来没有一个如此美好的产品和品牌遭遇如此大规模的误解、污蔑和诽谤"（2014）。在此，我们不谈论这句话的目的，只想提及一下它的出处，这句话确确实实是对《高级英语》（1993）第一册第十一单元《词典的作用究竟是什么？》（What's a Dictionary For?）中一句话的模仿。这句话的原文是：

"Never has a scholarly work of this stature been attacked with such unbridled fury and contempt."

参考译文:

还不曾有过一部鸿篇巨制遭受过如此谩骂和污蔑。

我们再看看被称之为"满分作文"的2006年TEM-8作文的范文（吴中东，2010）:

> In the second place, ambition can bring one's potentials to the full. Ambition may well serve as a catalyst activating one's dormant potentials. Without ambition one's potentials will remain slumbering like a dormant volcano. A case in point is Ms. Zhang Haidi, a Chinese Helen Keller. It was her ambition to be a useful person that has turned the almost paralyzed Zhang Haidi into a well-accomplished figure whose achievements would <u>dwarf</u> those of some normal people.

参考译文:

> 另一方面，抱负可以全力激发我们的潜能，它可以充当催化剂，唤醒我们休眠的能力。人若无抱负可言，则潜能如沉睡的火山，一直处于休眠状态。以被誉为中国的海伦·凯勒的张海迪为例，正因为她有远大的抱负，才得以从瘫痪之人变成了一位杰出的人物。其成就使那些四肢健全者相形见绌。

2006年TEM-8写作题目是Ambition，由于添加了美国作家爱泼斯坦的一段话而变得难度大增，致使当年的写作平均成绩直线下降。在这种情况下，这篇范文显得格外突出。其设计之巧妙、句式之优美、比喻之恰当、选词之用心等，无不令人膜拜。

我相信，能把tower和dwarf用作动词的考生，一定熟悉《高级英语》第一册第一篇课文《中东集市》结尾那段中的一个精彩句子:

> The pressing of the linseed pulp to extract the oil is done by a vast ramshackle apparatus of beams and ropes and pulleys

which <u>towers</u> the vaulted ceiling and <u>dwarfs</u> camels and their stone wheels.

参考译文：

榨亚麻籽油的是一套不停晃动的设备，它由绳索、大梁和滑轮组成。它们高耸至拱形屋顶，相形之下，骆驼和石碾显得非常渺小。

这两个词虽简短，却无比生动地表达了大小物体之间的反差，具有神似的效果。如果我们把它改成One is much bigger. The other becomes smaller.则称不上是高级写作了。

最后我们再来看一段美文翻译，是《人生是条漫长的河》中的一个片段。

人生是一条漫长的河流，从涓涓细流的上游到惊涛骇浪的中游，最后注入宽阔的海洋。

上游是美丽的童年，淙淙小溪从幽静的林间穿过，像一首浪漫的抒情诗。中游是沉重的中年，巨大的落差产生了飞流直下的瀑布；险恶的暗礁又使河面布满了龙潭虎穴，像一部惊险离奇的小说。

下游经过平静的入海口与海洋浑然一片，平静、辽阔、宽容、博大，像一篇淡雅厚重的散文。

许多学生在翻译这篇散文时，感觉无从下手。其难点有两方面：一是比喻；二是主要信息。比喻向来是翻译的难点，如果着手翻译的学生未能看出比喻所在，则翻译可能会失真。主次信息也是很多学生难以把握到位的一个翻译问题。

其实，熟悉大散文家罗素的人一看到这篇散文就会想到罗素的《如何平静老去》（How to Grow Old）。罗素就把人生比喻成一条长长的河流。让我们一起来温故一下罗素该散文的片段：

An individual human existence should be like a river—small at first, narrowly contained within its banks, and rushing passionately past rocks and over waterfalls. Gradually the river grows wider, the banks recede, the waters flow more quietly, and in the end, without any visible break, they become merged in the sea, and painlessly lose their individual being.

参考译文：

每一个人的生活都应该像河水一样——开始是细小的，被限制在狭窄的两岸之间，然后热烈地冲过巨石，滑下瀑布。渐渐地，河道变宽了，河岸扩展了，河水流得更平稳了。最后，河水流入了海洋，不再有明显的间断和停顿，而后便毫无痛苦地摆脱了自身的存在。（王佐良译）

我们可以看出，罗素先生的句式多么美，书面语体读来多么流畅。河流之后是形容词短语和过去分词短语small at first, narrowly contained within its banks，接下来是现在分词短语and rushing passionately past rocks and over waterfalls。河流特点明了，主要信息突出。

翻译《人生是条漫长的河》中的段落时，我们可以借鉴上面的句式：

Man's life is like a long river, trickling at the very beginning, then flowing down the middle part filled with torrents, and finally being merged in the vast sea.

The upriver, our early days of life, with lots of narrow streams threading its way among the forests and woods, gives us a romantic expression of lyric poems.

The midstream of the river, same as a man entering his tough middle age, is full of waterfall due to the different levels of lands and unknown risk under the submerged rocks, a real scene in a bizarre thriller.

When entering the downstream, the water loses itself in the ocean after rushing through the entrance of the sea, being peaceful and broad, profound and tolerant as an elegant prose containing some heavy contents.

诚然，这个译文还值得商榷，但它至少说明一点：如果我们善于阅读，并从中吸收我们需要的要素，则我们的译文处理起来会更加得心应手。

绝大部分学生把阅读当成应试的任务来完成。他们死记硬背，学得非常辛苦，效果却不是很好。阅读其实是一件非常有意思、非常享受的事情。但是，如果你缺乏阅读知识和相关技巧，很多东西你可能读不出来。从这本书里，你可以学到一些赏析文章的方法。希望借助这些方法，你可以读出更多内容来。

总之，要想写出好文章，就要养成看书的好习惯，因为阅读是写作和翻译的前提。唯有从阅读中吸收自己需要的氧分，写作水平才能提高。另外，阅读一定要先掌握正确的方法，否则，好的东西读不出来，也是枉然。

二
结构分布情况

（一）英语作文的常规

熟知英语作文的常规是很重要的，因为它可以帮助我们了解英语写作的基本脉络，以便在模仿的基础上多加练习，直到娴熟之后的创新。如果脉络都把握不好，则创新无从谈起。熟知作文的常规之后不能随意改动，并美其名曰"发挥"。

1. 结构的规范性

英语作文通常由三大部分组成，但不一定是三小段。因此，只写一段或者两段的作文是不恰当的。至于是写三段还是更多，取决于作文要求字数的多少：字数要求少的，有三段即可；字数要求在350词以上的，一般会有多个段落，通常开头和结尾各一段，中间部分可以写成几个小段。

广义而言，阐释文也是一种散文。但是，英语的阐释文和汉语的散文是不同的，它以说理为目的，不能过多掺杂情感，以免被误认为是煽情。此外，英语的散文不仅要文笔好，还要思想深刻。高级写作虽然可以归为散文类，但它具有严格的格式规范，不要随便改动。唯有先遵守规范，才有可能谈创新。

2. 开篇的直接性

英汉作文在开篇上存在着比较大的差异。有些英语作文让人皱眉头，经常就是因为不符合英语的表达习惯。既然开篇就可能让人感觉不知所云，我们对此就必须特别小心。

汉语的开篇比较随意，经常使用"螺旋式"手法，也就是一种绕弯的形式，比如题目是要求讨论电脑的作用，作者可能先谈改革开放或经济问题。英语则不然，不会随便绕弯。英语习惯采用"直线型"开篇，即开门见山，因为英语总是把重要信息放在前面，解释、说明、补充性的信息往往被看成次要信息放在后面。比如原因和结果，英语习惯先说结果，再说原因。只有搞清楚这一点，写出来的东西才不会让人感觉不知所云。

我们就以The Role of Computers Today为例。有的学生是这样开头的：

> With China's opening to the outside world and the development of economy, we become rich now. And most of us can afford computers, which were impossible to think of before.

评析：这显然绕得很远，说"随着中国对外开放及经济的发展，人们富裕起来了，大家几乎都买得起电脑了，这是以前不能想象的事情。"这可能是事实，但读者（尤其是以英语为母语的读者）会以为作者要讨论中国的改革开放成果，或者中国人民怎样摆脱贫困之类的问题。

那么，同样的题目，符合英式习惯的开篇会是怎样的呢?

> Computers take a very important role today in our work, study and life. They are used in almost all walks of life from office staff to factory workers.

评析：这样开篇让读者一眼就看出作者要讨论什么问题，这是最常见的开篇方法，它直截了当，简明扼要，不东拉西扯。

通常情况下，批改试卷的老师看到as...或者with the development...这类开篇句式，就先认定写作者习惯中式思维。如果衔接得好，还可以接受；如果衔接不好，则得不到高分。

我们再来对比一下Advantages and Disadvantages of Shopping on the Net的两个开篇。

开篇1

> With the coming of information age, shopping on the net becomes unusual, which enriches our life. However, it has advantages and disadvantages.

开篇2

Shopping on the net has advantages and disadvantages. Some people say that the disadvantages are more than the advantages. But others don't think so. I agree with the later.

评析：相比之下，开篇2更符合英语的表达习惯，它直接、流畅，为高分奠定了基础。而开篇1是我们尽量要回避的开篇方式。一方面，它不太符合英语的表达习惯；另一方面，迂回很容易导致偏题。

有个简单的方法可以防止我们绕得太远，那就是第一句就扣题。这样，我们就可以比较好地把握英式开篇法。

总之，汉语的"螺旋式"开篇法经常令以英语为母语的人看了皱眉头，因为它不符合英式思维习惯，英语的开篇要求"直线型"，也就是开门见山的方法。既然我们是学英语，就必须符合英语的习惯，因此，在这方面要尽快规范过来。

3. 切入点的选取

选择一个好的切入点也是我们提倡的一个应试技巧。我们再来看看下面这个情景。

Some people say that if we take away love from the earth, our earth will be a tomb. What do you think of this? Write a composition of about 400 words.

大部分人会从正面着手开始写作，也就是分析爱的作用，顺便提到其反面。有个学生是这样写的：

What Would the World Be?

When talking about love, some people say that if we take away love from the earth, our earth will become a tomb. I quite agree with that. What would the world be if we did not have love?

59

The world would be very cool and people would be very indifferent to each other. Nobody would care about what happened to other people. How were their family members? What were going on around? And how did people feel when meeting some difficulties or frustrations?

她写着写着就写不下去，因此她很烦恼，想知道这是什么原因。这个问题虽然不是很普遍，但也值得讨论，这就是选择切入点的问题。

就观点而言，批改试卷的老师并不在意你选择什么，因为主观性命题允许大家各抒己见，没有规定说只能有一种声音。那么，批改试卷的老师在意什么呢？批改试卷的老师只看你的证据，也就是看你在论证过程中能否拿出强有力的证据来支撑你的观点。证据充分，结论才可信或有说服力；反之，如果拿不出强有力的证据，结论就不可靠或难以令人信服。

让我们回到切入点的问题上来。为什么说这是个切入点的问题呢？既然批改试卷的老师不在意你选择了什么观点，那么我们当然首先选择好写的切入点。试想，考场上时间有限，稍不镇定，可能就会产生干扰因素，比如慌张、焦躁，这些情绪通常会影响我们正常发挥。

考场上和平时的练习场景截然不同。平常我们可以慢慢思考，可以不断改正、补充或完善。然而，在时间有限、精神紧张的考场，你必须能够静心地快速找到一个好的切入点，然后顺利完成写作任务。如果你迟迟不能下手，或者不断否定自己的思路，就会产生焦虑和急躁的情绪。越是不镇定，思路越乱，结果就可能找不到合适的切入点，写不出作文。由此可见，一个好的切入点是多么重要啊！

那么，怎样的切入点算是好的切入点呢？这个问题很难具体化，因为必须针对具体的命题，我们才能做出判断。笼统地说，任何影响你提出充分理由（不含因思维不足而提不出充分理由的情况）的切入点，都不是好的切入点。

我们再回到前文关于爱的具体问题上来，该学生选择的切入点就不好，因为爱是环绕我们周围的、无处不在的一种情感，我们处处可以感受到爱的温暖。以爱为主题的故事比比皆是，人们甚至把爱称为"永恒的主题"，谁都可以讲出几个关于爱的故事来。可是，写作者却撇开存在，从非真实条件入手，写一个没有爱的世界，这怎么可能写得好呢？谁知道一个无爱的世界会是什么样的？选择这个切入点，就只能提出假设，并在自己陌生的领域摸索。试想，在有限的时间内，你可能把一个自己不清楚、不了解的世界写清楚吗？几乎不可能。相信大家都有这样的体会，越是自己熟悉的领域，越写得流畅，写得得心应手。

在逻辑上，有一个谬误叫做"与事实相反的假设"（hypothesis contrary to fact），它是指以假设为前提，并试图得出一个结论。一个典型的例子是你没有参加考研，但你说假如你参加了，一定能够考上。这个结论是不可靠的，因为事实是你没有参加考试，如果参加了，结果有考上和没考上两种可能，你不能只强调其中一种。

由此可见，好的切入点应该是指我们相对更熟悉的领域。我们要尽可能避免写自己未知的领域，而那些基于非真实条件的论证最应该回避。

关于切入点，有个问题需要指出，那就是其信息可以是虚构的。比如，你其实很支持在校学生创业，但为了作文好写，你选择说你反对。

批改试卷的老师对于你所选的立场是真是假并不关注，他们只在乎你能否表达得流畅、合乎情理或逻辑。我们一起看看下面这篇作文，里面的人物是虚构的，其目的只是提供一个好的示范。

My Teacher Mr. Jiang

It seemed that some teachers in middle schools were very strict. My teacher, Mr. Jiang, was no different. He was not only a strict man, but also a man with little smile. When he stared at a student, the student might have a feeling of fear and would feel nervous. But Mr. Jiang only stared at those who made something wrong.

Mr. Jiang was middle-aged and he was short. He always wore dark clothes, which made him looked even more serious. Though strict and serious, Mr. Jiang was a wonderful teacher, I could say that.

Mr. Jiang taught us mathematics at that time, the hardest subject to most of us. Before Mr. Jiang came to teach us, it was Miss Zhang who taught us mathematics. Miss Zhang was young and beautiful. And she's kind, too. We all liked to listen to her nice voice. However, she always made us feel that mathematics was such a hard subject that nobody could expect to get to know it in a semester's time. After listening to her explanation, we did not become brighter. Sometimes we felt even more confused while Mr. Jiang made us understand what mathematics was immediately and how we could learn it well. We were attracted by his simple and easy words the first time when he started his lesson. And we were sure that no matter how hard the subject was, we could try to understand and grasp it. The way he taught showed that he had a good knowledge of mathematics and had good techniques in teaching. The way he taught also let us understand some other things. What made a good teacher? Was appearance so important to good teachers? Or was kindness enough to a teacher?

By the end of that semester, three students were among the best ten in our grade. Among them were three called by Miss Zhang the worst of all. I was one of them. Today, I am a teacher myself. I got my Ph.D. two years ago. And now I'm teaching mathematics in a university. I try to be kind to my students. But the one who taught me how to teach well is Mr. Jiang.

评析：信息是虚构的，但是作者通过对比和衬托等手法，把一个其貌不扬，但是却热爱教育、善于教学的老师形象成功地塑造出来了。这篇作文涉及的其他技巧，我们在后面会具体分析。

下面我们再看一篇关于品质的作文。

The Most Important Personal Quality of a University Student

In order to be successful in the present society, we need some good personal qualities. There are many things that can be called personal qualities, such as smartness, honesty, confidence, efficiency, etc. But what is the most important one for us college students? For me, persistence is the most important.

It is because persistence is something that everybody needs but most people cannot stick to the end. Persistence means one can continue to do something without losing confidence in spite of difficulties. Persistence means one can go on with his job without giving up before he fulfills it. Persistence also means one has a positive and firm attitude towards his career and would never quit until he wins.

In today's society, people suffer more and more pressure, face more and more difficulties. So, it's easy for us to give up something important but difficult to finish and to change something easier to do but less significant to our life. In today's society, everyone has some dreams which need us to make into reality. Without perseverance, we cannot insist them. Without perseverance, we cannot realize them.

So, for me, when I try to get the abilities that we need in facing the world, I value the personal quality of persistence and try to adhere to it no matter what difficulties I will meet in the middle of my goal and I'll go on no matter how long it will take me to my destination.

评析：在这篇作文里，作者选择的是"坚持"的品质。相信大家会觉得这个品质很好写，因为任何事情都需要坚持。从普遍性的角度入手写会比较快。对于什么品质更容易让人取得成功，其实每个人都有自己的看法，但是你选择的那个很可能不好写。比如，有人说机灵有助于快速取得成功，可是他就是下不了笔。如果考试时间到了，他的作文还没有完成，这就是件很糟糕的事。

综上所述，对于一个选言命题，我们如何选择并不重要，重要的是我们可以拿出充分的证据来支持自己的观点。应试的时候，为了不让情绪影响临场发挥，我们一定要注意选择好的切入点。

（二）作文的三大部分

1. 第一部分：开头

俗话说，万事开头难。好的开始是成功的一半。作文的第一部分，即开头，通常就是第一段。它通常包括两方面内容：一是提出问题；二是表明观点。二者缺一不可。

有的作文会对此进行提示，比如Your attitudes should be given in the first part。如果给出了情景，你就必须紧紧围绕情景来写，不能对情景只字不提。

我们先来看看2014年的TEM-8写作情景：

Nowadays, some companies have work-from-home or remote working policies, which means that their employees do not have to commute to work every day. Some people think that this can save a lot of time travelling to and from work, thus raising employees' productivity. However, others argue that in the workplace, people can communicate face to face, which vastly increases the efficiency of coordination and cooperation. What is your opinion?

Write an essay of about 400 words on the following topic:

My Views on Working from Home

In the first part of your essay you should state clearly your main argument, and in the second part you should support your argument with appropriate details. In the last part you should bring what you have written to a natural conclusion or make a summary.

Marks will be awarded for content, organization, language and appropriateness. Failure to follow the above instructions may result in a loss of marks.

我们先简单地审题。显然，作文是要让学生谈对在家工作的看法。审题时，我们通常会对几种选择作一个简单的估计。对于在家工作的看法无外乎两种可能：同意或不同意。

有的学生在第一段这样写道：

Everybody needs work. Work is one part of life. There are different kinds of work and the forms and places are different, too. I like to work at home.

评析：这个开头虽然表明了观点，但有两点不妥：第一，扯得比较远；第二，未提及所给的情景。

我们可以试着修改一下：

Nowadays, to work at home or in the workplace becomes a hot topic. Some people say that to work at home can raise people's productivity for the saving of time while others argue that to work face to face is more efficient. I agree with the latter.

鉴于能否在家工作取决于工作性质，不是想在家工作就可以在家工作的，我们可以这样写：

Nowadays, where to work causes people's attention. Most people think it a desirable place to work at home. They stress that under such a circumstance, one is more creative without any pressure from the managers and disturbance from their colleagues. For me, where to work depends on what our job is.

我们再来看看几个考生作文的第一部分：

例 1

In nowadays, with the developing of economy and the widely using of Internet, work-from-home is not a dream. Some companies even try to use the work-from-home instead of working in the company. What I want to say is that work-from-home is not a proper way in the financial society.

评析：作文占卷面分数的20%，该考生的得分为8分，按百分制计算就是40分，是TEM-8作文中比较低的分数，那意味着这篇作文从结构到思维都比较差。首先，前面我们提到nowadays是副词，无须加介词，而且它是个常用词，犯这样的错误说明写作者的英语基础较差。其次，先说因特网使得在家工作成为现实（可是，不是什么工作都因为有了因特网就可以在家做啊），而不是直接说现在有些公司采用在家上班的方式，这导致第三句和第二句之间缺乏联系。如果我们说"有些公司已经采用了在家上班这种方式"就好多了。最后一句表明态度是很好的，但是添加in the financial society显得莫名其妙。

例2

　　Recently, some companies have the policies of work-from-home or remote working. The policy means that the employees can work in home. But this action arouse widely lamented argument among the people. Some people think that this policy is very wise for the company and also for themselves. Because it can save a lot of time when they go to work. Staying at home to work can save many time and take advantage of these times can make more contribution to their work. It also promote their interest to work. But some people think that it is not very good for them. They work in company can communicate with their colleagues face to face. If they encounter the difficult problems, they can talk with each other. If they have any question about the work, they can also ask the supervisor directly. This can vastly increase the efficiency of coordination and cooperation. From my point of view, working in company instead of home is much better.

评析：该考生的得分为10.5分，按百分制计算就是52.5分，虽然也不高，但是基本达到历年TEM-8作文平均分水平。首先，作者直接开篇，这点不错，如果第二句变成第一句的从句会更书面化，可是里面in home的使用有误，应该是at home。其次，作者在结尾表明了自己的观点。但是，第一部分过长，有些句子显然没有必要，而且语法错误过多（见画线部分），给人凑字数的感觉。另外，各句之间的逻辑关系不够明显，比如第三句和第二句没有很大关系（如果第二句是定语从句，则有关系）。第四句和第五句应该是一句，because前面的标点符号也有误。

例3

Nowadays, working-from-home has been put forward by some companies and, at the same time, drawn the attention of a large number of office workers. As far as I am concerned, I believe that working-from-home, which possesses bunches of advantages, is totally feasible and promising, and will be a trend in the future.

评析：该考生的得分为13.5分，按百分制计算就是67.5分，在TEM-8作文中算不错的了。它读起来感觉流畅多了，而且行文简洁，几乎没有冗余的信息或多余的词。此外，该作文很书面化，逻辑关系也很强，结构非常规范。

例4

As the technology developing very rapidly, it seems a trend that working from home is becoming increasingly popular. Some people embrace this idea while others find it unacceptable. Despite what technology has brought us, it's time that we weighed the advantages and disadvantages of working from home. And in my humble opinion, I think it would be better if people stick to the traditional way of working.

评析：该考生的得分为15.5分，按百分制计算就是77.5分，在TEM-8作文中算是高分了。不过这个开篇没有例3的好，因为一旦用了as，with之类的词，就会减弱开篇的直接要求，但文章的结构规范、句式优美、内容紧凑。最妙的是选词，比如embrace，weigh，humble等，它们使文章显得既高级又生动。

例5

Small Office Home Office (SOHO) has always been tempting

and advent-guard concept of working style in modern enterprises. Advocates for SOHO champion that the flexible working style will vastly enhance both the quality and efficiency of completing tasks and benefit the society as a whole, which I strongly agree with for the following reasons.

评析：该考生的得分为18分，按百分制计算就是90分，这在 TEM-8作文中算是非常高的，它意味着文章从开篇到结尾都比较完美。该作文开篇非常直接，指出小公司家庭工作模式是吸引人的、前卫的企业工作模式（这一点不太公正客观，因为生产性质的企业基本上不能采用这种模式）。其结构规范，逻辑严密，用词高级，句式优美，行文简洁流畅。

小结：切记，你是在写英语作文，不是写汉语作文，不能简单地把汉语想到的内容翻译成英语，而是要按照英语的规范来写。在第一部分或者第一段，你要做的事情有两件：首先，提出问题；其次，表明观点。在做上述两件事的时候，还要注意下面几个小点：

- 直接提出问题，不要绕弯；
- 阐释文不采用叙述式，因为它是说理的文章，不要以讲故事的形式开头；
- 不要过度修辞，即不要文学气息太浓；
- 不要乱用标识词，比如 because，so，then，however 等；
- 字数不要过多，3~5 句话即可；
- 句与句之间必须有逻辑关系，不能前后无关联；
- 不要以假设开头；
- 不要轻易用 why 开头。

2. 第二部分：正文

作文的第二部分叫正文，可以是一段，也可以是几个小段，这取决于作文要求的字数是多少。通常基础作文字数比较少，这部分有一段即可；而高级作文由于字数要求多，这部分可能会有好几段。

第二部分是对第一部分提出的问题或表明的观点加以分析论证的过程。分析的侧重点是通过证据来说明问题或现象存在的合理性，或者支持自己对该问题的看法。

最突显作者思维能力的地方就在文章的第二部分，因为它不仅要说理，而且要说得理由充分，让人觉得可信，还必须符合逻辑规则，不能有逻辑谬误等，从而使读者接受或者认可作者的观点。

为了凸显这部分的逻辑关系，我们经常使用一些常见的连接词或者转折词（interjections or transitional words）。

我们再次以Some people say that if we take away love, our earth will be a tomb为例，这是上海经济贸易大学2005年商务英语专业研究生入学考试的写作真题。

例1

We Can't Live Without Love

When talking about love, some people say that if we take away love, our earth will become a tomb. I think there is no more reasonable than this. We can't live without love. And love is not the exclusive right between human beings.

First, you can't find a place where there is no love, no matter in man's family or in animal's family in which love is something instinct brought to us when we were born. Looking at the mothers of some fierce animals like wolves and tigers, we can feel their strong love for their babies.

Second, love is wide spreading for it is the meaning of our life in the world. Man's love to the world makes him different from common animals. Man has strong feelings and deliberate actions for loving others rather than some instinct passion. If we cannot be cultivated and educated to be kind to others beyond our instinct, we are not real man. A real man is one who does not only care about himself, but also care others, treating them as part of his life, seeing them as dear friends or family members.

From ancient time till today, both in China and in any other places in the world, we can hear numerous true stories about love not just between human beings but among all living things. With love, we live a happy and meaningful life, which will lead us to active and positive attitudes towards man and the world. Without it, we feel lonely and desolate and great disasters come along.

So we cannot live without love and love does not mean the exclusive right between mother and her children or between human beings. It means that to have a pleasant life, love must be given to the whole world, including all the species so that everything in the planet enjoys a happy journey in the world just like a saying on the net that the supreme happiness of life is the conviction that we are loved.

评析：作者在第一段就提出我们不能没有爱，爱不是人类的专属权利；接着，正文使用三段来分析为什么我们不能没有爱。首先，爱无处不在，爱是我们出生即有的一种本能，无论是人还是动物。其次，爱是人类生存的意义，它是超出本能的、刻意的情感，如果不能如此，人类就枉为人类。古今中外有很多这类故事。有了爱，我们会快乐充实；无爱的世界则让人孤立无援，灾难丛生。

这篇文章的第二部分使用了常见的关系词，因此逻辑分明，论证有力，爱的重要性得到了证明，结论可靠。不足之处是字数略微少了一些，而且第二部分第一小段的字数比后面的几段略少，显得不够协调。

例 2

We Need a World with Love and Care

The world where we live is a place full of love. Some people say that if we take away love, our earth will become a tomb. To testify whether it is true or not, we require to understand the real meaning of love and know how it influences people's life. Love is a kind of emotion expressing our likeness, happiness, our care or concern about someone or something we treasure, we like, we want and we need, not only between human beings, but also between man and other living things in the world, including animals, plants, our earth and our environment. We cannot live without love.

Some people do not understand this. They think love is the sole feeling among human beings so they care more about people around them while care less about the nature and environment related to them. It's a paradox that we depend on our earth so much but most of us ignore it. It is also a paradox that some people spend great efforts building up good relationship with other people but destroying the relationship between mankind and the place they rely on.

For relationship between mankind and environment, we have to understand all the factors that lead to a real meaningful life. The place where we live is not an isolated place, in which human beings mix together with a lot of other things like animals, plants and all the elements involved to make it a proper environment for us to live. In a larger sense, we can say that everything in this world is part of our life. If we want to have a good life, we have to keep good relationship with all those things by giving our care, our love, our concern to them. Animals are our friends. We should not treat them ill. Green trees, clean air and fresh water are things we should treat them as brothers. Our earth is our mother. We should give our true love and our best gratitude to it for her great generosity to provide us so much rich resource.

With love and care, children laugh and play. With love and care, people work and live. With love and care, the elderly enjoy their age. With man's love and concern to other living things, they give us a sound ecosystem in return. With man's love and concern to our earth, it gives us resource in return. With man's love and concern to our environment, it gives us a warm and comfortable home in return, decorated with green trees, beautiful flowers, fresh air and clean water. Paying no attention to all those things, we will not get what we want any longer. Ignoring those things, we will not enjoy our life any more. Destroying those things, we will pay for it forever.

So, love and being loved to ourselves, love and being loved to all those things. See them as our sisters and brothers. Treat them as our close friends. We need a world full of love. We never want a world without it.

评析：这篇文章的作者在第一段的写作方法上和前一篇文章的作者很相似，就是把love的外延扩大到了所有的生命体，提出我们不能没有爱，在正文中也使用三段来分析为什么我们不能没有爱。

尽管作者没有采用明显的连接词，但是逻辑脉络非常清楚。

在第二部分第一小段，作者揭示了某些人对爱的误解，指出人类的某些行为是一种矛盾。

在第二部分第二小段，作者解释了万事万物为一体的问题，它环环相扣，进一步强化爱的关系：想过上好日子，就必须与其他生命保持良好的关系，关心和爱护所有的生命。

在第二部分第三小段，作者采用排比的手法来强调爱的作用，使得观点进一步得到支持。

这篇作文在句式上也非常优美，而且字数足够，内容紧凑，结论也非常可靠。

第二部分通常是写作的核心，灵活性比较大，不像第一部分和结尾那样相对机械。对一个问题的分析直接反映出作者的思维能力，包括看待问题是否全面、主次是否分明、论证是否可靠等，所有这一切我们都需要逐步加强。我们将在后面的几个章节中更加详细地展开论述。

综上所述，第二部分是写作的核心，它通过具体的例子或证据来证明第一部分的观点能否成立、是否有可信度。鉴于高级作文的字数要求较多，这一部分通常会有几个小段，而不是一个小段。写作者不要机械地把作文写成三段，而必须根据作文要求字数的多少来合理分配段落。另外，要注意通过连接词或转折词来确定逻辑框架，因为英语最看重的就是逻辑关系。高分作文无一例外都有很好的逻辑框架。

3. 第三部分：结尾

在结构上，文章无论长短，其结尾都很短。我们先看看《词典的作用究竟是什么？》这篇文章的结尾，这篇文章的正文多达十几段，但结尾却很短。

The new dictionary may have many faults. Nothing that tries to meet an ever-changing situation over a terrain as vast as contemporary English can hope to be free of them. And much in it is open to honest and informed disagreement. There can be linguistic objection to the eradication of proper names. The removal of guides to pronunciation from the root of every page may not have been worth the valuable space it saved. The new method of defining words of many meanings has disadvantages as well as advantages. And of the half million or more definitions, hundreds, possibly thousands, may seem inadequate or imprecise. To some (of whom I am one) the omission of the label "colloquial" will seem meritorious; to others it will seem a loss.

But one thing is certain: anyone who solemnly announces in the year 1962 that he will be guided in matters of English usage by a dictionary published in 1934 is talking ignorant and pretentious nonsense.

评析：结尾通常是归纳，三言两语概述要点或得出结论，其写作要求正如这个例子，无论正文多长，结尾都很短小。

丘吉尔的演讲《关于希特勒攻打苏联的演讲》亦然，结尾只有几行。

The Russian danger is therefore our danger, and the danger of the United States, just as the cause of any Russian fighting for his hearth and home is the cause of free men and free peoples in every quarter of the globe. Let us learn the lessons already taught by such cruel experience. Let us redouble our exertions, and strike with united strength while life and power remain.

评析：英语演讲的结尾和汉语很像，经常采用排比的手法来加强气势，其内容类似于口号，但是字数总是很少。

任何一篇阐释文体的作文，其结尾都是用2~3句话对前文内容进行简单概括，简单重复正文中的主要内容。正文中未提及的内容，即便是事实，一般也不要再引入。还有一点要注意，结尾的标识词有so，therefore，as a result，in a word，all in all等。because和however这些用在分析部分的标识词则不适合出现在结尾。

最后，我们看一下前面在文章开头部分列举的五篇TEM-8作文的结尾，这有助于增强我们的辨别能力。

例1

So, in my point of view, that is not suitable for the people using the work-from-home way to instead the working in the company. Just like our President Zhu said, human nature is always important in each time. That is home alone, friendship away.

评析：我们可以看出，该学生的语法基础很差，结尾也出现了好几个语法错误。"以我之见"可以说in my opinion或者from my point of view，后者使用介词in的很少。句型it is suitable to do sth.用得比较多，而不是it is suitable doing sth.。此外，instead用作动词用法也不正确。至于介词like后面，要么说what President Zhu said，要么改成as。但有一点可以肯定，他的结尾很规范，使用了表示结束的标识词so，而且对前文内容进行了简短概括。

例2

In a word, I would rather work in the company rather work from home. Working in company give us a chance to communicate with other people and close to other people. It let us more sociable. Working in company has many benefits. It made us know more about the personality and improve the communication.

评析：这个结尾结构规范，标识词用得也不错，遗憾的是有几个语法错误。通常，语法错误扣分很多，因此，大家一定要尽量避免出现这样的错误。

例3

All in all, working from home is now plausible with various advantages, and will possess a bright future with information technology.

评析：这个结尾虽然很短，但它依然符合规范，而且标识词很清楚，没有语法错误，没有涉及其他的内容，整段就一句话，非常简短、书面化。

例4

All in all, working from home seems a tempting option due to the high technology today, but something should stay just the way it was, for as human beings, dealing things face to face can never fall out of fashion.

评析：这个结尾和例3有些相似，都使用标识词all in all，都用动名词短语作主语，整段也是一句话，而且句式很优美，连接词all in all，but，for用得非常自然，逻辑关系非常清楚，读起来也十分流畅。值得强调的是，流畅是好作文的一个外在表现，如果逻辑关系混乱，语法错误多，文章是不可能流畅的。

例5

As far as I am concerned, SOHO working style is a valuable invention for both companies and societies. With the advancement of information technology and Internet, people can communicate and interact with each other from homes as smoothly as they do at offices. Increasingly, SOHO is emerging as an inevitable trend and companies and employees will work out new ways of cooperation and coordination in the future.

评析：这个结尾的字数要比例4的多一些，但也非常流畅，概括得很精准，句式很优美，用词比较高级，如increasingly，emerging，inevitable。

综上所述，结尾部分相对比较机械，没有正文部分那么灵活，但同样可以看出写作者水平的差距，包括语法是否准确、句式是否优美、是否使用转折词等方面。作文要得高分，写作者就必须从头到尾都保持良好的写作习惯。

第3章

英语写作的高分要素及技巧

必备的逻辑要素

作文要得高分涉及各个方面的问题，其中最主要的是语法和思维，或者说是从结构到逻辑，再到修辞。这里需要重点强调的是逻辑的重要性，因为大部分学生在语法知识层面的意识要远远大于逻辑层面。

对于逻辑问题，与其说学生不讲逻辑，还不如说他们讲的逻辑通常是生活逻辑，而非逻辑学科所要求的知识。

生活的逻辑和逻辑学科所研究的逻辑不是相同的概念。生活逻辑主要是指生活中的行事规律，未必是只能这样而不能那样的思维规则；而逻辑学科是研究思维的科学，它以规则为表现形式，规则就是规定只能这样，不能那样，在论证问题时，我们只能遵守这些规则，决不能违反它们。在生活层面，很多东西是可以变通的，包括语言的使用，因此，很多时候，我们规定论证过程中必须遵守的逻辑规则在日常交流中是可以违反的，这个问题我们在第4章会具体讨论。

很多学生在写作过程中不考虑逻辑要求，或者他们缺乏逻辑观念。比如，在大型写作考试中，题目要求定义一个概念，我们强调必须给出它的逻辑定义。所谓逻辑定义，就是采用逻辑上的定义方法，比如"属+种差"的方法，而不是全凭自己的理解，甚至比喻。

事实上，在需要解释说明的文体中，比如阐释文中，对所有概念的定义都必须是逻辑定义。逻辑定义的其中一条注意事项就是不能使用比喻，因为定义的目的是让读者了解这个东西是什么，而比喻只能让他们了解这个东西像什么，对于这个东西是什么，读者无从知晓。比如，有人把诗比喻成"凝固的音乐"，这在文学作品（如小说和诗歌）中是可以的，但是在阐释文体中绝对不行。"诗"的逻辑定义是：a piece of writing in which the words are chosen for their sound and the images they suggest, not just for their obvious meanings. The words are arranged in separate lines, usually with a repeated rhyme, and often the lines rhyme at the end.

通常，我们建议学生养成查词典的习惯，看一个概念在词典中是如何解释的，这样就会把经验和常识规范化，而不至于用经验来取代科学。

在定义上，有的学生显得非常随意，或比喻，或感想，或诗情画意，唯独离逻辑要求相差甚远。这说明很多学生根本没有定义的概念，我们来看高级写作任务中的几个例子。

例1

考研，是当我们毕业时，不确定想做什么时，做出的一种决定。

例2

Going for business is like an adventure which some people eager to take. Actually, it is a job which we choose to do at our spare time.

例3

Helping others is a kind of feeling, which we use to express our kindness and our enthusiasm.

评析：这三个例子在高级写作任务中都是不符合要求的，属于

"诗情画意"类，这样的解释让人搞不懂这些概念的意思究竟是什么。"考研"是一种行为，不是决定。"经商"则是商业活动，不能说成是冒险，更不是闲暇时所选择的工作。"助人"是行为，怎么会是情感呢？

要真正写出高级作文，就要补充逻辑知识。然而，我们无法在有限的篇幅中把逻辑知识讲透彻，只能补充一些最基本的、直接影响我们写作的逻辑知识。

（一）逻辑的魅力

其实，逻辑是最美的学科，因为它确实会让人变聪明。

逻辑可以让人有好的推断能力；可以看出一个问题会引起什么结果；可以判断问题有多少种可能，并进行快速的策略调整。逻辑并非晦涩难懂的知识；相反，它渗透在我们的生活当中，使得我们的生活更加有趣。我们来看几个例子，领略一下逻辑的魅力。

例1

下课铃响了之后，后面来了一个人，他很年轻，手提电脑，站在上课老师身边等着。那位老师不好意思地说："对不起，老师，我动作慢了点。"等待的年轻人说："我不是老师，我是帮我们老师拿电脑的。我有那么老吗？"

"哦，你不老，可是我们有这么年轻的老师啊！"上课老师笑着回答。

例2

快下班的时候，有个人到储蓄所取钱，业务员听说他要取一万块，立刻说："没钱！"

那个人有些着急，于是嗓门就大了点，业务员因此说："你以为你声音大就有理了吗？"

那个人反问道，"难道声音小，就一定有理吗？"

储蓄所的负责人很快从里屋走出来，对业务员说，"赶紧把钱给她！"

例3

一对夫妇去邮局给孩子寄包裹，赶到邮局时是下午五点差几分，还没有下班。柜台前的服务员却说："今天不寄了，没有箱子了。"

男士说："哦，只能明天来了吗？"

女士则走到柜台前，看着上边摆放的工作牌说："我要投诉你！"

于是，服务员扭头朝她身后站着的两个工作人员大声说："还不去找箱子！"

包裹因此寄走了！

以上三个例子说明说话人思维敏捷，善于推理。例1说明老师里面确实有很年轻的人。例2说明声音太小主要和情绪有关，和有没有道理关系不是很大，因此"声音大就有理了吗"经不起推敲。例3说明没有箱子不是不营业的理由，经不起投诉。由此可见，逻辑其实是非常有趣的东西。学好逻辑，我们会变得善辩；学好逻辑，我们的思想才会深刻，提出问题时才能切中要害。知识装上逻辑的翅膀，原本枯燥的学习和生活会变得趣味盎然。

（二）逻辑的定义和功能

关于逻辑，我们必须先了解下面一些知识。

逻辑是研究思维的一门学科（Logic is the science of thinking.）。要正确思考，就必须了解逻辑规则。

逻辑这个词除了表示逻辑学科之外，在上下文中有不同的含义。比如，"你这是什么逻辑？"是口语里表示观点或看法的一种方式；在"我们研究该事物的逻辑"中，是指事物发展的规律或规则；在"合乎逻辑"中，是指人类总结的规律或规则。

而我们平常学习的是普通逻辑，它是研究思维的逻辑形式、逻辑规律以及简单的逻辑方法的科学（王向清，2006），其功能有以下四方面：

第一，普通逻辑是由已知到未知的必要工具；

第二，普通逻辑是人们论证思想和表达思想的必要工具；

第三，普通逻辑是揭露逻辑错误，批判诡辩的有力工具；

第四，普通逻辑是人们提高办事效率的重要工具。

（三）概念及其定义

1. 什么是概念？

概念是反映一个事物本质属性的思维过程。简单地说，概念就是万事万物的名称，它们用词语来表示，比如老师、学生、教室、桌子、椅子、电扇、黑板、粉笔等。所谓"本质属性"，是指一个事物区别于其他事物的特点，是一个事物特有的属性。比如，黑板和地板不同，一个是用来写字的，另一个是用来走路的。

既然事物的本质属性是指一个事物区别于其他事物的属性，那么，如果未能揭示出事物的本质属性，就可能引起歧义或被人钻空子。比如一位哲学家说："人，两足无毛也。"他的弟子就拎着一只拔光了毛的鸡给老师看，并笑称："老师，有人来探望你了！"

明确概念是写作中的一个至关重要的问题，因为写作中出现的一些重大错误，如跑题和偏题，都涉及概念。

我们在思考问题，继而进行写作时，要始终抓住概念，因为概念是思维的起点。只有明确了概念，才能正确思维，从而写出高水平的作文。但是，搞清楚概念不仅仅是为了写作文，它还能为我们的未来铺平道路，让我们生活得更有意义。

通常，一个知其然并知其所以然的人，生活得更轻松自在，因为他知道事情的原委；而要做到知其然并知其所以然，必定要有良好的逻辑知识和逻辑思维。比如，下面这条娱乐短信转发率特别高，因为编辑短信的人对概念的把握特别到位。

女：我想要两朵花。

男：什么花？

女：有钱花，使劲花。

男：你很美。

女：怎么美？

男：想得美！

评析：其实这是一个很简单的逻辑概念问题，使用了偷换概念的手法，用相同的语词表达不同的含义。"花钱"的花和"花朵"的花不是同一个概念。同理，"外表美"的美和"想得美"的美也不是同一个概念。

总之，只要我们把握好概念，就能解决很多问题。另外，在生活之路上，我们可以借助这个能力把事情做得更好。

2. 概念的内涵和外延

概念包括内涵和外延两部分。内涵就是概念的含义，外延是指概念使用的对象或适用范围。比如，"教师"的含义是"从事教书工作的人"，而它的外延是指任何以教书为职业的人；又比如，"食腐动物"是指以动物尸体为食的动物，比如秃鹫，其他动物则不算；再比如，"候鸟"是指随着季节迁徙的鸟类，其他的鸟则不算。我们再来看几个英语概念：a teacher is a person，an apple is a kind of fruit，a door is a material for opening or closing。

在写作过程中，我们首先要明确概念是什么，尤其要清楚它的外延，因为很多情况下我们会通过对一个概念外延的把握来凸显我们的写作意义。

对一个概念加以限定会使得该概念的外延放大或缩小。比如，上文说"教师"的外延是指任何以教书为职业的人，可是"清华大学的教师"外延就很小，它指的是在清华大学教书的人，别的学校的教师就不在这个范围内了。

概念明确，就是概念的内涵和外延明确。明确概念的内涵和外延对于准确地把握概念是十分重要的。

概念的内涵和外延是相互依存、相互制约的。确定了某一概念的内涵，也就相应地确定了这个概念的外延；反之，某一概念的外延确定以后，其内涵也就能确定下来。

但有一点我们要明确，随着客观对象的发展变化和人们认识的不断深化，概念的含义和适用对象是会发生变化的。

3. 概念的定义方法

定义由三部分组成：被定义项、定义项和定义联项。

定义概念通常有两种方式：一种是语词定义法；一种是"属+种差"的方法。

语词定义法是指通过解释语词的含义来揭示对象的特有属性，从而明确概念内涵的定义方法。比如，"舅舅"是妈妈的哥哥或者弟弟。这种概念比较少，我们就不介绍了。这里重点介绍"属+种差"的方法。

这种方法通俗地讲就是两点：第一，把概念放入它的最大范畴之下；第二，突出它与范畴中其他事物之间的区别。比如"教师"，首先，"教师"属于"人"的范畴；其次，教师与其他人的区别是教书。

鉴于阐释文写作中的定义都是逻辑定义，我们要养成查词典的习惯，因为词典里的解释大都属于这一类定义。

4. 概念的定义规则

解释概念必须符合逻辑规则，而不能违反逻辑规则，其逻辑规则主要有四条。

第一，定义项的外延和被定义项的外延必须完全相同，既不能大于被定义项，也不能小于被定义项，否则会犯"定义过宽"或者"定义过窄"的逻辑错误。比如，商品是用来交换的劳动产品。如果说商品是"劳动产品"则定义过宽，如果说商品是"用来交换的工业产品"则定义过窄。

第二，定义项中不能直接或间接地包含被定义项，否则就会犯"同义反复"或者"循环定义"的逻辑错误。这等于用不明确的部分去解释不明确的部分，结果还是不明确。比如，在《词典的作用究竟是什么？》一文中，如果作者对"门"的解释是a door is just a door，读者就搞不清楚a door到底是什么。

第三，定义项中不能用比喻，而且必须概念明确。定义的目的是要让读者知道某一事物是什么，而比喻只能让他们知道它像什么。比如，上面我们提到的"诗是凝固的音乐"，可是，诗到底是什么读者不得而知。

第四，对定义的解说必须是肯定的，不能用否定形式。其道理同第三，因为你的目的是要让他人知道某一事物是什么，而不是它不是什么。

（四）逻辑三律

同一律、矛盾律和排中律构成逻辑三律，是我们必须严格遵守的逻辑思维规律，尤其是同一律和矛盾律，我们必须特别熟悉，因为它直接决定我们论证的成败。

1. 同一律

同一律是指在同一个思维过程中，同一个概念或论题必须始终保持一致，不能中途改变，否则会出现"偷换概念"或"混淆概念"，抑或"偷换论题"或"转换论题"的逻辑错误。

偷换概念是一种故意的行为，也就是故意把一个概念的意思理解成另一个概念。比如，一个男老师看见女老师正在读《妇女之友》杂志，就说，"我就是妇女之友"。他显然是故意把该杂志的名字理解成了普通朋友的意思。

在张汉熙编写的《高级英语》第二册中，有一篇短篇小说叫 Love Is a Fallacy。它的主人公"我"的室友想得到一件浣熊皮大衣，他说，"I'd give anything for a raccoon coat. Anything!"而事实上，这位室友说的anything，双方都明白是自己拥有的、可以支配的东西，不包括不属于自己以及自己不能支配的东西，比如"我"的室友的女朋友，因为自己的女朋友不仅不属于自己，更不是"东西"。但是"我"就故意把anything理解成了天下所有的东西，因为"我"想用自己的浣熊大衣换室友的女朋友。

唐伯虎作诗为富婆祝寿的故事也属于这一类。当唐伯虎写第一句"这个老妇不是人"时，举座震惊，写第二句"好像南海观世音"时，大家就连连称颂。因为"不是人"三个字本来是骂人的话，有了第二句之后，它的意思就变成不是人类，而是神了。

混淆概念则是无意，或者出于无知，把一个概念搞错了。比如，小明的爸爸看到小明的评语里面写着"希望以后尊重师长"时，就着急地质问老师，"怎么可以给孩子灌输等级观念呢？师长要尊重，那么团长、连长、排长、班长就不要尊重了吗？"老师用的"师长"显然是老师、长辈的意思，而小明的爸爸理解成了职位，这就把不同的概念搞混了。

偷换论题或转换论题也是一样，故意转移话题就是偷换论题，我们在谈话或者讨论问题时经常会出现这类逻辑错误。

值得一提的是，我们必须对逻辑层面和修辞层面加以区别。当我们强调逻辑时，是指在说理或者论证的过程中必须遵守逻辑规则，任何违反逻辑规则的行为都是不允许的。而修辞层面则不然，在生活中，或者在说理以外的文体中，我们经常使用一些修辞手法，这些修辞手法可能是违反逻辑的，但是为了达到某一目的，它们也可以接受，因为修辞就是为了某一目的而故意采用某个词、结构或短语的过程，它可以是违反逻辑的。比如，有人喜欢开这样的玩笑，说自己一出门就下雨。没有人会说他违反逻辑，因为这是人们生活中调侃的一种方式，属于修辞层面。而在逻辑论证当中就绝对不允许，因为它属于"轻断因果"的逻辑谬误，天下雨是自然现象，与任何人无因果关系。又比如，在涉及某个令人尴尬的话题时，我们可能会故意把话题引开，这也算一种修辞技巧。生活中，这种偷换论题的方法被看成是一种语言艺术；而在逻辑论证过程中，偷换论题是一大谬误，凡是出现了逻辑谬误的论证，都是站不住脚的论证。写作中要求保持论题的同一性，如果转换了论题，作文就跑题了。讨论问题亦然，如果一方不停地转换论题，讨论就无法有效进行下去。

我们来看《高级英语》第一册中的一篇课文，它也是一篇短篇小说，叫Everyday Use for your grandmama（原文标题如此），它是著名黑人作家Alice Walker的作品。故事里的大女儿Dee非常自私，甚至不可理喻、胡搅蛮缠、无理取闹，当听说她改名为Wangero时，妈妈问她"What happened to 'Dee'?"女儿回答说自己无法忍受用压迫她的人的名字给她命名。原文是这样的："She's dead," Wangero said. "I couldn't bear it any longer, being named after the people who oppress me." 她妈妈回答说："你很清楚，你的名字是以你姨的名字来命名的，而她是我的姐姐。"这当然说明女儿改名字的理由站不住脚，可是女儿继续说："那她的名字是哪儿来的呢？"妈妈告诉女儿说她姐姐的名字是以她祖母的名字命名的。女儿就是不承认自己的无理，继续胡搅蛮缠地问："那祖母的名字又是以谁的名字命名的呢？"这已经和"压迫自己的人"完全没有一点关系了。相反，妈妈在一开始就已经否定了她给出的理由。可见，做什么事都必须有良好的逻辑思维。

2. 矛盾律

矛盾律是指在同一思维过程中，两个相互否定的思想不能同时为真，必有一假。

中国自古就有矛与盾的典故，因此我们对矛盾问题还是比较清楚的，包括言语之间的矛盾、言行之间的矛盾等。但是，根据我批改作文的经验，在实际写作当中，有的人似乎没有矛盾的意识。

以Should College Students Go in for Business?为例，前面我们谈到，对于一个命题，你持肯定或者否定的态度，批改试卷的老师并不在意，他在意的只是你能否拿出有力的证据来支持自己的观点。有力的证据首先是符合逻辑的证据。

对于这个命题，大部分学生都持否定的态度，因为这个角度相对更容易写，比较容易找到理由。首先，学生的主要任务是学习，学习需要时间和精力，而经商需要耗费他们太多的时间和精力等；其次，一般学校都不提倡学生经商。

有位学生选择同意大学生经商，遗憾的是，他论证的时候这么说，"以比尔·盖茨为例，他就是大学期间创业的，而且他成了享誉全球的成功人士"。这个证据就太糟糕了，因为这是自相矛盾，而自相矛盾是最明显的不一致，如果论证中出现自相矛盾，就彻底丧失了可信度。比尔·盖茨确实是在大学期间创业的，可恰恰是因为时间和精力不够，他才中途退学的。

论证的过程中一定要让读者觉得你的证据可靠。谷振诣（2007）指出："可靠论证的一个最主要的因素是保持论证的一致性，如果论证所提供的理由不但不能成为支持主张的证据，反而成为削弱甚至否定其主张的证据，这无疑是论证中出现的最糟糕的错误。如果在理论体系发现自相矛盾的观点，就等于宣告这一理论的破产。"

因此，我们在提供证据的时候，千万要注意，不要犯逻辑错误，尤其不要自相矛盾。

3. 排中律

排中律是指在同一思维过程中，两个相互否定的思想不能同时为假，必有一真。比如性别，我们不能说一个人既不是男的，又不是女的。

王向清（2000）在《逻辑趣话》中讲了一个百鸟朝凤的故事，说凤凰过生日，所有鸟，除了蝙蝠，都前来朝凤，蝙蝠的理由是自己有脚，是走兽，不算鸟类。后来麒麟过生日，所有的走兽，除了蝙蝠，都来了，蝙蝠的理由是自己有翅膀，不算走兽。这就违反了排中律。

排中律的错误虽然比较少，但是作为思维规律的一部分，我们也必须知道。

（五）论证及其规则

鉴于大型考试中的写作一般都是阐释文，必须通过证据来证明自己的观点，那么，我们就必须熟悉逻辑证明的要求。

任何逻辑证明都是由论题、论据和论证三部分组成的。

论题是在一个逻辑证明中需要确定其真实性的那个命题，它解决"证明什么"的问题；论据是在一个逻辑证明中用来确定论题真实性的那些命题，它解决"用什么证明"的问题；而论证是一个过程或者方式，就是论题和论据的联系方式，即在证明中所运用的推理方式，它解决"怎样证明"的问题。

既然任何逻辑证明都是由论题、论据和论证组成的，那么，我们就要清楚论题、论据和论证的规则。

1. 论题的规则

首先，论题必须清楚、明确；其次，论题必须始终保持同一。

论题必须清楚，否则他人就不明白你到底要讨论什么。比如，在讨论考试舞弊问题时，有个学生拟题Door with Windows，这个题目太具文学气息了，读者不知道他准备写什么，这种题目就属于不明确的题目；又比如，在讨论人的主要性格是遗传的还是环境决定的问题时，有学生拟题Environment，读者很可能以为他要讨论环境问题，这样的题目也属于不明确的题目。所谓明确的题目是指和所要讨论的话题直接相关，一眼就让人知道你要讨论什么问题的题目。

论题保持同一，就是要求我们不能违反同一律。论题是什么，就必须始终围绕这个问题来讨论，不能再去讨论其他问题，否则就会出现跑题或偏题的问题。

2. 论据的规则

首先，论据必须是已知为真的命题；其次，论据的真实性不能依赖论题来证明。

论据是用来证明论题的真实性的判断，如果论据本身不真，或者尚未被证实为真，则起不到证明论题真实性的作用。违反这条规则就会犯"虚假论据"或"预期理由"的错误。可以充当论据的判断一般有已经证实的关于事实的判断，以及科学概念的定义和公理、原理等。也就是说，不要用假设或者非真实的情景或判断来充当论据，比如小说、电影等。

论据除了必须为真以外，它还必须与论题直接相关，就好比你讨论的是李老师为人师表的问题，给出的却是张老师的事迹。虽然关于张老师的事迹都是真的，但无法证明李老师是如何为人师表的。

论题的真实性要靠论据来证明，而论据的真实性则要靠其他证据材料来证明。假如论据的真实性没有其他材料来证明，而是要反过来依赖论题证明，那么证来证去，等于没有证明。违反这条规则就会犯"循环论证"的逻辑错误。

"循环论证"是一个非常严重的问题，缺乏逻辑常识的人可能会不小心犯严重的逻辑错误。我们一起来看看下面这篇作文。为了强调学生和老师都要加强逻辑学习，我们把批改该作文的老师的评语也列在下面。

The More I Learn, the More Ignorant I Find Myself to Be

As soon as I was enrolled in college, I felt a big burden off my mind. So did my classmates. We just wanted to relax. But at our first English lesson on how to improve our study the teacher told us, "There is no end to learning. The more you learn, the more ignorant you will find yourself to be. The only way you can do is to work hard to learn more."

The teacher's words awaken me and remind me of the ignorant few who claim to have all of the answers to man and life but know less than you or I, and who, with their hands <u>held</u> up high, offer everything you may have wanted to know about life itself, but when pushed and pried know nothing but what they are told. Now I am a postgraduate, and life has taught me too many harsh lessons. <u>The more I learn and experience, the more I realize how little I know</u>. Therefore, bearing in mind the motto that there is no end to learning, I keep on my studies. I do not only learn from the books, but also from experiences, as practice makes perfect.

For all of my efforts, I am fully aware of how far I am away from the sea of knowledge. <u>The more I learn, the more ignorant I find myself to be</u> and the more I feel the need to learn. Art is long, and life is short.

老师评语：该文章比较简单，但段与段以及句与句之间衔接得很自然，文章一气呵成，不失为一篇好文章。作者以亲身经历的一件事开头，引出本文的中心论题：学得越多，越觉得要学的东西多，显得自然而不冗余；然后以 awaken me 过渡到第二段，进一步展开论述。首先，文章提到学术界有些人自以为什么都知道，什么问题都可以解答，但当被真正问及要点时，却哑口无言。接着，作者从自身的角度说明学习是无止境的。第三段重申中心论题，起到了画龙点睛的作用。

评析：讲老实话，这篇作文在结构上非常漂亮，短小精悍。批改作文的老师评论说"该文章比较简单，但段与段以及句与句之间衔接得很自然，文章一气呵成，不失为一篇好文章"。对于简单、自然、一气呵成，我都同意，对于不失为一篇好文章，我则不敢苟同。为什么呢？

论题的字面意思是越学越觉得无知，也就是学得越多，想知道的越多。有一句类似的中文，可以帮助我们理解，即"已知的东西扩大一寸，未知的东西扩大一尺"。

论题既然是学得越多，想知道的越多，当然需要我们拿出有力的证据来证明这一观点。可是，在第二段第一句，作者说，"老师的话让我猛然醒悟，并想起一些无知者，他们宣称无所不知，事实证明与你我无二；他们举起双手，仿佛什么都可以回答，被问及要点时却毫无新意。我们相信这一论据是真的，但是他人无知，可以证明自己什么呢？这不是和我们上面提到的证明李老师为人师表，给出的却是张老师的事迹同出一辙吗？而且这一部分就占据了作文一半的内容。

接下来，作者说Now I am a postgraduate, and life has taught me too many harsh lessons，我们相信这也是真的，可是这和论题又有多大关系呢？生活磨砺了你，你就觉得无知要读书了吗？博学多才的人也可能受到生活的磨砺啊！

我们重点提一下三个画线的句子，它们恰巧就是所要讨论的论题。作者用在第一段以引出话题，这是可以的，在结尾重复，也能接受。可是在第二段充当论据则不妥，因为这涉嫌"循环论证"，也就是用论题充当论据。通篇都重复一个论题，这样的论证怎么会有说服力？

文章的最后一句话"Art is long, and life is short."也很美，因为它采用了antithesis（对比）的修辞手法，其意思是"生命短暂，艺术长存"。可是，在这里起什么作用呢？它和论题有什么关系？

由此，我们可以看出，尽管作者的论据是真的，这篇作文却存在两大逻辑问题：一是论据相关性不足；二是违反了论据规则第二条"论据的真实性不能依赖论题来证明"，犯了"循环论证"的逻辑错误。这位批改作文的老师也可能因欠缺逻辑知识而无法识别学生的错误。因此，我们每个人都应该努力掌握一些逻辑常识。

3. 论证的规则

论证的规则就是指论题应是从论据推出的合乎逻辑的命题。违反这条规则就会犯"推不出论题"的错误。比如，一个论证的论据虽然是真的，与论题也有一定联系，但如果论题不是从这些论据中合乎逻辑地推出的，这些论据就是不充分的理由。同时，在论证过程中，如果论据与论题之间没有内在的必然联系，就不能成为证明论题的论据。

在学习对比手法时，有个学生写了这样一篇作文：

Class One and Class Two

There are two classes in our grade: Class One and Class Two. I am in Class One.

Our class is quite different from the other one. The students in Class Two are more active. We are inactive. They always speak aloud their opinions in class so that the teachers who teach them are very pleased to hear that while most of the students in our class keep quiet. They study harder than we do. In the morning when we are still in bed, they already read loudly in the campus. In the evening when we go to bed, they still read in the library.

Although there are so many differences between our class and the other class, I like our class better.

评析：这篇作文的对比手法用得还是不错的，写作者通过例子把两个班的差异表现得非常清楚。但最后那句话让人感觉太牵强，太突兀了，从逻辑角度来说，这属于犯了"推不出"的逻辑错误。假如我们把后面的话改成"这些差异有的需要我们改进，有的则是性格决定的"之类的句子，会显得更加顺理成章。

作文的审题和拟题及其技巧

审题是写作的第一个环节。审题意味着已经给出了题目。很多考试中作文都会给出题目，这样就无须自己拟题了。但有些考试的作文只给出情景或要求，需要自己拟题，在这种情况下，没有拟题是要扣分的，因为批改作文的老师总是根据写作者的题目来判断作文的好坏，包括作文是否跑题或偏题。如果连题目都没有，怎么知道好坏呢？因此，我们不能忽视这个问题。

（一）题目中的概念

从概念的数量上看，题目通常有三种类型：一是单概念题目，比如Ambition；二是双概念题目，比如Science and Religion，或者Morality and Law；三是多概念题目，即包含两个以上概念的题目。

请看看下面的题目，判断一下它们属于哪一种题目。

- My View on Terrorist Explosions in Some Countries
- My View on Job-hopping
- My View on Taking Part in the Postgraduate Entrance Exams
- My View on the Craze for Mo Yan
- Waste on Campus
- On Reading
- Graduation Means Unemployment?
- Not Living Together with Parents Means Unfilial Piety?
- Always Remember Your Next Door Neighbours

- The Role of Computers Today
- Competition or Cooperation
- Essential Qualities: Inherited or Not?
- Do Husbands or Wives Do Housework?
- Do Looks Really Count?
- Should University Students Go in for Business?
- Winning Sometimes Is Losing
- Work and Life
- Good News Is Bad News

1. 单概念题目

从审题的角度来说，单概念题目当然更好理解，因为它只涉及一个概念，但这不等于说单概念题目更好写。比如，从小到大，无论汉语还是英语，考试中经常让我们写的My Mother就是典型的单概念题目，但并不表示这个题目学生都可以写好，因为它同样涉及许多要素，包括语法规范、逻辑关系、修辞手法，等等。

我们一起来评析两篇关于My Mother的作文，看看好作文是怎样的。

例 1

My Mother

My mother is not same as millions of mothers. She's quite different from the mothers of my classmates'. Most of them look young and active. My mother is not.

My mother is only 42 years old. Yet she looks more than 50. And she's very dull. In addition, she never goes out of her native town in her life. However, she always meets my desire for travelling around during summer holidays every year.

She knows little about the world. She doesn't even know America. She does cleaning job, a job which we are very familiar with and where the workers do dirty and hard work with a little money.

She has two slanted eyes. When she looks at me, I often think she's looking aside. She seldom laughs. I usually make a judgment of her mood by listening to her speaking ways. If she speaks slowly and unclearly, she is in a bad mood. If she speaks in a fast and clear way, she has a good mood. Most of the slow people respond this way. The truth is that every time when I say to her I'd like to have a trip with my friends, she makes a quick response. "No problem. No problem." She always says this and gives me some money to enjoy my holiday.

When a boy I love stared at me after hearing this and turned away, and one day when I read in a newspaper the news that my mother not only did job during the day but also did work at night, I was astonished and realized how selfish I was. My heart trembled with shame and I cried aloud.

I'm going to ask for her forgiving my ignorance and my failure in filial and go travelling with her one day when I get the salary of my own.

评析：我们每个人都想过或者写过自己的母亲，可是为什么有的人写得平平淡淡，有的人含糊地回答没有什么可写？这是不懂写作的表现。写一个人，包括自己的母亲，不一定要写她有多好看的外表，也不一定要写她有多么了不起的成就，你可以把她的某一个点亮化，以便给读者带来某种启迪、思考或享受。

在这篇作文里，作者花了不少笔墨来写母亲残疾的一面，比如迟钝、眼睛有些斜视，然而，这篇作文的巧妙布局正是从这里展开的，因为这些外表的缺陷非但没有影响母亲对自己的爱，反而更加衬托了母亲高尚深沉的爱。她很少笑，作者必须通过她说话的方式来判断她的情绪。如果她说得缓慢不清，就说明她心情不是很好；如果说得流利而清晰，就说明她心情不错。大部分迟钝的人都是这样的，可是每次我说想和朋友外出旅行时，她都反应很快。大家想一想，对于一个这么辛苦的母亲而言，女儿的这种奢侈消费多让她为难，多影响她的情绪啊！可是母亲不仅反应迅速，而且回答得很干脆，"没问题，没问题！"作者通过这样一些小例子，达到了震撼我们心灵的目的："我母亲从来都没有走出过自己的家乡，她不了解世界，她甚至连美国都不知道！"

这个和大部分年轻、反应积极的母亲不同的母亲不会用大道理来教育作者，而是用实际行动来让作者醒悟。为了满足作者的享乐，妈妈不仅要上白班，还要上晚班。

有人可能会觉得文章的作者很自私，可是我们对作文的评价是针对论题来讨论和分析的，不能转换成对作者的品行进行评论。

其实作者是非常成功的，她深知自己的行为自私，为此她感到极度羞愧，甚至痛哭流涕。在这种铺垫、衬托之下，一个朴实感人的母亲形象脱颖而出。

作者的成功还在于她的英语思维习惯，她遵守了英语写作的规范：句式漂亮、主次分明、使用总分结构，让作文句与句之间的关系非常密切且自然，读起来特别流畅，因此，这绝对是一篇高分作文。

例2

My Mother

I was a naughty boy. I did many wrong things when I was young. My father was always angry to me and punished me every time when I made a mistake. But my mother treated me very kindly.

I remember one day when I broke an expensive plate, my

father hit me on the head which made me fall down on the ground. My mother stopped him and sent me to the hospital. I stayed in the hospital for three days. My father did not come to see me while my mother did not leave a minute, looking after me carefully. I always felt warm and grateful to her kindness to me.

That is my mother. She is a kind and gentle woman with big and bright eyes which make her look beautiful.

She is now fifty years old. I hope her to keep young and beautiful. I also hope her to live a happy life forever.

评析：读完这篇作文，我们首先感觉到它的中式思维很明显，而且很可能是随想随译的作文，作者没有想清楚就开始写。一位美国写作专家说过："想清楚了，不一定可以写清楚；但是没有想清楚，一定写不清楚。"这是很有道理的。

写作文时随想随写的现象非常普遍，我经常强调说，有的人写作的时候好像在做翻译，机械地把自己想到的一些内容变成了英语，丝毫没有考虑到写作不是把一个意思简单地翻译成另一种文字这么简单，而是通过修辞手法，把能够突出主题意义的内容组织成文字。所谓"作文"，就是把文字做成文章，其核心是组织，不是翻译。要组织成什么样的内容，达到什么目的，则是修辞的问题，我们在下一章将详细讨论。

这篇作文最大的问题还要算是偏题，文章的题目是My Mother，可是作者张口闭口我父亲怎样，尤其是第一段第一句，说我是个调皮的孩子，仿佛讨论的是"我"的所作所为，母亲只是陪衬而已。

对比例1和例2，我们就可以发现哪个写得好，哪个写得不好，因为我们可以根据好作文的要求来进行评价。

综上所述，单概念题目是指只有一个概念的题目，但它不意味着作文就好写。好的作文需要我们在下笔之前先构思好，再通过修辞手法把内容组织起来，最后翻译成另一种语言，而不是随想随译。

2. 双概念题目

双概念题目就是包含两个概念的题目，通常我们要注意这两个概念之间的关系，它们可能是对立关系，也可能是对立统一关系。只字不提二者之间的关系，我们会觉得很不好写。有时，把相互之间的关系搞反了也不好写。比如Science and Religion这个题目，有人张口就说它们是非此即彼的关系。这不准确，科学和宗教之间是对立统一的关系，有一句话可以给我们重要的启示："宗教是孕育科学之母"。

我们来看看下面这个情景：

Some people say, the trouble with most of us is that we would rather be ruined by praise than saved by criticism. Please discuss it. (800 words)

这是上海经贸大学商务英语专业研究生入学考试的写作真题，它只简单要求学生讨论，字数要求为800词。

我们先做个简单的分析。有人说，大部分人的毛病是宁愿毁于夸赞，也不愿被批评拯救。情景中给了"表扬"和"批评"两个概念，它们之间是我们熟悉的对立统一关系，关注它们之间的关系会让我们更好地整理思路。

我们一起来欣赏一篇考生的作文。

Praise and Criticism

Some people say that the trouble with most of us is that we would rather be ruined by praise than saved by criticism, which indicates a current phenomenon of praise everywhere but criticism nowhere.

It is true that praise is pleasant to our ears and most of us like it. It is also true that praise can be read and heard at any place from public speeches, work reports, work summaries, meetings, news reports to evaluations, etc. On the contrary, criticism, if any, is about some tiny things that do not matter.

It seems that everything in our work and in our society is now so wonderful that nothing needs to be improved. Is it really true that work in every field is good enough? And is it really true that we could be optimistic and feel safe about everything around us? If it is true, then what about those serious accidents like big fire here and there, building breaking now and then, killing the innocent by fake and inferior goods? If it is true, then how can we explain the unjustness in juridical and from enforceable organizations? If it is true, then how can we explain buying and selling a position, illegal exchanges in education, in academic and in almost all walks of life?

So monstrous a discrepancy in evaluation requires us to examine the relationship between praise and criticism and examine what criticism is for. In the process of evaluation, praise and criticism are two sides of it. The former evaluates a person, an object or an idea in terms of good words, while the latter, on the contrary, points out faults in terms of criticism or even severe words. Praise can motivate people to do things more and better. Praise expresses that something is good or acceptable or satisfactory. The gist lies in things are really good. For bad things or things not that good, people criticize. Criticism helps us find out what problems we still have and helps us correct them. We know that if we want to correct mistakes, we should first find out what those mistakes are. If we want to solve problems, we should first know what problems we have. Criticism also helps us make less mistakes, which means if we know someone will criticize us for failing to perform our duties properly, we'll try to do things better at the very start. In that case, criticism has the function of supervising, thus making sure that things will be done properly. The core of it is to show disapproval to what we have done improperly. To say everything is good, the value of the measure will lose, thus decreasing the reliability of the evaluation and the result cannot reflect the truth. To give praise to bad things or improper things is not praise but fake, fraud, deceit or concealment.

As to concealment，the consequence is serious and sometimes disastrous. Take SARS for example. When someone tried to cover the fact that SARS patients were found in China and things were grave, it caused very bad result: public fear, many victims lost their lives, great damage to China's image, followed by a lot of severe attack from all over the world. It was the sharp words that made Chinese government take immediate action against the illness. When it came to the end of the fighting, China regained a little of its prestige for the active support and aid to the SARS patients. Such kind of examples could be heard often in our work and life which became the main cause of many terrible events. So, in order to avoid tragedies like these, in order to ensure people's life and to protect a country's benefits, it is the government's responsibility to make sure that both praise and criticism can be heard at all levels.

For a country, or any country that claims to be democratic, that pursues development, different voices will be welcomed and accepted no matter it is good or bad, praise or criticism, so that a freer, safer and more prosperous world can be created.

To sum up, we are not difficult to find that, on the one hand, criticism is as important as praise in the process of evaluating something, an object or an idea. Neither can be ignored or overlooked. On the other hand, both praise and criticism need to be open, objective and appropriate. Overdoing any one of the two sides is not good for anyone, any organization and any country.

评析：作者把题目拟成双概念题《表扬和批评》，并在第一段先把情景给出来，然后再对情景进行解读，并指出处处有表扬无批评的现象。

在第二段，作者采用排比的修辞手法，交代赞美的言辞非常悦耳，大部分人都爱听，我们常常能在各种演讲、工作报告、总结中听到或看到，而批评的声音却都是无关痛痒的事情，这个过渡比较自然。

到了第三段，作者交代称赞意味着完美，然后连续采用多个反问句形成排比，引出赞美和批评的关系。这种分析法不仅顾及了双概念的两个方面，而且突出了它们缺一不可的关系。因此，尽管字数较多，文章条理还是比较清楚的，内容也比较紧凑。

3. 多概念题目

难度比较大的是多概念题目。多概念题目是指题目中有多个概念，通常比较长的题目都是多概念题目。我们看看下面一些题目：

- My Views on University Ranking
- Should Parents Send Their Kids to Art Classes?
- On the Importance of a Name
- How to Improve Students' Mental Health
- Will E-books Replace Traditional Books?
- A Letter Declining a Job Offer

- How to Reduce Waste on Campus

从上面的题目中我们可以看出，每个题目里面都包含好几个概念，这对于有些人来说会感觉无从下手。其实，不管是单概念题目、双概念题目或多概念题目，都要紧扣概念，把握概念的内涵和外延以及和概念相关的要素。

与单概念题目和双概念题目不同的是，多概念题目需要我们判断哪个概念更重要，也就是说面对多概念题目，我们必须抓主要概念，而不是次要概念，否则，很可能说不清楚问题，甚至可能会偏题。

很多人纠结的问题就是审不清楚题目，从而导致写作失败。因此，我们下面专门来讨论审题问题，尤其是多概念题目的审题问题。

（二）审题方面的问题

审题是写作的首要步骤，也是最重要的步骤，它决定我们要突出哪些信息，决定我们是否会跑题或偏题，决定我们能否把框架搭好。

如果题目是My Mother，而你大谈特谈你的父亲，这个题目就没有审清楚。

在审题过程中，我们通常就把写作提纲列出来了。审清楚题了，提纲就会比较有条理；反之，审不清楚题，往往会无从下手。

审题通常需要掌握两大要点：一是要确定主要概念，然后寻找相关信息；二是要做到有条理，不要思维混乱。

主要概念通常就是需要突出的概念，它也有两点需要注意：一是尽快交代要突出的信息，有时可以在作文第一句就把要突出的信息写出来，不要在其他信息上过多纠缠；二是需要突出的信息的字数要比其他信息的字数多，不要在次要信息上浪费过多笔墨。

1. 主要概念和相关信息

主要概念是作文要突出的信息，信息的相关性是指与主要概念相关的信息。

我们先举The Power of Language为例，该命题的主要概念当然是the power。作者只罗列出语言的作用是不够的，还必须在语言的力量上有所阐释，否则就有偏题的嫌疑，因为题目并不是简单地讨论语言及其作用，而是要突出语言的力量。

Power是我们需要花更多笔墨去描写的概念，language在语法关系上不过是the power的限定成分。如果侧重语言的功能，题目拟为The Function of Language更合适。

那么，与它们相关的信息有哪些呢？比如，什么是语言，其功能是什么。交代了语言的定义及其功能通常还不够，因为题目的侧重点不是讨论语言的功能。语言不过是一种工具而已，使用语言的人才是一大相关要素，比如，有的人把语言当作武器，间接杀人。善用语言的人有哪些呢？这样的例子当然不难找，关键是你会从相关性方面一步一步思考下去，比如诸葛亮骂周瑜就是个好例子。周瑜被诸葛亮骂了之后气得吐血，结果，诸葛亮不费一兵一卒，用语言就使得对方败下阵去，这就是语言的力量。当然，也有善用语言者，他们把语言当成是一剂良药，用来安抚受伤的人，鼓励受挫的人，这方面的例子也很多。

为了使作文思路清楚，并达到字数要求，我们可以从正反两方面来说明或论证。下面我们一起来看看下面这篇关于语言的力量的作文。

The Power of Language

Language is a tool used to communicate and to express our feelings or emotions and thoughts in our work, study and life. Language is the distinction of mankind from other species. It is so powerful that without it, man might not be the dominant of the earth and we cannot imagine what our world would be. I'll indicate the power of language from the following aspects.

First, it is because of language that human society can develop so quickly within hundred thousands of years, evolved from a primordial community to a modernized and civilized world, in which people enjoy life both in material and in culture.

Second, it is due to language, the relationship of men becomes closer, leading to the possibility of passing down the heritage from one generation to another.

However, language itself doesn't mean good or bad. It is the person who uses it can be called wonderful or not in using languages. Take Shakespeare, the master of language, for example, whose works are read even today. Readers feel profoundly enjoyable by appreciating his words. For some persons, languages can be a weapon. Take Kong Ming, the famous military counselor, for another example. He defeated his enemy, Zhou Yu, by using words instead of sword.

In real life, language can be used as placebo. We use it to comfort or inspire those who are hurt, embarrassed or frustrated. On the other hand, if it is not properly used, it might become a killer.

Therefore, language is powerful. With it, man is no longer common animals like monkeys or apes. With it, human society develops quickly and all the information can be descended down forever. If properly used, it can make us more harmonious. Let's have a good mastery of it. And let it help us live a better life.

评析：作者在第一段先对语言进行了简单的定义，指出它是用来交流和表达情感和思想的工具，然后提出与论题相近的观点：语言非常强大，没有它，人类称不上地球的主宰。

但作者不局限在语言的功能上。在第二部分第一段和第二段，他分析说正是因为有了语言，人类社会才飞速发展，在短短几十万年内，就由原始部落进化成了现代的文明社会，人们不仅在物质上，还在文化上享受生活。正是因为有了语言，人与人之间的关系才变得更加密切，文化遗产才可以代代相传。

接着，作者先笼统地写语言的强大功能，后面用两小段具体说明语言怎样强大，指出语言本身无所谓好坏，其不同在于驾驭语言的人。再从正反两方面举例说明我们可以借助语言来做什么。可见，作者非常擅于寻找相关信息，一点接一点，这样就不会毫无思路地凑字数。后面讨论流畅性的时候，我们还会提到这个问题，信息的相关度是决定作文是否流畅的主要原因；反之，信息不相关，作文读起来就不流畅。

接下来我们再看看2007年某校的研究生入学考试小作文，题目要求作者发现图书馆的某些不足后，给图书馆长写一封信。下面是一个学生的作文。

Dear Sir,

As you know, a library is the place the students often go to read. So I am writing to make some suggestions.

My first suggestion is that you should enhance the search scope so that students can find more information we want.

My second suggestion is that you should prolong the time of

the electronic reading room so we can have some more free time to come here to look for data.

We will be very happy if you pay prompt attention to our suggestions. That will be good to us.

评析：作者第一句话解释说图书馆是学生经常去看书的地方，这虽然可以，但不是很好，似乎是在说废话，谁不知道图书馆是学生看书的地方呢？就算它成立，它后面的内容应该是读书需要安静的环境之类的话语，可是作者却说"因此，我来给你们提建议"，这很突兀，显得前后很不相关。通常，提建议或意见之前应先说出某方面的不足，这二者是相关的，然而作者在没有提出问题之前，就提出了建议，显然不妥当。

因此，第一条要加强检索的建议就显得没来头，因为前面没有交代该图书馆是否在这方面有欠缺，可能人家有这项基本服务呢。第二条建议和第一条属于同一类问题，延长开放时间是好的，但作为写作，必须和前面的信息相关。

下面我们看看多概念题目中出现的同类问题，先看看下面这篇作文的开篇。

What's Your Opinions Toward the Rush for Post-Graduates' Entrance Exam?

The Post-Graduates' Entrance Exam is an exam or a choice when we don't want to look for a job after graduation. Many students make this choice before their leaving the college. I think it's a good choice. For myself, I attended last year's entrance examination for post graduates.

评析：这个开篇给人的感觉有些乱，作者没有按照常规来组织内容。照理来说，作者写出很多人考研的现状，然后再表明观点或分析其原因即可。但是，作者选择了写题目里面的次要信息，即研究生入学考试。之所以说它次要，是因为研究生入学考试是一个众所周知的概念，不一定要去解释或者强调它。一旦解释次要信息，主要信息就被掩盖了。即便写作者想交代一下，也要正确把握定义，先说研究生入学考试是an exam，然后补充说它是有人毕业时不想直接工作或想继续深造时做出的选择。把考研说成既是考试，又是机会，还扯到自己考研的问题，这样主次就不清楚，逻辑就乱了。

接下来我们看一个与是否救助他人有关的作文的开头。

Help or Not When Meeting Someone in Risk

Sometimes, when I meet someone who needs help, I want to give my hand to him. But my father says we'd better think twice before offering a help. Why don't other people offer their help? I am confused about that. Do we need to help those who are in risk?

评析：其实，该段落读起来感觉语言还是流畅的，里面也没有一个语法错误。但是，这一段文字里面涉及过多概念，"我""我父亲""需要帮助的人""其他人"，因此显得逻辑比较混乱，脉络根本不清晰。

写作时一次性把过多概念牵扯进来是我们必须要避免的问题，以保证作文思路清晰。思路清晰意味着思考问题要有层次和条理，意味着要清楚、准确地使用概念和语言。谷振诣（2007）指出，把事实问题、价值问题和情感问题交织在一起是导致思想混乱的根源。概念不清和语词滥用也会导致思想混乱。

总之，在审题时，注意抓住主要概念是非常重要的，主要概念很可能就是一到两个。试图把所有的概念都混在一起会导致思维和逻辑混乱。

2. 作文的条理

不混乱的反面就是有条理。条理是指思考、说话、做事有脉络、顺序清楚，好比画图时的线条一样，清晰可见，让人一目了然。有条理是良好思维的表现，所以，一般条理问题放在逻辑学科里学习。

那么，怎样才算是有条理呢？简单地说就是线条简洁。比如，分析一个问题的原因时我们把它分为两大方面，这样就比较简洁，条理就比较清晰。又如，在对事物进行分类时，一般分为两类或者三类是比较好的划分法。

条理清楚的文章读起来一定非常流畅；反之，过多线索或概念混在一起，条理就不清楚。我们来欣赏一下《大不列颠望洋兴叹》中的一段：

> The threat comes from two main directions: from the Russians and the Eastern bloc countries who are now in the middle of a massive expansion of their merchant navies, and carving their way into the international shipping trade by severely undercutting Western shipping companies; and from the merchant fleets of the developing nations, who are bent on taking over the lion's share of the trade between Europe and Africa, Asia and the Far East—routes in which Britain has a big stake.

参考译文：

　　威胁来自两大方面：一是来自苏联及东欧集团，他们正在大肆扩建商船队，通过拼命压西方船运公司价格挤入国际航运；二是来自发展中国家的商船队，他们试图在英国占大份额的欧洲与非洲航线、亚洲和远东航线分得一块肥肉。

评析：这是作者为《经济学家》杂志撰写的工业和劳资方面的

文章，在分析英国船运由繁荣走向衰败的原因时，他指出了上述两大方面原因，脉络十分清晰。

我们再来欣赏一下《沙漠之舟》中的一段：

> This century has witnessed dramatic changes in two key factors that define the physical reality of our relationship to the earth: a sudden and startling surge in human population, with the addition of one China's worth of people every ten years, and a sudden acceleration of the scientific and technological revolution, which has allowed an almost unimaginable magnification of our power to affect the world around us by burning, cutting, digging, moving, and transforming the physical matter that makes up the earth.

评析：这篇文章的作者是著名的环保人士阿尔·戈尔（Al Gore），即美国前总统克林顿的副总统。和《大不列颠望洋兴叹》一样，在分析复杂原因时，他也保持了最清晰的脉络，描述了两方面的变化。可见，好文章的作者都具有良好的逻辑思维，这是我们阅读时要认真学习和模仿的，以便我们也可以写出有条理的文章。

我们还要看一篇让小学生集体下跪以示感恩的作文。在作文的条理方面，它特别能说明问题。

Kneel Doesn't Mean Appreciation

Recently, I heard a news that some schools required their students kneel down to their parents to show their appreciation and claimed it is a part of traditional virtue education and we ought to pay more attention on it. My first thought is ridiculous when I knew about the purpose of the schools and their approaches to achieve it. Can you say for sure someone is appreciated for their parents simply through one simple behavior? <u>Of course not.</u>

<u>Appreciation</u> for their parents is indeed one of Chinese traditional virtues, and it is required for everyone <u>as a child.</u> It is good to remind us <u>pay</u> attention to <u>appreciation</u> because nowadays people care less about <u>appreciation</u> especially for their parents. But we don't have to show our <u>appreciation</u> for our parents by kneeling. <u>I think</u> such kind of daily behaviors, such as visiting and talking with them frequently or doing housework with them, are better methods to achieve this goal that let parents feel our <u>appreciation</u>. <u>And</u> their relationship <u>becomes</u> closer. <u>I believe</u> <u>they</u> must be very glad to see this kind of <u>phenomenon</u> take place.

<u>Kneel</u> in China means <u>appreciation</u> and respect. We also know many occasions that people <u>knelt</u> to show their <u>appreciation</u> and respect. <u>But we cannot define someone is appreciated for their</u> <u>parents just through this behavior.</u> <u>I think</u> students should have their own choice to decide whether <u>kneel</u> to their parents or not, but the arrangement of <u>schools</u> is compulsive. <u>I am afraid</u> this kind of behavior will upset some of the students. They are forced to do the things they are not willing to <u>because</u> some of them <u>perhaps</u> don't understand what <u>appreciation</u> is. <u>So</u> it will have not a good effect but very bad effect <u>to</u> students.

In a word, I don't think the schools' arrangement is appropriate. People usually dislike the things they are forced to. If they want to popularize the concept of appreciation, they can try many ways such as lectures instead of forced methods. <u>In my opinion, it should</u> <u>not be imitated by others.</u>

评析：有了画线部分的诸多问题，这篇作文足够让人云里雾里了。条理是逻辑范畴的一个问题，但是在结构方面，如果语法错误较多、用词不当，抑或词语摆放位置不妥，也会让人理解不透，从而感觉不知所云。读完这篇作文以后，我们可能会对随想随写的做法有更加深刻的了解。

画线部分有的是语法不当，有的是用词不当，有的是语体不当，有的是摆放位置不当，还有的是过多重复。但是，更主要的问题是句子间的关系比较混乱，条理不清楚。下面我们来逐一分析。

作文题目拟得不错，就是语法和选词不当，如果说Kneeling Doesn't Mean Gratefulness就很好，因为kneel是动词，动词不能用作主语，而appreciation虽然有感激之意，但更多人可能会以为是"欣赏"，这样，题目就不够明确了。

在整篇作文里面，appreciation重复了十多次，居然无一处替换，足以看出作者缺乏写作的高分要素意识。相同词义用不同词来表达是英语行文过程中的一大习惯，它是我们非知道不可的一个高分要素，我们将在第4章详细讨论。

从整篇作文来看，作者的主要问题是审题不清楚，条理有些混乱。前面我们说了，审题是为了建立写作框架，快速列出写作提纲。方法依然是抓主要概念，然后找与主要概念相关的要素，写作时要分清主次。在分类时，数量要少，条理要清楚。

题目里面有两个主要概念：一个是kneeling；另一个是appreciation。写作者首先要明确这两个概念，并看看它们之间有什么关系，进而把与它们相关的要素考虑进去。

我们先来看"下跪"这个概念。下跪是什么呢？下跪是古代经常使用的一种表达感谢、感激、尊敬的方式。而"感恩"是对他人的付出，比如爱、帮助、支持等，心存感激或报以感谢的一种行为。

与下跪相关的要素有时代变迁及其所产生的心理变化等。随着时代的变迁，感恩的方式多样化了，下跪这种方法逐渐消失。让孩子用一种过时的方法去表达感恩，一来并不一定能让他们了解什么是感恩，二来还可能会让他们觉得很别扭。试问，我们看见几个孩子给他人行下跪礼了？

与感激或感恩相关的要素有方式、方法，比如直言、问候、书信、探望、送礼物等。感恩的目的是让对方感到温暖或快乐，如果达不到这个目的，则没有意义。感恩的形式虽然多样，但它必须是发自内心的，是真挚自然的，而不是虚假的。

把概念理清，把要素罗列出来之后，框架就出来了，结果也就出来了。因此，如果你是持反对意见的，就可以提出这样的问题：下跪，尤其是集体下跪，有意义吗？这种过时的形式只不过是表面而不是发自内心的感激，会有多大意义呢？最后把这些思路翻译成英语即可。

我们当然也可以表示支持，方法是一样的，你必须先思考你觉得有利的一面，然后找出它的相关要素，把逻辑框架建立好，最后再翻译出来，这样就条理清楚了。

这篇作文另外一个比较大的问题就是主观因素过多，作者多处使用I heard，I think，I believe，I am afraid等来强化主观性，其实大可不必，因为即便是个人的观点，也必须有事实来支撑，否则这样的论据就不够强劲有力，因此，尽可能不要使用这类口头语。我们将在第4章详细讨论这个问题。此外，结尾画线部分其实就是作者的观点，观点通常在第一段，结尾的时候要改成结论句式，不要简单重复自己的观点，以免造成结构上的混乱。

下面我们以表格的形式再次强调一下审题问题。

表3-1　英语写作审题步骤表

步　骤	方　法
第一步	找到题目中的主要概念。
第二步	搞清楚主要概念的内涵和外延，包括彼此之间的关系。
第三步	找到与主要概念相关的要素，注意条理。
第四步	列出框架，把信息按主次排列。
第五步	翻译成英语。

（三）拟题问题

在这一节，我们讨论拟题问题。我们在前面说过，如果作文中已经给出题目，我们就无须再拟题了，命题作文的基本要求是不改动题目。但是很多时候，试题只给出情景，没有给出题目，这时，我们就必须自己拟题。

学习者一定要养成给作文拟题的良好习惯，因为批改作文时老师总是根据论题来进行评估的。是否跑题、偏题，是否论证充分，都必须根据题目来进行判断。

题目首先要清楚，不要让读者感觉不知所云，比如讨论考试作弊问题时，我们可以拟不同的题目：

- Windows or Doors
- Keep Going
- My Attitude Towards Cheating in Exams
- Cheating in Exams Should Be Blamed

前两个题目让人搞不清楚文章要写什么，而第三个属于中性题目，即不表明自己观点的题目。其实，使用中性题目是比较普遍的拟题方法，它的好处在于不容易出错。但是，较为高级的手法是使用表明自己观点的题目，让人从题目中一眼就可以看出你的态度，比如第四个题目。

让我们一起来看2003年TEM-8考试的作文真题，作文情景如下：

> An English newspaper is currently running a discussion on whether young people in China today are (not) more self-centered and unsympathetic than the previous generations were. And the paper is inviting contributions from university students. You have been asked to write a short article for the newspaper to air your views.
>
> Your article should be about 300 words in length. In the first part of your article you should state clearly your main argument, and in the second part you should support your argument with appropriate details. In the last part you should bring what you have written to a natural conclusion.
>
> You should supply a title for your article.
>
> Marks will be awarded for content, organization, grammar and appropriateness. Failure to follow the above instructions may result in a loss of marks.

我们先来审题。前面讨论过，你持什么观点，批改作文的老师并不在意，但是明确的论题和强有力的论证总是会让老师欣喜。这个题目是让考生提出对新一代人的看法，有人可能认为他们自私、以自我为中心，但不是所有人都这么认为。

反对者可以拿出什么样的证据来呢？比如，他们可能认为年轻的一代更加独立，因为他们就是这样成长的，尤其是独生子女，很多时候他们都是独自在家，没有可以一起玩耍的伙伴。遇到问题，没有人可以一起讨论或共同分担。他们可能因此认为凡事都要自己努力去争取成功，不能事事依赖他人。请注意，情景明确要求必须拟题。

下面我们一起来看两种不同的观点。

例1

A New Generation

It is said that young people today are not what they used to be. They are more self-centered and unsympathetic than the previous generations were. But is this new generation of teenagers really so different in qualities from their parents or grandparents? I don't think so.

About twenty years ago when China started to open the door to the outside world, people entered into universities without paying and when they went out of universities, permanent jobs were waiting for them so that they did not suffer any pressure from the society and they did not need to worry too much. All they should do was to try to focus their energy on their jobs. Words like contribution and dedication were commonly used once, which showed that people at that time cared more about their jobs, the society and other people than themselves.

However, the new generation, commonly referred to as "single child" generation, quite oppositely, had a quite different growing environment. In most cases they stayed at home with their mothers and fathers working all day long outside, during which they watched TV programs, read books or did homework without much time playing with companies. In this way, they formed their own way of thinking, a freer and simpler way to look at people and look at themselves, something that the previous generations could not imagine. And it made them less dependent on others. For them, going outside and facing the world is something everybody should do. If nobody could help you do that, you have to do it yourself. Accepting some of the Western ideas is another aspect that made them even more realistic: Live for yourself more than others, thus an expression that this new generation was more self-centered and unsympathetic was left.

Today's young people may not be what the previous generation used to be, but this generation has a free-minded and individualistic nature due to the facts mentioned above. They like to be left alone to solve problems. They have formed dramatically different ways of doing and thinking things than previous generations. And the changes will be profitable in many ways.

If we listen, there are a lot we can learn from them and the future will be a better place if we can mix harmoniously with them.

评析：作者使用"新的一代"作为题目，明确表明了自己的态度。新的一代不仅意味着和老一辈人不同，更意味着新思想、新方法，这样的题目是批改试卷的老师乐意看见的。

作者在正文中也不负众望，线条简洁，条理清楚，因果分明。文章内容紧凑，积极肯定了这一代人的思想和作风，并在结尾用了一句精彩的话：如果我们善于聆听，我们可以从他们身上学到很多东西；如果我们能和他们和谐交融，世界会变得更美好。

例2

More Self-Centered Youth

When talking about the differences between the present Chinese youth and the previous generations, we have a strong idea that the young people are particularly self-centered. They care more about their own feelings and benefits. For example, the young couples prefer having no child and living a life in which they will have double income and no child just because the child will cost too much of their money and vigor. We often read the news that an old mother is deserted by her four or more children for the reason that she will be a burden to them. Some phenomena <u>surprised</u> us while others go against the ethics of our society.

But this feature of today's youth has not come on to ground. Since the guideline of reform and opening has been established, the chances have increased greatly for young people to get to know the ideology of the Western countries. As is known, the Western world puts more emphasis on individualism. What's more, the youth accept the new thoughts more quickly than their seniors. These have resulted in the youth to believe in the importance of individual and in the virtues of self-reliance and personal independence. Another important factor in the youth's unsympathy is that the competition in our country has been intensified, and more and more people hope to succeed. One of the essential ways to be successful is to <u>be more self-reliant and dependent on oneself</u>.

In summary, <u>everything has its white and black sides</u>. What man can do is to develop the white aspects and check the black ones.

评析：我们先看题目，该题目也表明了作者的观点，只不过是从消极层面看待年轻的一代，这是可以的，问题在于作者没有用充足的证据来支持他的观点。

作者在第一段指出很多年轻夫妇只关心自己的情感和利益，比如结婚但不生孩子，怕花钱和耗费精力，甚至还指出有报道称四个孩子遗弃他们的老母亲，因为她成了累赘。这显然不行，我们探讨的是一代人，而非个别现象，这样片面的论据显然缺乏说服力。从古至今，难道还缺少不肖子孙的例子吗？如果这一点可以成为证据，那么每个时代的人都可以说是以自我为中心了。另外，一个国家越文明或越富裕，人口就会越少，这是社会发展的一个规律；反之，一个国家越穷，人口就越多。原本是社会发展的一个规律，却被说成是以自我为中心，这显然也站不住脚。

此外，我们还看见作者采用三段的一个不合理之处。第一段应该只有前三行，即提出问题且表明观点，后面几行都应该是第二段的内容，从标识词上就可以看出作者在提供证据了，虽然证据站不住脚。

而现在的第二段似乎和论题不相关，东拉西扯，显得很牵强。这一段结尾的画线处显示出作者对题目的概念理解不清楚，因为"自我为中心"不等于"自立"，把不同的概念混为一谈本身就是逻辑谬误，这样的论证怎么可能有可信度呢？

结尾也不符合要求，因为画线部分是进行分析时经常使用的一句话，预示着作者持中立态度，要分析事物的两个方面，可是作者的观点仅有一个方面，何来二者呢？这明显违反了论题的同一律要求。

总之，作文题目要明确，而且论题要保持同一。把题目审视清楚并拟出一个好题目才能更好地完成写作任务。

三
写 作 过 程

（一）不能跑题

对论题的逻辑要求之一就是要保持论题同一，也就是不能跑题或偏题。跑题是写作过程中一个致命的问题，有时批改作文的老师直接就给零分了。

在本章第一节里，我们补充了必备的逻辑要素，并对概念及其定义以及如何把握概念进行了解释。这样就不容易跑题了，因为跑题的原因就是把题目中的概念搞错了。为避免跑题，我们必须改进下面两点：第一，增加单词量；第二，把握概念在具体情景中的含义。

我们先看看与填鸭式教育方法相关的作文片段。

例1

I think this method is very good. All the students sit together to discuss problems. If we have only one or two people in one class, they cannot exchange their ideas.

例2

Cramming means the space we live is very crowded. It is true. In some places, the whole family live in a small house about nine square meters. That's awful.

评析：这是1999年一所大学英语专业研究生入学考试写作题的学生作品，当时很多人都不认识这个单词，有人因此就瞎蒙，结果闹了不少笑话。

出题人是要大家讨论填鸭式教学或死记硬背的学习方法，填鸭式教学是一种教学方法。在例1中，作者把它理解成是一起讨论问题的方法，称赞它很好，这显然是没有理解题目的意思。

而在例2中，作者则把它理解成了"拥挤"，其实这个单词确实有"塞"或"挤"的意思，在单概念题目中有时很难判断出题人的意图，这也许是作者开篇说cram意味着我们居住的环境非常拥挤的原因。

在这种情况下，上述两个学生的作文都可以不给分。但是，有一点必须指出，这个题目出得不好：首先，单一概念在缺乏语境的情况下是可以有不同的理解的；其次，作文的目的是考查写作者的语法运用能力和思维能力，用一个相对比较偏的单词就把大家考倒了，这不太合适。

接下来，我们再看一篇作文。

The Unexamined Life Is Not Worth Living

Through our whole life, we have experienced numerable examinations. In our young age, our parents send us to the kindergarten, in which we should have a test. Then at about six, before going the primary schools, we have to be tested. And testing will accompany us till old age.

评析：题目的意思是未经受过考验的生活就没有价值，换言之，有意义的人生必须要经历磨难。这是古希腊圣贤苏格拉底说的一句名言，写起作文来有一定的难度。

用名人名言作为考题还是比较常见的，但它们经常会给一部分考生带来困难，因为名人名言在理解上存在一定的难度。在这里，作者望文生义，把题目理解成人生的考试，这就明显跑题了，基本不能得分。

在具体的写作过程中，跑题的现象并不普遍，因为绝大部分题目都出得比较清楚，会回避一些生僻的词。我们需要注意的是跑题的原因，并尽可能提高自己的单词量，防止出现以上问题。

（二）不能偏题

与跑题比起来，偏题的问题就太普遍了，我们必须高度重视这个问题。偏题通常是指写作者对题目概念的理解基本正确，但是在正文写作过程中，无意间把概念的外延放大或缩小了，或者在正文中把次要的概念当成主要概念来写了。

我们先来看范例。

Is It Wise to Make Friends Online?

Recent decades have witnessed the increasing popularity of Internet surfing. More and more students spend many hours on it with the keenest interest. Many of them make boyfriends via the Internet. Personally, I think the merits of making boyfriends online outweigh its demerits.

On the one hand, as for students, it is no uncommon that people make friends online. Via the Internet, students can meet people from all walks of life. Maybe one of them can help you after your graduation. And you can learn a lot of things which you do not know through the book. On the other hand, you can make an online friendship over a long period of time. Moreover, it is a good way to help you improve your communication skill. At the same time, you will have more and more good friends. For example, if you have some troubles that you can not tell people around you, you may have another choice to talk to your online friends who do not know your name, your address and your phone numbers. It is an effective method to relieve your pressures.

However, every coin has two sides. Some criminals find a chance on online friendship. So students should be cautious to strangers. To sum up, making friends online does more harm than good.

评析：这篇作文的题目很明确，就是网上交友是否明智。但是，仔细思考一下，网上交友无所谓明智与否，关键看你交什么朋友。显然，题目中的make friends是主要概念，它的外延是任何朋友，男女老少都包含在内。

可是，在第一段最后一句话，作者认为交男朋友的坏处大于好处。这就无故改动了概念的外延。同一律要求概念必须在整个写作过程中保持不变，包括它的内涵和外延。对于论题也是一样，既然是讨论交友，就不能随便把交友变成交男朋友。当我们随便改变一个概念的外延时，作文就偏题了。

在结构方面，这篇作文也很不规范，看似三小段，而事实上最后一段的第一句依然是第二部分的分析。如果从To sum up这里看成是结尾，就太不协调了。

最后，作文的论据也很苍白无力，论题基本上没有得到支持。

我们再来看一篇作文，它所给出的情景是一则谚语。

An African proverb says "If you educate a boy, you educate an individual; if you educate a girl, you educate a family or a nation." Do you agree with this proverb? Write an essay of approximately 300 words on this issue to state your own opinion.

例1

The Importance of Women in Education

I think it's quite right. And I quite agree to this proverb. In the long history of China, we can find many stories about mothers who educated their children and made their children great men.

评析：如果情景是谚语，通常要对谚语加以解读。作者根据情景拟题为"妇女在教育中的重要性"，这个题目说明作者理解到位。

但是，从第一段来看，作者对于自己题目中的主要概念，即women的外延把握不到位。题目里的women是指任何妇女，而不是指具体哪个国家的妇女。在这种情况下，如果作文突然改成讨论中国的妇女，就属于偏题，因为概念的外延被无故缩小了。此外，education这个概念也太大，不仅指对孩子的教育，还可以指任何教育，而作者在第一段又变成了母亲对孩子的教育。由此可见，作者缺乏论证的逻辑知识或意识。

我们回过头来看情景。一则非洲谚语说："教育一个男孩，也就是教育了一个人而已；教育一个女孩，则教育了一个家庭或者一个国家。"

首先，我们理解一下"谚语"的含义。《牛津高阶英语词典》第四版给出的定义是a well-known phrase or sentence that gives advice or says something that is generally true。由此可见，谚语表达的内容通常是正确的或者普遍为人所接受的。还有一点我们必须清楚，那就是动态地看问题。动态地看问题有三个好处：思维更加有序，从过去到现代；观点更加全面；字数更加充足。

谚语往往是传承下来的东西，在当时可能是正确的，但随着社会的发展，情况可能会发生变化。那么，该谚语产生之时的情景可能是什么样的呢？古代社会，男人都外出打猎或觅食，妇女在家里照顾孩子，成为孩子最好的老师。接受了良好教育的女孩长大后，又去教育更多的孩子。读懂谚语的含义是一件不错的事，接下来就是要拟一个恰当的题目，把概念的外延控制在自己能驾驭的范围内，概念一旦确定，其外延就跟着确定下来，写作的过程中就不能随意改变它了。

例2

The Role of Women in Children's Education

There's an African proverb saying that if you educate a boy, you educate an individual; if you educate a girl, you educate a family or a nation, which indicates the great importance of females in children's education.

It is true that women take an important role in children's education, especially during the time when men were the only bread-owners of families while mothers' responsibility was to stay at home raising and nourishing their children. So a mother's manner and behavior influenced their children very much. Successful stories of a mother cultivating a future star or famous general, or a great statesman can be heard in almost every country. Take the mother of Yang's family in Song Dynasty for one example, and mother of Thomas Edison for another, which shows the great effect of mothers upon their children.

Although examples can be given here and there to testify that women are extremely important to the forming of characters or qualities of their children, we still have to consider two things. One is that a mother who wants to educate her child a future or potential figure usually has to have good qualities herself. She also needs to have good ways to teach them and good manner to influence them her own. That explains why some women failed to teach their children well. Another thing that we should bear in mind is that in today's society, things change very fast so that we should not insist in some old views of looking at things without thoroughly considering the factor of changing—change of our society, change of the way we work and live, change of the way we educate people, change of the agency involved, and change of the relationship between people.

With change, more people and factors are involved in the process of educating children. Some factors which might be the most important to the nurturing of children may become less important today, while some less important ones may become more important, and there may be some emerging, such as the role of a man, the environment like schools or colleges and everything around us, from which reasons can be found out why some children turned out to be prominent though the fact that they lost parents when young, or the fact that they were born of humble families, or the fact that they lived in orphanage.

So, women take a very important role in children's education, especially in ancient times. And one important thing for us is that we should look at this matter dynamically.

评析：与例1的题目类似，作者也看懂了谚语的含义。但和例1不同的是，这篇作文的作者拟题的水平较高，他把妇女的外延放大，却把教育的外延缩小了。这显然是深思熟虑的结果。作者在正文中写的是古今中外的妇女，而非非洲的妇女；而教育是专门讨论孩子的教育。这使得线条既简洁又清晰，比较好写。

可以这么说，能够保持论题的同一性的人，对于拟题时是否要限定一个概念一定会比较清楚；而明确题目的逻辑要求的人一定会在正文里面保持概念的同一性，以避免出现跑题或偏题问题。

总之，在写作过程中，无论是跑题还是偏题，我们都必须避免，以免被严重扣分。跑题是把题目里的概念搞错了；而偏题则是把次要的信息当成了主要的信息，偏离了原来的主线。此外，学生经常犯的错误是把概念的外延随意放大或缩小，这也是偏题的一个方面，我们要高度重视这个问题，从一开始就奠定好高分作文的基础。

四
写作目的、意义及高度

（一）写作目的

有一次，我们学校发生了一件令人痛心的事情：一个男生因故跳楼自杀了。我的一个学生因此写了一篇作文，题目是A Letter to the Dead Boy。当我问及他的写作目的时，他说他不知道。也许从未有人提醒过他，写作必须是有目的的。

写作的目的相当于一个目标，比如我们想指出某人的一些不当言行，于是就给他写了一封信。看完作文后，我问他是不是想通过给轻生的学生写一封信来教育活着的学生，他点头称是。

由此可见，他还是有写作目的的，只是自己没有意识到。在写作之前，我们要想清楚自己为什么要写一篇作文，这样我们就可以有一个清晰的目标，从而思考采用什么手法来实现这个目标。目的明确对于我们组织文字、选择用词、采用修辞都是非常重要的。

（二）写作意义

判断一篇作文是否是高分作文的一个重要标准就是要有写作意义，没有意义的作文，不可能进入高分作文的行列。

写作意义通常意味着自己写作的内容或者角度与他人不同，能给人带来一定的启发性，具有一定的新意。它不是具体的某一个东西，在结构上也没有固定的位置和形式。不过通常在第一段，大家就可以看出一篇作文的写作意义了。

很多学生说自己想不到什么与众不同的东西，有些则强调说自己习惯采用模板，很难有新意。对于大部分学生而言，要发现一个事物的不同之处确实比较难。但是，这不等于我们不可以逐步改变这一观念。如果我们学会一些方法，就更容易找到事物之间的差异。

我们先来看看下面的文章：

Most Americans remember Mark Twain as the father of Huck Finn's idyllic cruise through eternal boyhood and Tom Sawyer's endless summer of freedom and adventure. Indeed, this nation's best-loved author was every bit as adventurous, patriotic, romantic, and humorous as anyone has ever imagined. I found another Twain as well—one who grew cynical, bitter, saddened by the profound personal tragedies life dealt him, a man who became obsessed with the frailties of the human race, who saw clearly ahead a black wall of night.

参考译文：

在大多数美国人的心目中，马克·吐温是一位伟大的作家，他描写了哈克·费恩永恒的童年中充满诗情画意的旅程以及汤姆·索亚在漫长的夏日里自由自在地探险的故事。的确，这位美国最受人喜爱的作家的探索精神、爱国热情、浪漫气质及幽默笔调都达到了登峰造极的境界。但我发现还有另一个不同的马克·吐温 —— 一个由于深受人生悲剧的打击而变得愤世嫉俗、尖酸刻薄的马克·吐温，一个为人性的弱点而忧心忡忡、清楚地看到前途是一片黑暗的人。

评析：《马克·吐温——美国的一面镜子》是《高级英语》上册中的一篇课文，我们学习它的主要目的就是培养写作意义方面的意识。马克·吐温是赫赫有名的大作家，他和他的作品为世人所熟悉。如果你只是介绍他人知道的信息，写作就毫无意义，可以说根本不用去写。

作者一定是有所发现，才会决定写这么一位大名鼎鼎的文学界人物，比如一些不为他人所知的内容。实际上正是如此，作者先交代一个大家熟悉的马克·吐温：他是这个国家最受人爱戴的作家，是个具有冒险精神和浪漫情怀的人，是个饱含爱国热情又笔调幽默的人。然后，作者告诉大家，他发现了另一个完全不同的马克·吐温：他变得愤世嫉俗、尖酸刻薄；他在生活中饱受了人世间的苦难；他身上满是人性的脆弱，看不见世界的未来。这样一来，就有了写作意义。

如果你是一个爱好写作的人，又喜欢投稿，那么，请谨记，编辑首先看你的作品有没有什么新意，新意就意味着有意义。对于我们写英语作文而言，这可能有难度，但如果我们增强了这方面的意识，我们就一定会做得更好。

我们再看看下面的两个例子。

例 1

Human Migration

Human migration: the term is vague. What people usually think of is the permanent movement of people from one home to another. More broadly, though, migration means all the ways from the seasonal drift of agricultural workers within a country to the relocation of refugees from one country to another.

例 2

We Need a World Filled with Love

Love is a kind of emotion expressing our likeness, happiness, our care or concern about someone or something we treasure, we like, we want and we need, not only between human beings, but also between man and other living things in the world, including animals, plants, our earth and our environment.

评析：在介绍概念的内涵和外延时，我们提到了例2。对于绝大部分概念，我们在它们的含义上很难突出写作意义，因为大部分作文中要我们写的概念都是大家熟知的事物，也就是众所周知的事，它们不需要解释，就算解释了也没有太大意义。相反，如果我们观察概念的外延，可能更容易发现新意。

在例1中，如果写作者解释migration，就没有意义。《牛津高阶英语词典》第七版提供的解释是the movement of large numbers of people, birds, animals from one place to another。正因为此，写作者没有对这个概念的内涵进行阐释，而是对它的外延表示了不同的看法。平常人们认为永久性的搬迁才算迁移，而他认为迁移的范围可以更大，季节性的、地方性的，以及跨国的都算。

例2也是一样，写作者没有必要去解释爱本身，因为爱是无人不知、无人不晓的一种情感，但爱的外延却值得重视。大部分人只在意人与人之间的爱，忽略了人与其他生命体之间的爱，而只有关注整个系统的健康，人类才会幸福。这样，写作意义就出来了。

例1和例2还有另一个相同点，就是在把握概念外延的时候，刻意突出了句式美。

综上所述，写作意义通常是指自己所写的内容与他人的不同，或者发现了他人所不知的东西，或者有了看待事物的不同方法或角度等。从逻辑角度来看，就是写作者对概念的外延有不同的看法。关注概念的外延，经常可以让我们有所发现。

（三）作文的高度和深度

作文的高度或深度是高级英语写作中最需要也最难实现的，这就是每年TEM-8考试作文的平均分都很低的原因。

所谓作文的高度，通常指写作时分析问题的起点高。比如谈教育的重要性时，我们把问题提到国家或民族的高度，说教育是利国利民的大事，或者是造福后代的大事，这就有了高度。如果从个体说起，说教育可以让我们读书认字，其高度就不够。又比如说环保问题，也同样可以把高度提到关乎人类存亡的层面，说保护环境是造福人类的大事，是为后代着想的大事等。

简单地说，高度就是要向上看，向前看，不要始终关注自己。作文的深度也是一样的道理，就是你可以挖出比较重大的意义来，以此引起大家的关注。

谈及作文的高度和深度，有一点必须明确，那就是我们在这里讨论的作文能够有高度就不错了，不要求也未必能够同时既有高度又有深度，因为作文的深度受字数的限制，越有深度的问题，就越需要更多的笔墨来分析。通常初级写作没有高度和深度的要求。但是，写作训练过程中，我们要培养这方面的意识，因为提高写作的能力不仅仅是为了完成当前的学习任务，更是为了培养自己未来所需的能力。

我们先看一篇关于富裕的作文。

My Attitude Toward Richness

One of our dreams is to live a rich life. Most of us study hard and work hard for this reason. For a student, he studies very hard in order to enter a good university, during which he can be educated well. The ultimate purpose of this is to get a good job. And good job means earning a good salary.

For a country, things are the same. Take China for example. It has taken some new policies and measures to improve people's life. Since the reform and opening to the outside world, China's economic growth has increased very quickly. More and more people get rid of poverty. They have their own houses. They have their own cars. And some of them have their own businesses. Recently, many successful businesses are private-owned. And that is a standard of being rich.

Typically, the richness of a country represents the richness of its people and vice versa. To me, to be rich is a wonderful thing. That means we can not only get what we need, but realize what we want. Richness is also a symbol of development and a symbol of civilization.

But there's one thing that we should not forget. The richer we are, the more generous we must be—generous to those who give us the opportunity to be rich, generous to those who are still in poverty. The richer we are, the kinder we must be—kind to the earth which gives us so much rich resource, kind to our environment on which we live for a better life.

评析：这篇作文虽短，却极有高度。在谈富裕问题时，写作者把它分为个人和国家两大方面，这样线条就非常清楚，让人一目了然。无论是个人还是国家都是大概念，因为这里的个人不是具体的某一个人，而是指一类人。

最精彩的要算最后一段，读起来感觉特别温馨。富裕了以后不要忘记：越是富裕越要慷慨，对给予我们机会的人慷慨，对依然贫困的人慷慨；越是富裕越要友善，对给予我们无数资源的地球友善，对给予我们更美好生活的环境友善。

值得注意的是，这篇作文的体裁不完全是阐释文体，它更像一篇演讲稿，和我们前面一直强调的先表明观点然后论证的写法略微不同。它没有固定一个情景，只是谈自己的感想，因此结尾也没有明显的概括，而是表明态度，这在写作中是允许的。

接下来，我们再看看2009年TEM-8考试的翻译真题。

We, the human species, are confronting a planetary emergency—a threat to the survival of our civilization that is gathering ominous and destructive potential even as we gather here. But there is hopeful news as well: we have the ability to solve this crisis and avoid the worst—though not all—of its consequences, if we act boldly, decisively and quickly.

However, despite a growing number of honorable exceptions, too many of the world's leaders are still best described in the words Winston Churchill applied to those who ignored Adolf Hitler's threat: "They go on in strange paradox, decided only to be undecided, resolved to be irresolute, adamant for drift, solid for fluidity, all powerful to be impotent."

So today, we dumped another 70 million tons of global-warming pollution into the thin shell of atmosphere surrounding our planet, as if it were an open sewer. And tomorrow, we will dump a slightly larger amount, with the cumulative concentrations now trapping more and more heat from the sun.

评析：虽然是翻译题，但翻译也是他人的作品，也能表达作者的思想。这篇短文讨论环境污染问题，我们一眼就可以看到它的写作高度——人类正面临着一场关乎文明生死存亡的星球危机。试想，还有什么比生死存亡更严重的问题吗？

我们再欣赏一下《大不列颠望洋兴叹》的开头部分，看看它的高度又是怎样的。

Britain's merchant navy seldom grabs the headlines these days; it is almost a forgotten industry. Yet shipping is the essential lifeline for the nation's economy. Ninety-nine percent of our trade in and out of the country goes by ship—and over half of it in British ships.

Shipping is also a significant British success story. It earns over £1,000 million a year in foreign exchange earnings: without our merchant fleet, the balance of payments would be permanently in deficit, despite North Sea oil. But, today this vital British industry is more in peril than ever before. On almost all the major sea routes of the world, the British fleet risks being elbowed out by stiff foreign competition.

参考译文：

近来，英国商船队已经很少见诸报端，它快成为被人们遗忘的产业了。然而，船运业是英国的经济命脉，99%的进出口贸易都靠船运，其中一半以上是英国船运。

船运业是个兴旺发达的行业，它每年创10亿英镑的外汇。没有我们的商船队，那么，就算有北海石油，国家财政也永远是赤字。可是，如今英国这一重要产业正面临着前所未有的危机。在几乎所有国际航线上，英国商业船队都面临着被来自其他国家残酷竞争挤出市场的危险。

评析：这是《大不列颠望洋兴叹》里面的开头，它是一篇阐释文体的经济类文章。它首先提出论点，并通过例子分析因果关系，最后得出结论。在高级阅读课程中，我们主要是学习它的写作高度和分析的深度。作者把英国船运业称为英国的经济命脉，并用几个具体数字来凸显它的重要性。这样的产业如何能够不受重视呢？文章的高度因此就出来了。

最后，我们看看关于"语言的力量"的另一篇作文。

The topic of whether the language is powerful or not causes great attention. I quite agree that language is powerful.

First, we use language to communicate with others. If we do not have language, how can we understand each other? Second, we use language to order people to do something. If they cannot understand each other, how will things be done? Third, we use language to differ man from other animals. We all know that only man has language, which other animals don't.

So, language is important and powerful. We should learn it well.

评析：撇开字数不说，这篇作文在结构方面还可以，分成三段，先提出问题，然后列出三点，最后结尾，前后都使用了适当的标识词。可是从深度或高度方面来看，则无从谈起，因为它仅仅是一篇套模板的作文，其字数决定它不可能有深度地探讨问题。

作为初级作文，它还不错。然而，作为高级作文，它还存在一些问题。首先，第一段的说法就不合适，因为语言的强大功能是公认的事实，把事实当成自己的观点本身就是不妥当的；事实就是事实，无所谓同意或不同意。这一点我们会在后面详细讨论。其次，第二段第二点和第一点重复，在逻辑学上叫概念交叉。"命令他人做事"也是交流的一种，这部分跟在第一点后面，作为第一点的补充可以，单独作为一点，就不妥当。第三点不错，但鉴于证据比较单薄，说服力还不够强。不过它没有什么语法错误，句式也还不错。

总之，高级写作必须有高度或深度，不能总是平平淡淡。加强这方面的意识对于我们思维能力的提升具有重要意义。所谓高度或深度，就是要我们尽可能从大处着眼，突出问题的严重性，以此引起他人的高度重视。

第 **4** 章

英语写作技巧及方法运用

结构方面的技巧和方法

（一）常见开篇法

写作的几种常见开篇法我们必须了解，因为很多学生无论写什么文章，都用千篇一律的开头方法。这样的开头很单调，也很难有新意。

常见开篇法有定义法、背景法、反问法和引言法。

要特别注意的是，无论用哪一种方法总是有目的的，不能盲目使用。英语写作水平高的人对要做什么、为什么要做一般都十分明确。

1. 定义法

定义法是对命题中的主要概念进行解释的开头方法。定义必须是逻辑定义，不可以用比喻或者自己的感想。通常，有三种情况会用到定义法。

第一，大家对某个概念不清楚，甚至不知道，你想让他们了解这个事物。

第二，大家对某个概念存在认识上的差异，你想在讨论之前先确定这个概念。

第三，你准备在这个概念，尤其是它的外延上，做点文章，以突出你的写作意义，因为你有与众不同的发现。

第三点经常意味着你的观点与他人的观点不一样。我们前面列举的Love就是一个经典例子。对于一些大家熟悉的概念，我们一般不采用定义法，因为大家都知道的东西，你解释一通没有意义，甚至可能会显得多此一举。比如前面提到的"研究生入学考试"，写作时对研究生入学考试加以解释毫无意义。

汉语写作和英语写作其实是一回事。在汉语写作中，老师经常让学生注意观察，观察什么？其实就是看你能否发现他人没有发现的事物。目的是什么呢？当然是为了突出写作意义或价值。你写的东西与他人不一样，才会有意义、有价值。

在高级写作中，对于熟知的概念，如果你采用定义法，一般是想强调你对概念的外延有新的认识。就像在Human Migration和We Need a World Filled with Love里面一样。

我们重申一下：对于熟知的概念，我们采用定义法一般只是在这个概念的外延上有所把握，基本上不会在内涵上有什么创新。你若是有一大发现，当然是了不起的事情，可是在考试过程中，基本上不会出现这种现象。试想，大家都不知道的东西，怎么写啊？写什么呢？

事实上，高级写作中一般是让大家写一个熟悉的现象，比如救助他人、玩手机、垃圾信息等。我们来看几个例子。

例1

Do Husbands or Wives Do Housework?

Housework refers to work done at home, including cleaning, washing, and cooking, etc. Women who stay at home doing housework are called housewives. Why don't we have househusbands?

例2

Do College Students Still Need Good Qualities?

Everybody needs good qualities no matter who you are and what you are. Good qualities of a person refer to good nature or characters like honesty, kindness and generosity, etc, which indicate man's mental needs. The development of man's needs from a lower level to a higher level, from physical to mental is a regularity which nobody can deny. No one can counter to it and no one can surpass it.

例 3

Work and Life

Work and life are something that we cannot separate for people to work for a living. When mentioning work, some people always put it together with a permanent or regular job. But in fact, work means to do something by using our bodily or mental power, including housework, farm work, etc. Today, with the development of the society, people work not only for a living, but also for improving the standard and quality of their life. That's why some people from rich families still work hard.

评析：在例1中，家务虽然是大家再熟悉不过的事情，但是作者采用定义法有两个目的：一是为了让大家知道，家务其实也是工作，只不过是在家里做的工作；二是为了使句式更加美观。

在例2中，作者对优秀品质进行解释，是因为有的人可能不清楚什么是quality，它具体包括哪些内容。对它进行解释后，就等于与大家达成了一种共识，告诉大家作者讨论的优秀品质是这些内容。

由此可见，使用定义法就一定要明确使用的目的：我们是想告诉别人他们不清楚的东西，还是想在概念的外延上发表不同的看法？只有这样，我们才能更好地发挥定义法的作用。

例3和Human Migration很像，作者认为别人把工作理解为职业的说法不准确，他认为工作就是用体力或脑力做的事情，可以是家务，也可以是农活。他采用定义法的目的很明确，就是要突出自己的写作意义，这样的开篇方法非常好。

2. 背景法

背景法也叫情景法，是指在作文的开头给出一个情景，或者表明存在某个现象的开头方法。

TEM-8作文，确切地说是阐释文写作，一般都是采用背景法，也就是基于某个现象提出自己的看法。关于The Monitors on Campus的开篇有人就是这样写的：

> Nowadays, many monitors can be seen on campus, from the teaching building to the dormitory. Some students say that it is a good thing to be done. There are some people to say no. As far as I am concerned, I support the latter.

接下来，我们一起来欣赏一下怀特先生的散文《林湖重游》（Once More to the Lake），也有人把它翻译成《缅湖重游》，因为这个湖在美国缅因州。这篇散文被称为世界上最美的散文之一，然而能读懂它的人并不多。

怀特先生是美国当代最伟大的散文家，他的散文有两个特点：一是文字简洁，风格清新，读起来令人特别愉快；二是思想深刻，一般人很难看得懂。

> One summer, along about 1904, my father rented a camp on a lake in Maine and took us all there for the month of August. We all got ringworm from some kittens and had to rub Pond's Extract on our arms and legs night and morning, and my father rolled over in a canoe with all his clothes on; but outside of that the vacation was a success and from then on none of us ever thought there was any place in the world like that lake in Maine. We returned summer

after summer—always on August 1st for one month. I have since become a salt-water man, but sometimes in summer there are days when the restlessness of the tides and the fearful cold of the sea water and the incessant wind which blows across the afternoon and into the evening make me wish for the placidity of a lake in the woods. A few weeks ago this feeling got so strong I bought myself a couple of bass hooks and a spinner and returned to the lake where we used to go, for a week's fishing and to revisit old haunts.

参考译文：

　　大约是 1904 年的一个夏天，我父亲在缅因州一个湖区租了一个露营地，他带着我们全家，到那里度过了为时一个月的假期。

　　我们从小猫咪身上染上了虫子，从早到晚忙着往手臂和腿上涂抹旁氏止痒药膏，我父亲痒得在筏子上和衣打滚。不过除此之外，假期非常成功，那之后，谁也没有想到世界上有比缅湖更美的地方了。

　　我们每个夏天都去，总是在八月一日，然后待上一个月。

　　后来，我成了盐湖人，可是有时候，在夏天，从下午到晚上，海潮不断，海水奇冷之时，我就想起那幽静的林中之湖。

　　几星期之前，这种思念与日俱增，于是我买了鲈鱼钓具，重回那让我魂牵梦萦的地方，悠然垂钓，为期一周。

评析：作者在这篇美丽的散文中，采用了情景开篇法，为的是告诉读者他为什么故地重游。他父亲曾经带他们去那里度过假，那是一个非常幽静的地方，由于换了工作地点，不能每年都去了，他对缅湖的思念越来越无法抑制，因此，他买了钓具后就赶了过去。

大型英语考试中的写作一般不会考散文，欣赏怀特先生的散文也有一定的难度，我们也不是要求大家都能够写出这样的作品来，欣赏这篇散文的目的是体验一下情景法的开篇。

现在，我们来看看采用情景法开篇的阐释文。

例 1

The Fake and Inferior Goods

Nowadays, one can find different kinds of fake and inferior goods almost anywhere, from little stalls along the side of roads to big shops, even supermarkets, including small goods like stationery pupils use to big brand things, such as famous clothes, electric appliance, cigarette, wine and even medical apparatus. I resolutely suggest fighting against them.

例 2

Noise Problem

We can hear unpleasant noise easily around us, like loud hawking in the street or market, music in some big shops, horn of vehicles, and the hitting and banging of building sites. Noise refers to loud, unpleasant and unwanted sounds, which disturb people's life and are harmful to people's health. Studies show that people living in an environment of much noise are irritated and upset often. The continuity of this situation can make them suffer a lot both in physical and mental health. I support the severe punishment of the noise makers.

评析：例1和例2很像，二者都是先提出了一个现象，例1是关于伪劣产品的，例2是关于噪音的。此外，他们用的手法也很像，二者都在概念的外延上做文章，从而使得结构美观漂亮。

例1说伪劣产品随处可见，然后用from...to...来突出范围，接下来又用including引导的现在分词短语来突出种类。例2用around us来表示范围，然后用like来突出这个范围。作者还对噪音进行了解释，这样就可以明确要讨论的噪音具体指哪些声音。

接下来我们看看2015年TEM-8的写作真题，它所给的情景如下：

> There has been a new trend in economic activity—the sharing economy. The biggest sector of the sharing economy is travel. You find a potential host through the website. If you both get along and they are available during your planned trip, you stand a chance of getting a place for free. In addition, people also use website or apps to rent out their cars, houses, tools, clothes and services to others. *Time* magazine has included this trend in a list titled "ten ideas that will change the world." It said, "in an era when families are scattered and we may not know the people down the street, sharing things—even with strangers we've just met online—allow us to make meaningful connections." What do you think of *Time*'s comment?

题目是统一的，考生无须自己拟题。我们先来分析一下题目的要求。分享经济其实就是对"拼车、拼房"等概念的概括，在旅游业体现得最为明显，它确实是互联网的产物。这一趋势被收录在《时代周刊》的"十大改变世界的点子"里。它说，这个时代，家庭分散，互不相识，分享事物，甚至是与陌路人分享，也会让我们建立有意义的关联。

一定要注意，题目问的是考生是否同意《时代周刊》的言论，不是对分享经济的直接看法，也就是说，写作者在第一段必须表明是否认同《时代周刊》的观点。接下来，我们来看几个考生的作文。

例 1

My View on the Sharing Economy

There has been a new trend in economic activity— the sharing economy. *Time* magazine has included this trend in a list titled "ten ideas that will change the world." It said, "In an era when families are scattered and we may not know the people down the street sharing things—even with strangers we have just met online— allows us to make meaningful connections." However, some people don't think so. In my view, every coin has two sides. I think the sharing economy has more advantages than disadvantages.

评析：例1的第一段包括两方面内容：一是完全重复了题目的要求；二是表明了自己的观点。作者说了两句话，"我认为，凡事有两面，分享经济的利大于弊"。这个开头属于典型的背景法。

这个开篇无论是语法还是结构都非常规范。规范的最大好处是保险，不会被扣分。当然，如果作者直截了当地说认同《时代周刊》的观点，那样会更保险，因为情景只要求写作者回答是否同意《时代周刊》的评论，没有提及他人的观点。

例 2

My View on the Sharing Economy

With developing of world's economy, a new trend in economic activity has come into sight—the sharing economy. As is known, travel is the biggest sector of the sharing economy. What else, people also can use websites and apps to rent out their cars, houses and so on to <u>one other</u>. And *Time* has claimed that it is one of the ideas that can change the world for in an era when families are scattered and we may not know the people down the street, sharing things—even with strangers we have just met online—allows us to make meaningful connections. As far as I am concerned, it is not only a kind of economic activity, but also brings people closer and closer. So, I agree with *Time*'s comment.

评析：从第一句就可以看出，这个作者习惯绕弯式的开篇。前面我们说过，在高级写作中，这种习惯要改正，尽量采用直接的开篇方法。采用with开头，一般都是绕弯式，它有时会给人偏题的感觉；另外，它很容易让人钻空子。

分享经济的趋势主要是互联网发展的结果，无须提及世界经济的发展。恰恰相反，正因为经济不景气，或者收入不理想，人们才更愿意和他人分享事物。你见过几个富人愿意和陌生人拼住一间房，或同乘一辆出租车的？所以，掌握规范，改变不良的思维习惯，对于写作大有好处。

除此之外，例2的开头还算规范，既提出了现象，又表明了观点。不过标识词用得比较乱，感觉整篇文章的内容都集中在开头了。

例 3

My View on the Sharing Economy

<u>In</u> the age of Internet, the global economy has been redefined <u>by</u> new phenomenon developed <u>by</u> new generations. The sharing economy, as part of the Internet family, has the potential to shape connections <u>between</u> people into a new level. *Time*'s comment on the sharing economy about its meaningfulness, while truthful to its positive influence, is ignorant of its security issues and its impact on people's privacy. In my humble opinion, the positive position of the sharing economy can be threatened by the following aspects.

评析：例3的开头一句和例2很像，是绕弯式，扯得比较远，

（而且还出现了语法错误in the age of，两个by也有些别扭），说全球经济被新的一代人重新定义了。那么，这个新的一代人是指什么人呢？我们要讨论的分享经济难道只限于年轻人吗？另外，第二句说"作为网络一族的分享经济，有加强人们之间联系的潜在作用"，这句本来是《时代周刊》的观点，怎么变成事实了呢？再说，它和第一句的关联是什么？二者似乎关系并不密切。

开门见山是最好的开篇方法和习惯，不会丢分；相反，你一扯远，立刻就会给别人反问的机会。以我多年批改作文的经验来看，采用绕弯式开头的作文，十有八九是相关性欠缺的，因为写作者不了解英式思维习惯或写作能力不足才会采用这样的开篇方式。

例3中，作者的观点还是不错的，显然他不同意《时代周刊》的观点，因为它忽略了人的安全问题和隐私问题。

写作是对综合因素的考察，从2015年TEM-8写作真题的三个例子中我们可以发现，同样是背景法，开门见山最好，不要绕弯，以防别人认为作文与主题关系不密切，让人挑出问题。

背景法的最后一点，就是必须扣住情景所给的问题，不要偏题。我们一起评价一下下面这篇作文的开篇，作文的情景如下：

Some people think that college students should get higher salary when they undertake work because they have got good education. What do you think of it?

例4

College Students Should Get Higher Salary

With the extreme expansion of higher education consumers in China, more and more college students roll in colleges. As a result there are millions of graduates every year and the market cannot absorb them. <u>So</u> most of the graduates have low salary. In my opinion, college students should get higher salary.

评析：这篇作文的开篇就忽略了所给的情景。情景是有人认为大学生应该得到更高的工资，因为他们受过良好的教育。而作者说的是扩招以后，每年的毕业生数量众多，市场无法消化，这样容易偏题。必须紧扣情景，才不容易偏离主题。

另外，标识词不要随便乱用，as a result和so的意思相同，不要连着使用，而且它们是用来表示结论的词，通常出现在结尾部分，偶尔也会出现在第二部分，但不要轻易出现在第一部分。

综上所述，背景法是TEM-8写作或其他高级写作里面经常采用的方法之一，因为题目经常给出一个情景，让考生分析其因果关系。但是，这不意味着考生不能采用其他方法。

3. 反问法

反问法一般是指采用反问句作为作文题目，或者在作文第一段使用反问句的方法。反问或设问是我们非常熟悉的一种修辞手法，使用起来并不难，但是，在英语写作中要注意，采用反问法通常意味着作者不同意他人的观点。

采用反问法开篇的好处在于，读者一看就知道你的观点是反对什么的，它是另一种表明立场或观点的方法。多样化的开篇方法也是避免雷同的有效途径。雷同意味着没有新意，因而也就没有很大的意义，它是追求高分者要极力避免的。

下面这个例子虽然是中文的，但它是一个非常典型的范例，对于反问法的学习非常有益。接下来我们来欣赏反问法的标题及其文章的第一段。

钱锺书能够与鲁迅比肩?

八十年代末，九十年代初，《围城》被众"考"们捧得沸反盈天，不仅誉为现代小说的经典，而且在文学史排行榜上硬是加了一把交椅，险险乎乎地伴在鲁迅的身旁——钱鲁比肩。钱鲁可能比肩吗?

评析：钱锺书先生是学贯中西的大学者，他的小说《围城》还被拍成了电视剧，引起了广泛的关注。大家发现这部小说写得实在精彩，尤其是里面的几百个比喻，有些让人拍案叫绝。然而，写小说毕竟不是钱锺书先生的专长，他也就是写过这一部小说。对小说更有造诣的研究者指出，小说中的有些笔墨有些过当，超过了小说的要求，甚至给人显摆学识的感觉。这些评价都是比较切中要害的。一个作家能否在一个国家的文学史上占有一定位置，通常不是一部小说能决定的。鲁迅先生凭借对文学的巨大贡献被排放在当代中国文学史第一位是当之无愧的。因此，外行人认为钱锺书先生伟大到可以和鲁迅先生比肩并不重要，重要的是小说评论家们是怎么看的。

作者显然是不同意钱锺书与鲁迅比肩的看法，于是他用了反问法，以此来表示不同的看法。

我们再来看一篇关于品质的作文，它的题目也是反问句。

Good Qualities Are Not Important for Advanced Students?

Some people argue that advanced students don't necessarily need good qualities. They say that advanced students are rare resource and we should not demand them too much. Is that true? I don't think so.

评析：作者在肯定句后面加问号表示反问，意思是"优等生就不要好品质吗?"作者只是说有人认为优等生不一定要有好的品质，他们认为优等生犹如稀缺资源，我们不该过分要求他们。然后，作者再次使用问句说"这是真的吗？"，最后提出否定。虽然简单，但是反问法确实用得恰到好处。

总之，使用反问法通常表示写作者不同意他人的观点，因而采用反问句来表明自己的观点或立场。另外，使用反问法表达的情感一般要比使用肯定句表达的情感更强烈。

4. 引言法

引言法也叫引语法，它是指引用名人名言开头的写作方法。

这种方法是开篇法中最简单的，但引言一定要和文章的主题直接相关，并且可以支持文章的观点。无关的引语即使再美也没有意义。另外，要注意，引言要引用名人名言。之所以必须引用名人的话语，是因为这些人的智慧大多经过实践的检验，经得起推敲，有说服力，可以充当论据。就像谈教育与学习，有人经常引用孔子的话，如"三人行，必有我师"。只要命题恰巧与你知道的某个著名人物说过的话有关，你就可以采用引言法，用名人名言来支持你的观点。

引言法一般都在文章的开头，它可以分为直接引言和间接引言两种。我们来看下面的例子。

例 1

People Are Never Satisfied with What They Have

Some people say that people are never satisfied with what they have. And they criticize the great desire or lust of man to which caused a lot of the world's tragedies and disasters. However, everything can be divided into two. We should look upon it objectively.

It has been claimed that workers over 50 are not responsive to rapidly changing ideas in the modern workplace and that for this reason younger workers are to be preferred. This may be true in some aspects but not exact in all the aspects.

例 2

Ambition

Ambition is the decision one makes and the resolution with which he carries out that decision. It provides us with the required driving force to accomplish any undertakings in our life. Just as Joseph Epstein, a famous American writer put it, "And as we decide and choose, so are our lives formed." Indeed, once we make up our minds to choose to do something, then our life becomes meaningful and specifically orientated. This notion of life, as far as I observe, is closest to truth and does apply to almost all aspects of life.

例 3

The Role of Women in Children's Education

There's an African proverb saying that if you educate a boy, you educate an individual; if you educate a girl, you educate a family and a nation, which indicates the great importance of females in children's education.

评析：例1中的间接引言"欲望不止"其实是人的需求规律。根据马斯洛的需求理论，低一级的需求一旦满足，就会产生高一级的需求。一个人如果连最基本的需求都满足不了，就没有工夫去考虑其他的需求了。但是，你可以对"欲望不止"进行反驳，它表示一种过度的欲望，甚至贪欲。因此，作者提出要客观看待这个问题，这是合理的。

例2中，作者先对ambition进行了解释，也就是对这个概念进行了界定，然后引用了美国作家爱泼斯坦关于人的命运形成的观点，最后加上了作者的巧妙解读。他把爱泼斯坦的话解读成近乎真理，表示自己同意他的观点。如果把他的话说成是真理，当然不正确，会招来非议；说成近乎真理就不仅具有可信性，又不会遭到非议。

例3中，作者把非洲谚语作为引言，然后加上了一句自己的理解，作为文章的第一段，既简洁又精准。

总之，引言法是使用很普遍的一种开篇方法，目的是使用引言来增强文章观点的可信度，它的唯一难点是要求我们能够记住什么人在某个领域说过什么话，这就要求我们平时多阅读、多积累。

（二）标识词的用法

1. 标识词及其用法

标识词也叫转折词或过渡词，常用的有firstly，secondly，because，then，in addition，as a result，so，therefore等。

所谓"标识"，就是说看到某个词，读者就知道你在进行哪一部分的写作，比如first，second说明你在写第二部分，分析论证问题，而as a result，therefore说明你在写文章的结尾。

标识词问题很简单，因为这些词都是我们很熟悉的连接词或副词。但是，在写作中这个错误很常见，很多人完全没有正确使用标识词的意识。

要知道标识词，就要知道连接词或转折词。通常，连接词或转折词中也包括标识词，比如currently，nowadays，first，secondly，first things first，furthermore，moreover，in addition，however，as a result，consequently，so，therefore等，它们的主要作用是确定逻辑

框架，因为英语是形合的语言，文章的逻辑关系主要靠连接词和转折词来表达，这就是我们一眼就可以看出一篇作文是否整齐规范的原因。

大部分人对开篇和结尾的连接词比较熟悉，但在第二部分，标识词经常使用得不是很恰当。

连接词或转折词使用得好，文章能给人留下线条分明的好印象；不用或者不恰当地使用这些关系词，文章经常会给人一种线条模糊的感觉。大家可以留意一下，凡是高分作文，作者在关系词的使用上都特别到位。

我们一起来看一个例子，它短小精悍，关系词的使用令文章增色不少，逻辑框架既分明又美观。

例

Comparison of Cars and Motorcycles

Compared with cars, motorcycles have their advantages and drawbacks.

Both cars and motorcycles are the convenient means of transport, enabling the driver to move around freely. But a motorcycle is cheaper, so more people can afford it. In addition, a motorcycle needs smaller parking place. However, traveling by car is more comfortable and safer, especially in rough weather. Besides, a car can carry bulky packages as well as several additional people.

评析：这篇作文短小精悍，读起来非常流畅，主要原因是逻辑关系密切，而逻辑关系密切是通过连接词来实现的。由此可见，标识词在写作中非常重要。

为了便于记忆，我们把常用的连接词和转折词列出来，供大家参考：

表4-1　常用连接词和转折词用法表

开篇常用连接词：	提供理由时的常用转折词：
• in my opinion	• first
• I believe	• to begin with
• I think	• second
• I feel	• next
• I prefer	• another reason
• my favourite	• finally
• nowadays	• lastly
• currently	• most importantly
提供例子或细节时的常用转折词：	用于总结的常用转折词：
• in fact	• all in all
• in particular	• as you can see
• in other words	• in conclusion
• additionally	• so
• for example	• to sum up
• for instance	• therefore

2. 使用标识词的常见错误

使用标识词时注意别乱用，用来分析的词不要用于结尾部分。同理，表示结论的词，不要随便用于开篇或正文部分。

文章的第一部分很少使用标识词，但是有的学生在开篇部分就把该用于正文部分的标识词用完了，让人感觉一段即全篇，无须再写第二部分和第三部分了，这样是不对的。

我们先来看一篇一段即全篇的作文开篇，它的情景如下：

A girl student was caught to be cheating in the middle of a test. She was asked to quit school as punishment. She was sad because it was common to cheat in almost every exam and it was not her first time to cheat in exams. She did not know what to do and who she could ask help for. What's your opinion on cheating in exams?

例 1

Results of Cheating in Exams

Nowadays, cheating in the exams becomes more and more spreading <u>because</u> most students don't take serious attitude towards testing in colleges. <u>However</u>, it is necessary to have exams after a lesson is finished. <u>Moreover</u>, in the middle of a lesson, students are often tested. <u>So</u> exams are still important and students have to make them. Exams need us to follow exam rules. <u>Therefore</u> cheating is against the rules and those who cheat in exams should be punished and I quite agree to that.

评析：这篇作文除了内容不相关、话题扯得很远等问题外，拟题和内容也有问题。所拟题目是Results of Cheating in Exams，可是作者在第一段里面没有明确给出结果，而情景里面则提到"女孩很难过，不知怎么办，也不知向谁倾诉"。

该作文还有一个问题是乱用标识词。作者在第一段差不多把开头、正文、结尾部分的标识词都用上了，似乎已经没有必要继续写下去了。其实，我们完全可以这样开篇：

A girl student was caught to be cheating in the exam. She was asked to leave school as a punishment and she was very sad. I think the result is what she should suffer.

再看一篇关于大学生高薪的作文。

例2

College Students, Higher Salary?

Now, there are more and more college students in our society as the enlargement of higher education in our nation. So, there are more college students <u>get</u> the job than ever before. I think the college students should get a high salary.

评析：这篇作文问题也比较多。首先，它的题目采用反问，段落里面却不是持反对意见。我们在作文的开篇方法部分提到，采用反问法通常意味着作者不同意这个观点。其次，标识词用得不合适。最后，前后逻辑关系很别扭，最后一句和前面一句关系不够密切，画线部分还有语法错误。

如果写作者说的是现在大学生读书成本很高，出来就业时的工资却普遍偏低，没有体现他们的价值，大学生应该得到更高的工资，读者就会感觉好得多。虽然这样未必有说服力，但至少逻辑关系密切。

规范问题看似简单，但就是有很多人始终不注意，因此，在教学过程中，我们反复强调的一件事情是，哪怕还有一个人没有搞懂某个知识点，我们都要重复讲。对于写作的规范问题，我们要始终头脑清楚。

阐释文体的标识词非常明显，因为它是说理的文体。鉴于连接词的作用是体现逻辑关系，那么它们就不仅仅使用在阐释文体中。为了更好地从阅读中吸收这个知识点，我们也举几个其他体裁的例子。事实上，它们在开篇时和阐释文体有着相同的习惯，即开篇中标识词的使用不是很多。

例 3

The Middle Eastern bazaar takes you back hundreds—even thousands—of years. The one I am thinking of particularly is entered by a Gothic-arched gateway of aged brick and stone. You pass from the heat and glare of a big, open square into a cool, dark cavern which extends as far as the eye can see, losing itself in the shadowy distance. Little donkeys with harmoniously tinkling bells thread their way among the throngs of people entering and leaving the bazaar. The roadway is about twelve feet wide, but it is narrowed every few yards by little stalls where goods of every conceivable kind are sold. The din of the stall-holder crying their wares, of donkey-boys and porters clearing a way for themselves by shouting vigorously, and of would-be purchasers arguing and bargaining is continuous and makes you dizzy.

评析：《中东集市》是一篇描述文，这一段是它的开头。英语的描述文体包括三大部分，第一部分交代要介绍什么，通常采用开门见山的方法，直接告诉读者要介绍的内容。

这段话一共六句，句与句之间逻辑关系密切，但几乎看不到一个连接词或转折词。

别的体裁是怎样的情景呢？

例 4

"Hiroshima! Everybody off!" That must be what the man in the Japanese stationmaster's uniform shouted, as the fastest train in the world slipped to a stop in Hiroshima Station. I did not understand what he was saying. First of all, because he was shouting in Japanese. And secondly, because I had a lump in my throat and a lot of sad thoughts on my mind that had little to do with anything a Nippon railways official might say. The very act of stepping on this soil, in breathing this air of Hiroshima, was for me a far greater adventure than any trip or any reportorial assignment I'd previously taken. Was I not at the scene of the crime?

评析：《广岛——日本"最快乐"的城市》是一篇报告文学，属于叙事文体。作者是参加第二次世界大战的一位飞行员，也是投放原子弹的机组成员之一。战争结束后，他成了新闻工作者，再次来到广岛时，他已经是一个深刻反省战争的人。除了first of all和secondly，我们看不到其他标识词，而这两个词只是为了解释他为什么听不明白铁路官员说的话。

例 5

The storm of abuse in the popular press that greeted the appearance of *Webster's Third New International Dictionary* is a curious phenomenon. Never has a scholarly work of this stature been attacked with such unbridled fury and contempt. An article in the *Atlantic* viewed it as a "disappointment," a "shock," a "calamity," "a scandal and a disaster." The *New York Times*, in a special editorial, felt that the work would "accelerate the deterioration" of the language and sternly accused the editors of betraying a public trust. The *Journal of the American Bar Association* saw the publication as "deplorable," "a flagrant example of lexicographic irresponsibility," "a serious blow to the cause of good English." *Life* called it "a non-word deluge", "monstrous", "abominable," and "a cause for dismay." They doubted that "Lincoln could have modeled his Gettysburg Address" on it—a concept of how things get written that throws very little light on Lincoln but a great deal on *Life*.

评析：《词典的作用究竟是什么？》是一篇论辩文。论辩文通常是对某个或某些观点持反对意见的一种文体，是通过解释、说明、证明、反驳来论证自己观点正确的文体。

英语论辩文通常包括五个部分（引言、说明、证明、反驳、结尾）和三大要素（理性的，道德的，情感的）。

第一段通常就是第一部分，告诉读者要辩论什么问题。我们可以看出，这篇文章是要讨论一部词典的好坏，各大媒体认为它不好，甚至使用了很多谩骂、侮辱的言辞。在陈述的过程中，同上面其他体裁的例子一样，标识词用得很少，这是我们可以借鉴的。

综上所述，标识词是用来表明段落所处阶段的连接词或转折词，有些词如recently，nowadays等是用在第一段里的标识词；有些如firstly，secondly，then等则是在第二部分分析时用的；而so，therefore，as a result等一般是在结尾使用的标识词。

（三）总分结构法

总分结构是指from general to specific或者from overview to details的一种表达方式，即从整体到具体的一种结构。通常总和分是连在一起使用的，而不是有总没有分。

总分结构有两大好处：第一，它是典型的英式思维习惯，按照这个习惯写出来的内容比较地道，因此，英语学习者一定要掌握；第二，它特别好增加字数，纠结字数的学生可以好好借鉴一下。

既然是典型的英式思维习惯，那么老师在阅读课上就应当把这个知识点传授给学生。

有些词经常使用在总分结构中，比如性质形容词以及一些表示范围的短语，如good，bad，wonderful，awful，beautiful，ugly，same，different，anywhere，in any place等，大家可以留意。

我们先来看一些例子。

例 1

　　Peanut was a dachshund with a long list of dislikes. He didn't like people taller than he was. He didn't like bicycles or cars. And he had tried to attack so many people that he was now confined to our yards.

参考译文：

　　"花生"是一只德国犬，有一大串不喜欢的东西。它讨厌比它高的人，讨厌比它跑得快的自行车和汽车，它试图攻击过太多的人，结果现在它被关在院子里了。

评析：这是《三人出游记》里面的一个小片段，是典型的总分结构。前面用的是表示范围的短语"一大串不喜欢的东西"，后面则具体展开，列出了它不喜欢的东西。

例 2

　　The only thing that Montmorency and I disagree about is cats. <u>I like cats. Montmorency does not.</u> Every time when I meet a cat, I say hello to it. Then I bend down and I stroke it gently, behind the ears and along the side of its head. The cat likes this. It puts its tail up and it pushes itself against my legs. And there is love and peace. When Montmorency meets a cat, everybody knows about it, and a lot of bad words are used.

参考译文：

　　我和"元帅"之间唯一的分歧是猫，我喜欢猫，"元帅"讨厌猫。每次我见到猫，我就跟它打招呼，然后弯下身子，轻轻地抚摸它的耳朵和头的两侧，猫很喜欢这点。它会竖起尾巴蹭我的腿，于是我们之间洋溢着爱与和谐。"元帅"则不然，它一见到猫，邻里都被惊动，于是骂声不绝。

评析：这也是《三人出游记》里面的一个小段落，非常有意思。"元帅"是狗的名字，主人和它关系很和谐，他们之间只有一个分歧，就是二者对待猫的不同态度。请注意，画线部分既是前面的具体内容，同时也是对后面的概括。因此，作者继续交代自己和"元帅"对待猫的不同态度，前后加起来就成了一段。

小说显示出作者良好的思维能力，包括看待事物的角度，小说里处处可见幽默和诙谐之趣味。英式思维习惯也是一样的，时常可以让我们领略到总分结构带来的喜悦。

例 3

Many people believe that their economic prospects are gloomy. They believe they will not do as well financially as their parents or grandparents. They know that the average income for young people has declined significantly over the past generations. Many feel their chances for finding the job and salary they want are bleak.

参考译文：

许多人觉得经济前景渺茫。他们觉着不如长辈们赚得多了，他们清楚年轻人的平均收入在过去的几十年间大幅度下降了。许多人感到要找到好的工作，获得好的薪水，可能性很小。

评析：这个例子和上面两个例子似乎不太一样，它的侧重点好像是动词。其实，仔细分析一下，它的概括还是在形容词上，也就是gloomy，后面的具体内容都是为了说明前景不佳。

例 4

My hometown is wonderful. It is small with only five thousand people. The sky is blue and the air is clean. You never have the feeling of dark and grey clouds in the sky during the day as in some big cities.

参考译文：

　　我的家乡妙不可言。地方小小的，仅有五千居民；天空碧蓝，空气清新；白天的时候，绝对不会像有些大城市那样，感觉天空灰蒙蒙的。

评析：在今天工业带来严重环境污染的情况下，大部分城市天总是灰蒙蒙的，这个地方真的是很美了。在写作时，我们先说这里很美，然后说具体哪里美，这就是总分结构。

例 5

　　Today's workers want to be a valued part of the whole. They want to know that their work is important and how it fits into the corporate strategy. They want to know not only how the work they do affects others and the organization's goals, but how they as individuals can make an impact. Employees will contribute their knowledge enthusiastically in a corporate culture that values the individual.

参考译文：

　　今天的工人想成为整体中有价值的一部分。他们想知道自己工作的重要性，以及它是怎样融入公司战略的。他们想知道自己的工作对他人及组织目标产生什么样的影响，还想知道他们作为个人的作用。在尊重个人的企业文化中，员工会热情地奉献他们的才智。

评析：这一段写得很美，但手法很简单，就是采用总分结构。

前面说工人想成为有价值的一部分，后面则展开他们想要体现自我价值的心愿。

例 6

From the sidewalk outside the station, things seemed much the same as in other Japanese cities. Little girls and elderly ladies in kimonos rubbed shoulders with teenagers and women in western dress. Serious looking men spoke to one another as if they were oblivious of the crowds about them, and bobbed up and down repeatedly in little bows, as they exchanged the ritual formula of gratitude and respect: "Tomo aligato gozayimas." Others were using little red telephones that hung on the facades of grocery stores and tobacco shops.

参考译文：

从火车站外面的街道看，这里和其他城市没有什么区别。穿着和服的小姑娘和上了年纪的女士，与穿西服的年轻姑娘和女士们擦肩而过。严肃的男子旁若无人地和他人聊着天，还不停地鞠躬，说一些感谢之类的礼节性话语。还有人正在使用装在杂货店和烟草铺墙面上的小小的红色电话。

评析：这是《广岛——日本"最快乐"的城市》中的第二段。作为原子弹投放机组成员之一，作者内心纠结，负罪感让他感到极度压抑。他再次来到广岛时，以为这里的人和事与其他地方不同，可是他发现这里的一切和日本其他城市没有什么区别。same是对总体的概括，后面三句是关于相同点的具体表现。

其实作者想要表达的是，曾经遭受过核武器毁灭性打击的广岛，在其外表、人的态度和现代化程度上，都和其他城市没有两样。人们的心态或生活方式不是他想象的那样留有战争的痕迹；相反，那里的人已经非常现代，非常开明。作者的写作手法很简单，不过是采用了总分结构而已，但却让读者对广岛的现状一览无余。

总之，总分结构是最大的英式思维习惯，是我们必须要掌握的一种结构。一来这样写出来的内容会关系密切，读起来很流畅；二来它在帮助我们增加字数方面是一个很好的方法。有时，写作者可以根据需要进行二级扩展，也就是一个句子既是前面的具体内容，同时又是对后面的概括，这样不仅可以增加字数，而且可以使文章环环相扣，逻辑关系更加密切。

二
逻辑方面的技巧和方法

（一）论据要充分

我们在第3章第一节里补充了一些逻辑知识，因此，这里就不重复前面提到的知识点，而是侧重说一下错误较多的几个方面。

第一就是论据充分问题。前面我们提到，论据不仅要相关，还要充分。论据充分是指所提供的论据有说服力，令人信服。这就是为什么我们强调，你是什么观点不重要，重要的是你可以提出强有力的证据来支持自己的观点。

论辩最需要拿出强有力的证据，只有强有力的证据才能让读者放弃原有立场，变得信服作者。我们先看《词典的作用究竟是什么？》中的例子。

例 1

The broad general findings of the new science are:

First, all languages are systems of human conventions, not systems of natural laws. The first—and essential—step in the study of any language is observing and setting down precisely what happens when native speakers speak it.

Second, each language is unique in its pronunciation, grammar, and vocabulary. It cannot be described in terms of logic or of some theoretical, ideal languages. It cannot be described in terms of any other languages, or even in terms of its own past.

Third, all languages are dynamic rather than static, and hence a "rule" in any language can only be a statement of contemporary practice. Change is constant—and normal.

Fourth, "correctness" can rest only upon usage, for the simple reason that there is nothing else for it to rest on. And all usage is relative.

From these propositions it follows that a dictionary is good only insofar as it is a comprehensive and accurate description of current usage. And to be comprehensive it must include some indication of social and regional associations.

参考译文：

新学科的成果概括如下：

第一、所有的语言都是约定俗成的，不是自然法则，研究语言第一个，也是最重要的一个步骤就是观察并准确记录本族语者是怎样说的。

第二、任何一门语言的发音、语法、词汇都具有独特性，不能按照逻辑，或者理论或理想的语言来描述，也不能按照其他语言来描述，甚至也不能用这门语言的过去来描述。

第三、语言是动态的，不是静止不变的，因此，任何语言的所谓"规则"只能是当前的用法，变化是不断的，是正常的。

第四、关于准确，它只能依赖运用，因为别无其他东西可以依赖，而所有的用法都是相对的。

根据以上这些观点应该可以得出这样的结论：一部词典只有当它能全面而准确地描述词语的当前的用法时才算是好词典，而要做到全面，它就必须包含对一些社会性和区域性等方面情况的描述。

评析：这是《词典的作用究竟是什么？》里面的一段介绍新学科成果的段落。当时，各大媒体都说这部词典不好，作者要拿出什么样的证据才有说服力呢？有什么比科学发现更让人信服的？

我们打个比方，甲乙两人在争论地球的形状。甲说地球是平的，乙说地球是圆的。甲的证据是主观的，他说怎么走都在平地上走；而乙的观点是客观的，他说，"地球是圆的，因为它是科学事实，科学已经证明了这一点，只是你不知道而已"。所谓不争的事实，强调的就是问题的客观性，它具有最大的说服力。

在这篇文章中，作者拿出科学事实来充当论据，就成功地达到了说服他人的目的。

我们看看2010年TEM-8写作真题，它的情景如下：

Recently newspapers have reported that officials in a little-known mountainous area near Guiyang, Guizhou Province, wanted to turn the area into a "central business district" for Guiyang and invited a foreign design company to give it an entirely new look. The design company came up with a blueprint for unconventional, super-futuristic buildings. This triggered off different responses. Some appreciated the bold innovation of the design, but others held that it failed to reflect regional characteristics or local cultural heritage. What is your view on this? Write an essay of about 400 words. You should supply an appropriate title for your essay.

例 2

The Benefits of Bold Innovation

It is reported that officials in a remote mountainous area near Guiyang, Guizhou Province intended to transform the area into a "central business district" for Guiyang and invited a foreign design company to carry out a plan for unconventional buildings with an entirely new look. This news aroused a heated discussion, with some speaking highly of the bold innovation of the design while others suggesting that this practice would bring a dark side to the local cultural heritage. On considering the case in an all-round way, personally, I am more in favor of the former.

The first reason to support my standing is the abundant merits brought by the bold innovation to the local residents. In the first place, the building of "central business district" in that area can promote the process of urbanization advanced in China to some extent. So, local people have an opportunity to get access to the lifestyle of urban people, which broadens their horizon and enjoys the convenience of urban life. In the second place, the bold innovation of the design is capable of attracting investment from home and abroad, which, in turn, boosts the working situation in the area. Local people have no need to go out for making a living. They can manage a job at home, so that they can take care of their family, especially their children. If managed and guided under a feasible plan, the remote mountainous area is able to develop into a prosperous area like Shenzhen which is originally a small village.

评析：首先，题目就表现出了作者的观点。另外，文章从拟题到开篇，从句子结构到文章的整体布局，都把握得非常好，而且证据比较有说服力。

在第一段，作者间接引用了所给的情景，但不是完全复制，然后就表明自己的观点。我们会注意到作者使用的句式很漂亮，语言也很书面化。

第二段中作者采用了几个总分结构，在第一个总分结构中作者先是概括了项目对当地居民有巨大的好处，从这里我们可以看出作文的高度，因为一个项目是好是坏，当地人最有发言权了。然后，作者具体说了两大好处。接下来作者再次使用总分结构，先说当地居民无须外出谋取生计，在家里工作即可；又说这样还可以在家养育孩子。整段内容条理清楚、逻辑关系密切、主次分明，读起来非常流畅。可见，这是一篇高水平的文章。虽然我们没有把结尾拿出来欣赏，但从证据来看，结论是站得住脚的。

例3

Protecting the Regional Characteristics or Local Cultural Heritage

Recently, there is no consensus among the people as to the view of a report that a foreign design company invited by Guizhou Province came up with a blueprint for unconventional, super-futuristic building without any regional characteristics. Some people hold that they appreciated its design. They point out that this wonderful design reflects this area a new look. However, others have different opinions. They argue that the design didn't reflect regional characteristic or local cultural heritage. Personally, I am in favor of the latter opinion.

Many remarkable reasons contribute to this opinion. In the first place, a design for unconventional, super-futuristic buildings is in need of a large amount of money to build. A little-known mountainous area near Guiyang may be a quite small city. So its economical condition cannot suit the requirement that a lot of money should be needed. Secondly, a city's regional characteristics or local cultural heritage should be protected. As we all know, China has a long history. In the meanwhile, many cultural heritages also have been reserved. A city's regional characteristics or local cultural heritage reflect a city's condition and means its symbol. It is really important for everyone to protect their countries' local cultural heritage. Finally, a blueprint for unconventional, super-futuristic buildings is essential, but we cannot abandon a city's regional characteristic or local cultural heritage.

评析：从例3的语法上，我们就可以看出写作者基本功还不是很好。时态用得比较乱，前后没有保持一致，有的用一般现在时，有的又用过去时，有的词用得也不是很准确，比如protect characteristics搭配不是很好。

不过，题目拟得不错，直接表明作者对项目持反对意见。然而在第二段分析时，写作者给出的理由之一却是需要钱，而且还花了不少笔墨说城镇很小，经济条件无法满足，这就属于偏题，因为题目只是强调要保持传统的文化特色而已。搞建设肯定需要钱，如果是偏远的小城镇，可能经济比较落后，财政会比较紧张。但是，我们需要紧紧扣住主题来完成写作任务，达到以论据支持主题的目的。对于主题之外的信息，即便是真实的，也不该无故涉足。也就是说，有钱没钱不是我们要讨论的问题，否则写作的背景应该是类似"偏远小镇大搞建设，合适吗？"这样的。可是，写作者上来就说钱的问题，这样的证据，无论真假，都属于不足以使人信服的证据。

总之，证据是关乎我们的论点是否为他人所接受的关键，证据不仅要真实，要有相关性，而且一定要强劲有力，要能够支撑观点。与主题无关的证据，即使是真实的，也不要随便扯进来。

（二）区别个别现象和普遍现象

要使得证据有说服力，还有一个问题是很重要的，那就是区别个别现象和普遍现象。在论证过程中，以特例或非典型事例为根据概括出关于一类对象的一般结论的错误，被称之为"轻率概括"或"以偏概全"的逻辑错误，它是使用简单枚举法进行论证时常见的错误类型，有很多人因为缺乏这方面的逻辑知识，常常犯一些令人啼笑皆非的错误。

我们先来看1994年TEM-8写作真题，其情景如下：

Personal Appearance: Looks Really Count. Or do they? Looks aren't everything, the saying goes. Write a composition about 300 words agreeing or disagreeing with the topic.

例 1

Looks Really Count

Looks refer to our appearance. I think looks are important. However, some people don't think so. I'll give my reasons to refute them.

In a cinema, it is broadcasting a film. The film stars are beautiful and the audience like the film very much. If the stars were not beautiful, do the audience love the film? I'll give another example. It is my own experience. I can't forget it. It was last year. I went out to look for an odd job. The boss looked very strict. I thought he was not a kind person. To my expectation, he looked at my face, my body. As a result, I failed in the interview. After that, I realized that personal appearance is so important that if we are not good-looking, we will fail in our work and life.

评析：这篇作文问题比较严重。首先，作者在开篇采用定义法，说长相就是我们的外表。定义本身没有很大的问题，可是定义这个概念的目的是什么呢？难道我们不知道长相是什么吗？抑或作者发现长相有什么新内容可以补充吗？显然都不是。事实上，我们根本看不出作者定义的目的。第二句说长相很重要，这句和前一句之间的关系显然不密切，不如直接说I think looks are important，这样既符合英语开门见山的开篇习惯，又不会出现与前一句缺乏关联的错误。另外，从基础写作到高级写作，我们反复强调作文的第一段应包含两个内容：提出问题和表明观点。而在这篇作文里，观点似乎有，但问题却不见，区区几句话，都是简单句。

第二段，作者举了两个例子。第一个例子是影星，作者说她们是银幕上的美女，因此，大家喜欢看她们演的电影，并反问"如果影星不好看，大家还会喜爱这部片子吗？"这个论据主观性太强了，而且牵强附会，有点让人哭笑不得。你怎么知道别人一定是冲着美女去的？喜欢美女，就一定喜欢她们演的电影吗？再说，有很多演员长得不好看，甚至还有一些"丑星"，他们却有很多影迷，因为他们是演技派；相反，有些演员很漂亮，可是并不受人欢迎。由此可见，这样的证据经不起反驳，根本没有说服力。

第二个例子谈到自己的亲身经历，不仅句与句之间严重缺乏关联，读起来非常费劲，而且极其片面。感觉作者不是在写作文，而是对着某个人在回忆一个故事，断断续续，没有条理。

前面我们说过，英语写作首先要注意规范，规定写什么就写什么，规定怎么写就怎么写，不能随意发挥。另外，写作过程中一定要讲逻辑，论据必须具有普遍性，不能犯"轻率概括"这类论据不足的逻辑错误。

例 2

Looks Really Count

Recently, there is a heated discussion on whether personal appearance counts or not. Some people think personal appearance is quite important, others don't think so. In my opinion, looks really count.

First of all, when you are looking for a job, personal appearance counts a lot. The first impression is extremely significant when having a job interview. A good appearance can give the interviewer a good impression, thus an opportunity might be got. Compared with common people, those who have beautiful appearances can have more chances to obtain a job under the same condition.

评析：题目表明作者认同这个观点。第一段写得非常规范，作者先提出现象，然后表明自己的观点。在论据方面，作者先举求职为例，说外表很重要，面试的时候第一印象很关键，外表好会给面试官留下好印象，从而增加获得工作机会的概率。与常人相比，外表好的人，在同等条件下，得到工作的概率更大。这个论据是比较有说服力的，因为这是一个普遍现象。

例2之所以比例1有说服力，是因为例1只是个别现象，而例2是普遍现象。我们要特别注意，用个别现象充当论据是片面的，没有说服力，而用普遍现象充当论据是很有说服力的。

有一句话大家要知道，那就是"普遍现象不排除反例"，意思是说在一个普遍的现象中可以有例外。这充分说明普遍性有说服力，而个别现象没有说服力。在一个普遍存在的现象中，就算你找到了几个例外，也不能说明什么问题。

综上所述，个别现象和普遍现象本来不是一个复杂的逻辑问题，但是如果我们对此不加以区别，把个别当成整体，就犯了"以偏概全"的逻辑错误。普遍现象中允许存在反例，发现几个不同的例子，也无法否定既存的事实。

（三）巧用全称概念

性质判断（断定对象具有或不具有某种性质的判断）按量划分，可分为全称判断和特称判断。全称即全体或所有，比如人人、每个人等，无一例外。特称则是指部分，比如有些、某些。全称作为论据，既简单又有说服力，不善说理的人可以特别留意。

我们来看看《词典的作用究竟是什么？》里面的几个例子。

例 1

All languages are systems of human conventions, not systems of natural laws. The first—and essential—step in the study of any language is observing and setting down precisely what happens when native speakers speak it.

评析：这篇论辩文之所以巧妙，有说服力，其中一个原因就是我们可以处处领略作者的高级思维，包括全称概念的使用。既然所有的语言都是约定俗成的，它们都必须准确记录本族语者说话的真实情况，那么英语也就不例外了。既然新版词典只是准确地记录了本族语者真实的讲话情况，何错之有呢？

例 2

All languages are dynamic rather than static, and hence a "rule" in any language can only be a statement of contemporary practice. Change is constant—and normal.

评析：这句话的方法和例1一样，使用了全称概念。既然所有语言都是变化的，而不是静止不变的，怎么可能用三十年前那部词典（第二版，新版是第三版）来做比较呢？第二版词典解释得更简洁，就等于说第三版的词典不好吗？三十年间出现了多少更复杂的新生事物，又多了多少以前没有的词？因此，第三版词典在解释一个变化了的事物上，怎么可能会更简洁呢？

例 3

Anyone who attempts sincerely to state what the word "door" means in the United States of America today can't take refuge in a log cabin.

参考译文：

在今天的美国，任何人试图诚挚地把"门"解释清楚，都不能龟缩在小茅屋里面。

评析：这一句话是针对媒体谴责新版词典把一个"如此简单的门解释得这么晦涩难懂"而进行的反驳。意思是久远的过去连门都没有，而现在有多达几十种门，怎么可能字数不会更多呢？

Anyone这个全称概念包括了第三版词典，既然第三版词典只是做了其他人在这种情况下也会做的事，那么，它何罪之有呢？

例 4

The new dictionary may have many faults. Nothing tries to meet an ever-changing situation over a terrain as vast as contemporary English can hope to be free of them.

参考译文：

新词典可能还存在许多错误，当代英语领域宽阔且不断变化，要满足这种需求，无论是谁犯错误都在所难免。

评析：即使在承认错误的时候，作者也很巧妙地使用了全称概念，也就是谁都会犯这样的错误，新版词典也不例外。

总之，很多方法让文章的论据强劲有力，其中一点就是学会使用全称判断。全称判断穷尽了所有，所以特别有说服力。这个知识点其实比较容易，只要在阅读过程中注意any，all等全称概念的使用情况即可。值得一提的是，虽然全称判断非常有说服力，但用起来必须特别小心，因为只要找到一个反例就可以把你的论点推翻。

（四）密切逻辑关系

逻辑关系有两层意思：一层意思是指前后句子有联系，或者指事物之间具有前因后果的关系；另一层意思是指在论证过程中，结论是由前提按照推理的一般规则从论据合乎逻辑地推出来的，即在论证过程中，论据与论题之间应当有必然联系，从论据能够合理地推出论题。

其实，我们已经举了不少例子来说明这一点，尤其是在补充逻辑知识一节，这些都是逻辑关系问题。

有的老师在批改作文时，会写上"读不通"一类的话语，因为学生的作文缺乏逻辑关系。

我们来看两个例子。

例 1

In the end, British companies could be driven out of shipping altogether. Some, such as P & O, have already moved into other fields, from house building to oil. Smaller shipping lines do not have the resources to diversify. They face extinction. And when they go, so does a huge slice of the few traditional industries worth keeping.

参考译文:

最终,英国公司可能会被挤出船运业。有些公司,比如东方远洋船运公司,已经转型到其他领域,从房地产领域到石油领域。而小公司,由于缺乏资金转型,只能面临倒闭。它们一旦倒闭,一大批值得保留的传统产业就要随之倒闭。

评析:这是《大不列颠望洋兴叹》一文的结尾。最后一句我们在前面分析时已经看过了。英国曾经是海上霸主,船运是它的主要财政收入来源,可是后来它逐渐失去了霸主地位,作者在分析各种原因之后,指出了英国船运业的结局,前后因果关系分明,逻辑关系密切。

例 2

But the real solution will be found in reinventing and finally healing the relationship between civilization and the earth. This can only be accomplished by undertaking a careful reassessment of all the factors that led to the relatively recent dramatic change in the relationship. The transformation of the way we relate to the earth will of course involve new technologies, but the key changes will involve new ways of thinking about the relationship itself.

参考译文:

真正的解决方案在于重新找到和最终修复人类文明与地球之间的关系,而且只能建立在认真评估导致当前破坏的所有要素之上。转变我们依赖地球的方式,自然需要引入新科技,但是,关键的变化还是对相互之间关系的思维转变。

评析:这是《沙漠之舟》的结尾。作者通过考察,科学地分析了导致环境破坏的根本原因之后,提出了解决问题的方案。换言之,这个方案是建立在正确的因果关系基础之上的,不是随便高呼几句空洞的口号。

（五）加强句与句之间的关系

句与句之间关系密切始终是逻辑的基本需求。

思维也好，写作也罢，关键是要使句子之间具有一定的关系。然而，从初级写作教学到高级写作教学，句与句之间的关系一直都是一个大问题。

写作文和平常思考不同，和日常对话也不同，它要求句子流畅，前后相关。

思维的跳跃在文学作品里属于常见的现象，但高级写作和文学作品不一样，思维不能随便跳跃。

在逻辑层面，尽管我们反复强调句与句之间要有关系，但实践证明，效果并不是很好。要不然，这个问题也不会一直都缠着我们，难以摆脱。那么，什么方法能最有效地解决这个问题呢？最简单的方法是记住一句话：后一句与前一句必须相关。

我们再来看两篇1994年TEM-8作文范例，其情景见本章的前面部分。

例 1

Looks Don't Play a Decisive Role in Success

Nowadays, more and more people do plastic surgery. This phenomenon leads to a puzzle: Does personal appearance really count? Some people attach great importance to it while others think that it is not so important. In my opinion, there is no doubt that people with good personal appearance are easier to do things, but inner beauty, instead of personal appearance, plays a decisive role in one's success. Personal appearance, to some degree, can contribute to one's success, but it is a short term influence rather than a long time one. When applying for a job, people with good personal appearance are more likely to be hired. Generally speaking, the employers put a high value on the employees' first impression. In this way, they get an easier access to what they desire. However, as time went by, good appearance will vanish and will not bring you any advantage any longer. Personal appearance is only the driving force to success, but not a decisive factor.

People with inner beauty are the group most likely to achieve great accomplishments. Inner beauty, such as integrity and faithfulness, can withstand any examination, no matter whether it is time or any difficulty. A person's inner beauty is a decisive factor in his or her success. With the qualities that others don't possess, the people with inner beauty can keep a positive attitude towards their life and are more confident in their work. There are numerous successful people in the world, but not everyone has a beautiful face or figure. It is their intelligence and perseverance that push them to success. Only when a person <u>realize</u> the importance of inner beauty and <u>learn</u> to approach it will he succeed.

All in all, personal appearance has <u>some influence</u> one's success, but the most important factor to achievements is inner beauty.

评析：只要瞥一眼就可以看出这篇作文在结构上头重脚轻，因为作者在第一段花了过多的笔墨。

第一段为什么这么长呢？是因为作者把外表和内在美糅合在一起了，结果要表述的内容太多。

我们在前面说过，一次性把过多的概念糅合在一起，线条就会变得很模糊。虽然主线出现了偏离，但这篇作文在句子之间的关系上还是比较密切的，因此它读起来让人感觉比较流畅。画线部分属于语法不当或词语使用不准确，大家在行文过程中应当注意。

在立场上，有一点我们必须说明：如果你是赞同的，就不要同时接受反对者的意见；如果你是反对的，就不要同时接受赞同者的观点；除非你持中立的态度，而且你在题目中或第一段就应该表明你的态度是中立的。

例 2

Looks Are Important in Some Ways

Some people believe that looks really count. They hold that in no matter what chances, looks take the most important role. I just think that looks are important in some ways, not in all the ways.

It is true that everyone, especially women, hope to have a good-looking face because it is the nature of man to be noticed. A good-looking face can attract more people's attention, which in return brings satisfaction to their mind. No wonder there is a saying that everyone has the desire for beauty.

It is also true that, in some fields, appearance seems so important that without a good-looking face, you cannot enter it. Take film stars or models for example. They choose a job which needs beautiful appearance to attract the audience.

However, man's desire for beauty does not mean it really counts. On the one hand, to be good-looking or not does not mean that good-looking faces can decide anything in the world. The world we live is not decided by ourselves, but by different kinds of people who are in charge of different fields among which there is little relationship with appearance. On the other hand, appearance changes quickly with age. The more we rely on it, the more disappointed we will be. Many tragedies happened in the history of mankind, both in China and in other countries, especially in the struggle of courts. Those who domineered and tried to elbow others out by having the advantage of good appearance usually did not have a good result.

If we want to have a meaningful life, our inner beauty must be expressed. People may like beauty, but they care more about good quality which is something lasting and will lead to a better life.

Therefore, looks don't count that much. They are just important in some ways. We can pay some attention on our faces. But it's improper to focus on that too much. Good qualities are much more important than one's appearance in our life. The former disappears quickly while the latter lasts long.

评析：从头至尾我们都可以感受到作者的精工细作。整体来看，文章写得很规范，句与句之间联系密切，读起来让人感觉无一词多余，无半句冗余。

他选择的角度和例1相同，但有两点比较突出：第一，他直接从题目中表明了自己的观点，让批改试卷的老师一眼就能看出他要写什么；第二，他在第一段突出了写作意义，他人觉得外表很重要，作者却不这样认为，外表不过在有些方面比较重要而已。这个开篇准确地扣住了自己的题目，既没有放大也没有缩小概念。

第二段和第三段是排比，表明了两个事实：一是爱美之心人皆有之；二是有些职业，比如影星和模特，需要看外表。排比的最大好处是句式优美，采用段落排比还能让字数更多一些。

在第四段，作者进行转折，他说人爱美，并不意味着外表就是那么重要，然后采用on one hand...on the other hand...的句式，让意思紧密关联。文章显得条理清晰，脉络分明。作者指出，一方面，好看与否不意味着就能够支配整个世界，世界是由不同人掌管的，其中与外貌相关的甚少；另一方面，外表随着年龄快速变化，越是依赖外表，我们就会越失望。纵观历史，例子比比皆是，借助外貌飞扬跋扈者以及试图借着外貌排挤他人者，大都没有好下场。

文章的每个句子都和前面的句子紧密相连，读来甚是流畅，而且整篇作文的论据充分，主次分明。

总之，在写作过程中，我们要始终把握句子之间的关系，这样，整篇文章的逻辑关系就会很密切。任何文章，越是紧凑，越说明前后信息相关。换言之，文章要紧凑、要流畅，就要加强句与句之间的关联。

（六）信息必须按主次排列

缺乏主次是学生写作时常见的问题，这和他们的知识背景有关，很多问题他们都不知道，怎么可能切中要害呢？

通常情况下，对于一个现象或问题，我们有两方面要清楚：一是我们要尽可能多地掌握这个问题的相关要素；二是对于所有的相关要素，我们要分清主次，这也是因果方面的逻辑要求，因为"诉诸远因"是一个常见的逻辑谬误。

当然，生活中有太多的问题，谁都不可能对所有问题都熟悉。因此，越是大家熟悉的问题，作文会越好写；越是大家感觉生疏的话题，作文越不好写。但是，即便面对熟悉的问题，有的人也会遗漏相关要素，或者颠倒主次。

我们在这里强调主次的目的，一是让大家清楚，有条理意味着主次分明，写作一定要把握主次；二是促使我们多读一些课外书籍，多了解一些社会问题，看看别人是怎么看待这些问题的，这对于我们的写作大有好处。

对此，我们强调一下写作时应注意以下问题：第一，尽可能涵盖更多相关要素；第二，主要信息放在前面，笔墨多一些；第三，次要信息放在后面，笔墨少一些；第四，可以用last but not the least，但不能使用last but the most important。

下面我们来看一篇CET-6的作文真题，它的情景如下：

> While some people claim that a person's essential qualities are inherited at birth, others insist that the circumstances in which a person grows up are principally responsible for the kind of person he or she becomes. Which view do you agree with and why? You should write a composition about 250 words.

很多人在写这篇作文时选择了遗传因素。按照我们前面讨论的内容，选择哪种观点并不重要，那么，选择遗传因素当然是可以的。但在这里其实不然。选择遗传因素这个观点说明作者无知，无论他怎么论证都站不住脚，因为研究表明，决定一个人品质的因素是环境因素，而不是遗传因素。事实上，影响人品质形成的因素很多，遗传因素排在后面。从这个角度来看，这个题目有问题，它犯了"遗漏子项"的逻辑错误。在选言判断中，要求穷尽子项，也就是说选项里面必须包括所有的可能，否则就是逻辑不当。好在题目中没有缺少最重要的因素，否则这个命题就不成立。

心理学研究已经证明，人的主要特征是环境决定的，而不是先天的。事实上，遗传因素在决定个人品质方面的作用是次要的。许多人不知道这个科研成果，就凭自己的意愿选择了遗传因素。那么，选择遗传因素的学生可以给出有说服力的证据吗？我们一起来看下面的例子。

例1

Inheritance Takes the Most Important Role in a Person's Main Quality

Many people argue that the circumstances in which a person grows up are principally responsible for the kind of person he or she becomes. I don't agree with them. For me, a person's essential qualities are inherited at birth.

Take myself for example. I am the only child in my family. My mother is a gentle woman while my father is strict with severe appearance but actually he's a kind man. Our neighbours always say that I look the same as my father. I am a boy who looks serious. But I know my heart is soft and kind. So do my classmates and friends.

The same evidence can be found in books and films, where the evil father had a wicked son, where the daughter committed the same cruelty to her kind as her mother did. No one can refuse to accept the fact and we have to agree that they are the reflection of the society.

As to the circumstances, I think, it is also important to the forming of our quality but not that important than the inheritance.

So, the quality of ours is the result of our heritage rather than the circumstances. To have realized this, we can have a better understanding what people do and what they say.

评析：上面我们提到，如果选择遗传因素，我们就很难论证，因为事实证明，人的品质主要是环境决定的。下面我们一起看看这位学生是怎样论证遗传因素最重要的。

第一部分，即第一段，很是规范，表明了作者的观点。第二部分包括两小段：第二小段和第三小段。在第二小段，作者举自己为例，说自己是独生子，母亲很温柔，父亲貌似很严厉，却有一颗仁慈的心。邻居们说他和父亲很像，看起来很严肃。但他很清楚，自己内心很温柔，很善良，其同学和朋友也是这么看的。

我们在前面谈到，普遍现象才有说服力，个别现象没有什么说服力，因为普遍现象不排除反例。因此，作者以自己为例并不意味着这种理由可以支撑观点。在主次上，我们也看不出它有什么代表性。

在第三小段，作者举了另一些个别的例子，分别是书和电影里面的。句式还可以，说邪恶的父亲生了个邪恶的儿子，恶毒的女儿做了母亲做过的坏事。我们都知道，文学创作里出现的未必是普遍的事情，而且文学作品的内容大都是虚构的，根据论据的逻辑要求，证据必须为真，虚假的东西不能用来充当论据，不能够说服读者。最后一句作者突然改成全称，说"没有人可以否定他们折射出的社会现象"，这是很突兀的，仿佛我们"被代表"了。你怎么知道没有人否定？故事里面的人物怎么就一定反映了社会现象呢？我们前面说了，使用全称是很有说服力的一种写作方法，但是必须特别小心，找到一个反例就可以把你驳倒。把个人的观点或猜测放大成大家的观点，甚至说成是事实，是严重缺乏逻辑的表现。

在第四段，作者提到了环境的重要性，却强调没有遗传因素重要，鉴于遗传因素的重要性没有得到合理的证实，这个说法就不能让人信服。

最后，作者就得出了结论，尽管结尾在形式上很规范，但从逻辑角度看可以称得上是"草率判断"。

例 2

Which Is More Critical to a Person's Essential Quality: Inheritance or Circumstance?

When it comes to the factors which influence people's essential qualities like talents, intelligence, especially characters, there are two main different views. One focuses on the factor of inheritance. The other puts emphasis on the circumstance. I support the latter.

The first view is right in explaining why some people can be great scientists, prominent writers, actors, translators, excellent musicians, politicians or top athletes and most people can not because it has been proven that those abilities can be inherited.

However, studies do not say that a person's essential qualities are inherited. Rather, studies show that the circumstances are critical elements to the form of a person's essential quality. Nothing is more evitable than scientific findings. I'm quite sure that those who support the former are ignorant of the fact that the circumstances in which a person grows up are principally responsible for the kind of person he or she becomes.

I still remember the Indian film called *The Fugitive* which is about a young man who turned out to be the son of the judge. He stole things with some bad boys after being abandoned by his father when he was still a baby.

So, believe in science which will throw light on what we want to know. And to know that a person's essential qualities are determined by circumstances, we must pay attention to the surroundings so that we can choose good companies to be a good person.

评析：题目中立，未体现作者的观点。作者在第一段表明认同环境决定论。第二部分由三小段组成，设计得比较巧妙。

在第二小段，第一句作者看似肯定遗传论的观点。他说，"在说明有些人能够成为伟大的人而另一些人不能方面，是有道理的，因为已经证明这些能力是会遗传的"。既然都被证明了，那就无须多费口舌了。在第三小段，作者用一个however进行转折，然后说，"研究并没有表明人的主要品质是遗传的，研究表明它们是环境决定的"。这确实很巧妙，因为二者之间形成了强烈的反衬。作者强调，有什么比科学事实更让人信服的呢？要突出一方的重要性，反衬是一种很好的方法。如果要增强说服力，则没有什么比科学事实和科学发现更有说服力的了。

作者在第三小段举了印度电影《流浪者》作为补充例子。

作文的结尾不是太好，因为作者前面说相信科学，科学为我们提供答案。后面却说知道了我们的品质主要是环境决定的之后，我们就可以关注周围的事情，从而选择有利于我们成长的伙伴。这一点在第二部分没有提到，出现在结论里就不太合适。始终要记住，结论是重申自己的观点，而不是提出新的观点。

顺便提一下，在逻辑证明过程中，没有规定一定要反驳。但是在证明的过程中，对不当的言论进行批驳是一种值得借鉴的方法。如果是论辩文，在论证过程中一定要加以反驳，这是论辩文体的结构要求。

总之，选言判断中，要求题目穷尽子项，否则就犯了"子项遗漏"的逻辑错误。而我们在思考问题的相关因素时，则必须涵盖主要的因素。鉴于高级写作讨论的问题大部分是我们熟知的问题，它们的主要因素我们应该知道。此外，主次信息必须合理排列，重要信息要放在前面，笔墨多一些；次要的东西放在后面，笔墨少一些。有的人在写作时布局非常巧妙，可能会通过衬托的方法来突出主要信息，还有的人会对对方的不当言论加以批驳，这都值得我们借鉴。不过，衬托属于修辞手法，不是逻辑层面的问题，我们在修辞层面还会继续讨论。

（七）区分主观性命题和客观性命题

1. 主观性命题及其主要特征

命题有主观性命题和客观性命题之分，这是我们必须要注意的问题。

在讨论问题时，有的学生喜欢说"公说公有理，婆说婆有理"。其实，这是不对的。不是什么命题都可以拿"公说公有理"说事，这一点大家必须铭记在心。在主观性命题中，"公说公有理"有一定的道理，但也不尽然。

主观性命题也叫经验性命题，通常是指根据自身的感受对人或事物发表看法的命题。主观性命题的观点可以因人而异。

总之，尽管高级写作基本上是主观性命题，我们也需要特别注意，即便是主观性命题，也不能随心所欲地发表站不住脚的观点。

2. 客观性命题及其主要特征

与主观性命题相对应的是客观性命题。客观就意味着不以人的意志为转移。《震惊世界的审判》里面有几句特别精彩的话，我们一起来欣赏一下。

例 1

"There is never a duel with the truth," he roared. "The truth always wins—and we are not afraid of it. The truth does not need Mr. Bryan. The truth is eternal, immortal and needs no human agency to support it!"

参考译文：

"与真理无所谓斗争，"他大声吼道，"真理永远是赢家，但我们无须畏惧。真理不需要布莱恩先生，因为它是永恒的、永存的，它无须任何人的支持。"

评析：这是哈佛大学教授，同时也是天主教徒杜德利·菲尔德·马龙反驳布莱恩的话，他说得铿锵有力，展示出了真理的无限魅力。

对于客观存在，学过哲学的人会比较清楚。但在写作中，很多学生欠缺这个意识，错误主要表现在I think的使用方面。在使用这样的主观表达方式时，写作者有时候会忽略现象的客观性。比如，I think the atmosphere was formed for a long time and we can't change it.在这句里面添加I think这样的词就不妥，因为I think是用来表示不确定信息或者主观意志的一个短语，而"我们的生存环境是几十亿年才形成的"，是客观存在。写作时，要求信息尽可能确定，除非是表达个人的主观意志，否则就不要使用它。我们再来看看下面的例子。

例2

Should We Compare Ourselves with Others?

In our culture a lot of times people advise us to compare ourselves with others. "You should be like your father," "You can win; the others aren't as good as you," "You must be the best of your class," etc., and this is not always the best way of thinking. There are many reasons to change this way of thinking and begin to compare ourselves only with ourselves. The following are the most important ones in my mind.

The first reason to avoid comparing yourself with others is

that it makes you unhappy. There will always be someone better than you. It does not matter in which aspect, but it is always true. Therefore, you could feel inferior to others and maybe without a real reason. For example, you can be an incredible architect and the best of your generation, and this can make you feel incredibly good, but if some day someone is better than you are, you could feel sad although you are still the same incredible architect that you were before.

The second reason to elude this kind of comparison is that it projects an illusory self-image. In life, you will also always find someone worse than you, but as opposed to the first reason, this can make you feel better than others, and this feeling can turn into a horrible pride. For example, if you are the second best student of your class, and one day the very best student leaves the school, you will then be the best one although you are still only as good as you were before. In this case, you are likely to overestimate your abilities and achievements.

The last but most important reason to stop comparing ourselves with others is that it causes us identity crisis. When we compare ourselves with others, we can be tempted to copy them, to do the same things, and to act and think like them. The problem with this is that if we copy someone, we will never know who we really are and what we really want, and then we will never grow spiritually.

For all these reasons and because we are unique, we should not compare ourselves with others, but only with ourselves. The only comparison pattern that we really have is our consciousness. So, if we use this pattern, we will not feel less or more than others and we will accept ourselves as we really are. In other words, we will live happier.

评析：这显然属于真理性命题，因为世界是相对的，一切都是相比较而言的，不存在应不应该比较的问题，比或不比都是比的结果。因此，无论什么论据都不可能支撑这个观点。况且，文章提供的论据是自相矛盾的，作者的主张是不应该和他人比较，可是所有的例子都是比较的结果。不通过比较，作者怎么知道自己是好还是不好呢？

其实，仔细思考一下，我们就会发现，这不是应不应该比较的问题，而是个人的心态问题。比较后的结果有两种可能：其一，和他人比较后感觉不好，有的人可能因此丧失信心，甚至变得消极被动；其二，和他人比较后感觉很好，因而信心倍增。然而，作者只说了不好的一面，这就犯了"遗漏子项"的逻辑错误。而且作者给出的三个理由属于同类，没有也不可能支持他的观点。因此，无法顺理成章地得出结论。

另外，"身份危机"（identity crisis）的概念使用不当。对自己和人生目标感到迷茫的现象称为"身份危机"。和他人比较了，就一定会有身份危机吗？至于作者说we are unique简直有些莫名其妙。The only comparison pattern毫无依据可言，纯属自己杜撰的，因为比较有很多形式，比如横向比较和纵向比较等。而且，心理因素往往是我们不能把握的，你不可能决定采用哪一种比较模式。

此外，the last but most important reason的用法我们是反对的，因为最重要的信息要放在前面，而不是后面。

批改这篇文章的老师评语是这样写的："通过细致的对比论述突出了'虽然个人情况未变，但因为与不同人相比，感受或好或坏'这一事实。在谈'避免与他人比较'时用词灵活，避免了枯燥的重复，分别使用了avoid，elude，stop。"

我们评价一下这位老师的评语。首先，相同词义用不同的词来表达，"避免了枯燥的重复"，这是事实。可是，"通过细致的对比论述突出了'虽然个人情况未变，但因为与不同人相比，感受或好或坏'这一观点"是什么意思呢？似乎让人搞不清楚。这篇作文的题目明明是"不应该跟他人比较"，我们应该围绕着这个论题来论证才对。

如果确实要提建议，我们可以把题目修改成The Possible Influence of Comparing with Others，或者干脆说Advantages and Disadvantages of Comparing with Others。它们未必很好，但至少很明确，不容易被人钻空子。

综上所述，审题时，我们需要特别注意题目的主观性和客观性问题。不要把客观存在当成主观的东西，添加一些如I think之类的词语。

另外，主观性命题也不意味着可以无事实根据地乱说，而是要求写作者拿出可信的证据来支持自己的观点。在增强可信度方面，没有什么比客观事实、科学研究成果等更有说服力的了。因此，如果想让人信服，写作时就要增加客观因素，减少主观因素。

（八）明确争论的前提

谷振诣（2007）指出，日常生活论证中，争论是不可避免的。以经验性命题作为论题时，争议就不可避免，这主要是由经验性论题的可争议性决定的，因为经验性命题的真理性是有局限的。

争论的关键在于争论的前提。如果争论双方不能在争论的前提上达成共识，则无法争论问题。所谓共识，就是争论双方在问题的起点、相关范围、基本概念、主要事实等方面应有一致的看法。

有一个例子很说明问题。当我让学生讨论"为什么物质越来越丰富，很多人却觉得越来越不幸福"的话题时，一个学生说她觉得自己很幸福，另一个学生就说，"那就不用讨论了，写作文的时候你写上'我很幸福'，就完事了"。

这是个有趣的例子，因为这个问题的讨论前提是我们认定"不幸福"是一个普遍问题，从自身或个别出发来断定这个事实不存在，这就没有在要争论的问题上达成共识。

当我强调英语重语法而汉语不重语法时，有个女生反驳我说，"汉语有语法啊！"我提醒她我们是在讨论重视与否，不是讨论有或没有语法的问题。

在共识点上，常常存在理解上的差异，也就是误解。因误解发生的争议没有什么认识价值（谷振旨，2007）。

由此可见，在争论之前，我们首先要明确概念的含义及其使用范围，包括对题意的理解，这样争论才有意义。而且一定要牢记，达成共识之后，概念或者论题必须保持同一，不能转换。如果偷换概念或转换论题，则会引出新的问题，这一点我们后面还会讨论。

（九）分清观点与事实

观点和事实是个非搞清楚不可的问题，有的写作书上会告诉大家"Don't make a fact your idea"，即不能把事实变成自己的观点。

观点和事实的主要区别是：观点是人的主观看法；事实是客观存在。有时我们也说是这两者的出发点不同，前者的出发点是人，后者的出发点通常是一个事物或者现象。

请大家特别注意，如果作文考查的是你的观点，你谈的却是众所周知的事实，就没有意义。另外，要让你的证据可信度高，就要尽可能多一些客观事实，少一些自己的观点。

（十）了解逻辑谬误方面的问题

逻辑谬误是指论证过程因违反逻辑规则而出现的错误，论证或者说理过程中不能出现逻辑谬误。逻辑谬误如同交通规则或者语法，它们是规定性的，一个人有没有犯逻辑错误，不是人为认定的，而是由这些规则来判定的，评判者通常要指出犯错者具体犯了哪一条错误。

1. 最严重的逻辑谬误

自相矛盾是最严重的逻辑错误，因为自相矛盾是最尖锐的不一致，如果发现论证过程中有自相矛盾的现象，则该论证立刻丧失了说服力，可以立刻被驳倒。同理，如果我们发现对方的论证中有自相矛盾之处，则可以立刻推翻对方的论证。

我们看两个例子，第一个例子前面我们从别的角度看过了，在这里，我们从逻辑谬误的角度再分析一下。

例 1

Do College Students Go in for Business?

Recently, there is a heat discussion on whether college students go in for business or not. Some people say that students should not go in for business. Others suggest that it is a good thing for students to go in for business. I quite agree to that. Students should have a chance to do some work after class.

My first reason is that students are young and energetic. Some of them are extremely talented. Take Bill Gates for example, who was a smart student at university and he went for business. Later he became a well-known businessman all over the world and got very rich.

My second reason is that students need to put their knowledge into practice. What can be better for a chance to go in for business?

评析：首先必须明确的是，go in for business 是经商的意思，不是做普通的兼职工作。如果这个概念把握不到位，就会跑题。

文章的第一段很规范，作者先说经商现象引起了热议，有些人认为大学生应该经商，另一些则认为不应该，再说自己支持大学生经商。作者的观点无可非议，但是最后一句话是不妥的，它显示出作者对于go in for business这个概念的错误认识，因为他说的是"我赞同大学生经商，他们应该有机会在课后做点工作"。

在第二部分，作者列出了两个理由。第一个理由是大学生年轻有朝气，这是事实，可是，年轻就一定要经商吗？事实恰恰相反，经商风险莫测，需要有经验，不是年轻就一定好。作者还说到学生中有些天才人物，这也是事实，因为任何时代任何学生群体中都会出现一些天才人物，但他们毕竟是个别现象，用个别例子充当证据，就很难有说服力。

作者给出比尔·盖茨作为例子就是自相矛盾，因为比尔·盖茨为了满足自己经商的愿望，不得不从哈佛大学退学，这应该证明学生不合适经商才对。换言之，如果你的论据非但没有起到支持你的观点的作用，反而削弱了你的观点，这种论据就是不恰当的。自相矛盾会彻底摧毁自己的观点。

作者给出的第二个例子是大学生应该将理论运用于实践中。这一点没错，可是实践就一定要经商吗？这很难让人信服。

最后，我们再看看下面的例子中，作者是怎样指出对方的自相矛盾的。

例 2

For example, in the issue in which *Life* stated editorially that it would follow the Second International, there were over forty words, constructions and meanings which are in the Third International but not in the Second. The issue of the *New York Times* which hailed the Second International as the authority to which it would adhere and the Third International as a scandal and a betrayal which it would reject used one hundred and fifty-three separate words, phrases, and constructions which are listed in the Third International but not in the Second and nineteen others which are condemned in the Second. Many of them are used many times, more than three hundred such uses in all.

评析：各大媒体对第二版词典褒奖有加，对第三版词典却极力批评，声称自己只会用第二版词典，不会用第三版，但却使用第三版才有的词或短语等，这就是自相矛盾。指出对方自相矛盾的逻辑错误会让对方哑口无言，从而达到驳倒对方论据的目的。

综上所述，自相矛盾虽然是我们熟悉的问题，但它是最严重的逻辑错误，这个错误一旦被发现，就等于彻底否定了自己的观点。因此，在写作时千万不能犯自相矛盾的逻辑错误。

2. 最常见的逻辑谬误

写作中最常见的逻辑错误是因果关系方面的错误，包括"假因果""轻断因果"和"诉诸远因"等。

哲学课里面讲得很清楚，世界上没有什么无因之果，因果关系是维系事物的主要方式。只有找到正确的因果关系，问题才能得到妥善解决。科学探索的主要目的就是探索事物的因果关系，这也是科技、社会不断发展的原因。

任何涉及因果的错误，如"倒因为果""混淆因果""轻断因果"等，都是极其不当的。

我们一起看看温室效应的原因分析。

例 1

I think global warming is the result of the change of the atmosphere. Everything will turn into its doom like a candle.

例 2

There are different reasons for the warming of the earth, our burning of things in the world, like trees and woods, our destroying of the atmosphere.

例 3

There are many reasons for the warming of the earth. First, the sun may release more heat. Second, we destroy the environment.

评析：这三个例子都是在分析导致温室效应的原因。对于温室效应的真正原因，很多人都说不清楚。他们要么没有说到点子上，要么凭自己的感觉，没有揭示出真正的因果。

例1就说明作者不清楚原因，他使用了I think短语。但他的第一句还是很不错的，因为这是一句概括，如果后面有具体内容就非常好了。遗憾的是，作者却说了一句，"万事万物都会像蜡烛一样走向灭亡"。这样一来，不仅原因没有说清楚，而且两句之间的关系也不密切了。

在例2中，作者也采用了总分结构。第一句说地球变暖有很多原因，例如焚烧和破坏环境。这个不错，但焚烧就是破坏的一种，所以这样说不妥当，如果说引起温室效应的原因是"一系列破坏环境的行为，包括焚烧等"，这样会更符合逻辑。

例3和例2很像，采用总分结构，先概括说地球变暖的原因很多，然后具体说了两点：第一是太阳释放了更多的热量；第二是我们破坏了环境。第一点本身可能是对的，但是它未必是地球变暖的真正原因。事实上，人类文明是导致地球变暖的真正原因。

从例1到例3，我们可以看出，在原因方面，我们缺乏相关的专业知识，致使理由要么过于笼统，要么诉诸远因。我们要逐步改变这个习惯，不要一说到原因就笼统概括，笼统通常是缺乏说服力的。

接下来，我们再看看下面关于温室效应的解释。

例 4

But the most significant change thus far in the earth's atmosphere is the one that began with the industrial revolution early in the last century and has picked up speed ever since. Industry meant coal, and later oil, and we began to burn lots of it—bringing rising levels of carbon dioxide (CO_2), with its ability to trap more heat in the atmosphere and slowly warm the earth.

评析：这是《沙漠之舟》里面对温室效应的解释。阐释文体的特点之一就是提供的知识是专业的、公正客观的，而不是片面和外行的。我们不仅可以领略到作者写作的文体美，更能感受到作者的专业性，他给出了产生温室效应的根本原因。我们当然不可能轻易做到这么专业，但是，增强这方面的意识并养成尽可能挖掘深层原因的习惯是我们每一个人都必须努力做到的。

3. 其他一些常见谬误及其含义

逻辑学科给人的总体印象是抽象难懂，一些逻辑谬误的定义很难把握，让我们通过几个有趣的例子来掌握这个内容，它们都来自小说 *Love Is a Fallacy*（《爱情是谬误》）。虽然是小说，其主要内容却是围绕逻辑谬误展开的，对于我们增强逻辑谬误知识大有好处。

例 1

Seated under the oak the next evening. I said, "Our first fallacy tonight is called Ad Misericordiam."

She quivered with delight.

"Listen closely!" I said. "A man applies for a job. When the boss asks him what his qualifications are, he replies that he has a wife and six children at home. The wife is a helpless cripple. The children have nothing to eat, no clothes to wear, no shoes on their feet. There are no beds in the house, no coal in the cellar, and winter is coming."

A tear rolled down each of Polly's pink cheeks. "Oh, this is awful, awful," she sobbed.

"Yes, it's awful," I agreed, "but it's no argument. The man never answered the boss' questions about his qualifications. Instead, he appealed to the boss' sympathy. He committed the fallacy of Ad Misericordiam. Do you understand?"

参考译文：

第二天晚上，我们坐在橡树下，我说，"今晚第一个谬误叫'诉诸怜悯'。"

她高兴得发抖。

"听仔细了！"我说，"一个男人申请一份工作。老板问他有什么资历，他回答说家中有妻子，还有六个孩子。妻子残疾，是跛脚，孩子没饭吃，没衣穿，没鞋穿。家里还没有床铺，地窖里没有煤了，而且冬天就要来了。"

波利粉红色的脸颊上落下两行热泪，"哦，这太糟糕了，太糟糕了！"她哭泣起来。

"是的，确实很糟糕，"我同意道，"但这站不住脚。这位男子没有回答老板关于资历的问题，相反，他企图获得老板的同情。他犯了'诉诸怜悯'的逻辑错误。明白吗？"

评析：所谓"诉诸怜悯"就是企图用怜悯打动对方，替代所需的理性需求，而这根本不是所需要的理由或证据。《爱情是谬误》里面的所有例子都很棒，既有趣又浅显易懂，比其他一些逻辑书上的例子更好记忆。

例 2

"Next we take up a fallacy called Hasty Generalization. Listen carefully: You can't speak French. I can't speak French. Petey Burch can't speak French. I must therefore conclude that nobody at the University of Minnesota can speak French."

"Really?" said Polly, amazed. "Nobody?"

I hid my exasperation. "Polly, it's a fallacy. The generalization is reached too hastily. There are too few instances to support such a conclusion."

参考译文：

"下一个谬误是'草率判断'。仔细听好了：你不会说法语，我不会说法语，皮悌·伯奇也不会说法语。我因此可以得出结论，明尼苏达大学没人会说法语。"

"真的吗？"波利吃惊地问，"没人吗？"

我压住怒火说，"波利，这是'草率判断'的逻辑谬误。样本太少，无法支撑结论。"

评析：我们学习《爱情是谬误》这篇短篇小说的目的是了解逻辑谬误相关的知识点。

依赖过少的样本得出的结论就叫"草率判断"，这个例子有趣又好记。

例 3

"Next comes Post Hoc. Listen to this: Let's not take Bill on our picnic. Every time we take him out with us, it rains."

"I know somebody like that," she exclaimed. "A girl back home—Eula Becker, her name is, it never falls. Every single time we take her on a picnic..."

"Polly," I said sharply, "it's a fallacy. Eula Becker doesn't cause the rain. She has no connection with the rain. You are guilty of Post Hoc if you blame Eula Becker."

参考译文：

　　"接下来我们学习'轻断因果'。听好了：别带比尔去野炊，每次带他去，就下雨。"

　　"我也认识这样一个人，"她惊叹道，"我们家乡的一个女孩，叫娥娜·贝克，一次都没有例外，每次一带她去野炊……"

　　"波利，"我严厉地说，"这是谬误。下雨并不是娥娜·贝克造成的，她和雨之间毫无关系。你怪罪于她，就犯了'轻断因果'的错误。"

评析："轻断因果"的逻辑谬误是指结果不是认定的原因导致的。它和我们日常调侃不是一个层面的问题，就好像有人说："我一出门，就下雨，没一回落空。"逻辑谬误是规定论证和说理过程中不能犯的逻辑错误，而日常调侃属于修辞范畴，通过故意违反逻辑规则达到搞笑的目的。

　　在修辞的讨论当中，我们会重申修辞与逻辑规则的冲突问题，鉴于它们是写作的两个不同层面，有些违反逻辑的做法在修辞层面是可以接受的。这一点大家在英语阅读中要加以注意。

例 4

"First let us examine the fallacy called Dicto Simpliciter."

"By all means," she urged, batting her lashes eagerly.

"Dicto Simpliciter means an argument based on an unqualified generalization. For example: Exercise is good. Therefore everybody should exercise."

"I agree," said Polly earnestly. "I mean exercise is wonderful. I mean it builds the body and everything."

"Polly," I said gently, "the argument is a fallacy. Exercise is good is an unqualified generalization. For instance, if you have heart disease, exercise is bad, not good. Many people are ordered by their doctors not to exercise. You must qualify the generalization. You must say exercise is usually good, or exercise is good for most people. Otherwise you have committed a Dicto Simpliciter. Do you see?"

参考译文：

"我们先来学'绝对判断'的逻辑谬误。"

"那就赶紧吧！"她急切地说，睫毛闪动。

"'绝对判断'是指论据未得到限定。比如，锻炼身体有好处，因此人人都应该锻炼身体。"

"我同意！"波利急切地说，"我的意思是锻炼身体是很棒的事，可以塑身什么的。"

"波利，"我温柔地说，"论据是错的，'锻炼有好处'这个命题没有被限定。假如你有心脏病，锻炼就不好，医生会建议你不要锻炼。这个命题必须加以限定，你应该说，'锻炼通常是有好处的'，或者说'锻炼对大部分人有益处'，否则你就犯了'绝对判断'的错误，明白吗？"

评析：这个例子对"绝对判断"的谬误解释得特别清楚。"锻炼有好处"的外延太大了，但事实上并非所有人都适合，也就是说你可以找到反例，因此这样说不合适。

例 5

"All right. Let's try Contradictory Premises."

"Yes, let's," she chirped, blinking her eyes happily.

I frowned, but plunged ahead. "Here's an example of Contradictory Premises: If God can do anything, can He make a stone so heavy that He won't be able to lift it?"

"Of course," she replied promptly.

"But if He can do anything, He can lift the stone," I pointed out.

"Yeah," she said thoughtfully. "Well, then I guess He can't make the stone."

"But He can do anything," I reminded her.

She scratched her pretty, empty head. "I'm all confused," she admitted.

"Of course you are. Because when the premises of an argument contradict each other, there can be no argument. If there is an irresistible force, there can be no immovable object. If there is an immovable object, there can be no irresistible force. Get it?"

"Tell me some more of this keen stuff," she said eagerly.

参考译文:

"好吧, 我们来学习'相互矛盾的前提'。"

"好的!"波利眨着眼睛欢快地说。

我皱了一下眉,还是挺住了。"这是一个'相互矛盾的前提'的例子:如果上帝是万能的, 他能够制造一块自己搬不动的石头吗?"

波利迅速回答:"当然能。"

"可是他是万能的啊!"我指出。

"是哦,"波利若有所思,"嗯, 那我猜他就无法制造出这样一块石头。"

我重复提醒，"可是他是万能的啊！"

她挠着可爱的、空空的脑袋，承认道："我搞不清楚了。"

"你当然搞不清楚，因为当前提相互矛盾时，主张不成立。具有万能的能力，就不可能有移不动的物体。如果有移不动的物体，就不具备万能的能力。听明白了吗？"

"多讲点这些好玩的。"她急切地说。

评析："相互矛盾的前提"是和前提有关的问题，在争论问题时很有借鉴性，它可以帮助我们快速提高逻辑意识。有一个类似的说法是：如果前提是假的，永远找不到真答案。

例6

One more chance, I decided. But just one more. There is a limit to what flesh and blood can bear. "The next fallacy is called Poisoning the Well."

"How cute!" she gurgled.

"Two men are having a debate. The first one gets up and says, 'My opponent is a notorious liar. You can't believe a word that he is going to say.'... Now, Polly, think. Think hard. What's wrong?"

I watched her closely as she knit her creamy brow in concentration. Suddenly, a glimmer of intelligence—the first I had seen—came into her eyes. "It's not fair," she said with indignation. "It's not a bit fair. What chance has the second man got if the first man calls him a liar before he even begins talking?"

"Right!" I cried exultantly. "One hundred percent right. It's not fair. The first man has poisoned the well before anybody could drink from it. He has hamstrung his opponent before he could even start... Polly, I'm proud of you."

参考译文：

再试一次，最后一次了！血肉之躯总是有个限度的。"下一个谬误叫'井底投毒'。"

她咯咯地笑着说："太有意思了！"

"两个人正在争论。第一个站起来说，'我的对手是无耻的骗子，你们一个字都不能相信他'。好了，波利，想想，好好想想，哪儿不对了？"

我仔细地看着她，她米色眉头紧锁，专注地思考。突然，我头一回看见她眼里闪现出一丝智慧。

"不公平，"她气愤地说，"太不公平了。如果第一个人在第二个人说话之前，就说他是骗子，那人家还怎么有机会呢？"

"太对了！"我兴奋地叫了起来，"百分之百正确！不公平，第一个人在对手喝水之前，往井里投毒了，对方还未开始，他就伤害了他。波利，我为你骄傲。"

评析：这个例子对"井底投毒"这个逻辑谬误解释得特别生动。对他人进行人身攻击就属于"井底投毒"。

例 7

"Next," I said in a carefully controlled tone, "we will discuss False Analogy. Here is an example: Students should be allowed to look at their textbooks during examinations. After all, surgeons have X-rays to guide them during an operation, lawyers have briefs to guide them during a trial, carpenters have blueprints to guide them when they are building a house. Why, then, shouldn't students be allowed to look at their textbooks during an examination?"

"There now," she said enthusiastically, "is the most marvy idea I've heard in years."

"Polly," I said testily, "the argument is all wrong. Doctors, lawyers, and carpenters aren't taking a test to see how much they have learned, but students are. The situations are altogether different, and you can't make an analogy between them."

参考译文：

　　"下一个，"我努力遏制自己的声音说，"我们讨论'错误类比'的例子：考试的时候，应该允许学生看书本。不管怎么说，外科医生做手术时可以参看 X 光片；律师在庭审过程中可以看案例；木匠建房子时，有建造指南。那么，学生考试时怎么就不能看书本呢？"

　　"哎呀，"她兴奋地说，"这可是这些年我听过的最棒的主意了。"

　　"波利，"我不快地说，"论据完全错了。考试不是检查医生、律师和木匠所学的内容，是检查学生掌握的内容。情景不同，二者之间无可比性。"

评析：这是关于"错误类比"的例子，简而言之，强调的是两个事物之间要有可比性，无可比性的比较非但起不到支撑观点的作用，反而会削弱自己的主张。比较是论证过程的常用手法，我们不仅要学会使用，还要注意比较的事物之间必须有可比性。

　　例 8

　　"My dear," I said, favoring her with a smile, "we have now spent five evenings together. We have gotten along splendidly. It is clear that we are well matched."

　　"Hasty Generalization," said Polly brightly.

　　"I beg your pardon," said I.

　　"Hasty Generalization," she repeated. "How can you say that we are well matched on the basis of only five dates?"

参考译文：

　　"亲爱的，"我笑着说，"我们已经在一起五个晚上了，我们相处得好极了，显然我们很般配。"

　　波利立刻回答："草率判断。"

　　"你说什么？"我问。

　　"你草率判断，"她重复道，"怎么可以仅根据五次约会就得出我们般配的结论呢？"

　　评析：在例2里面，我们已经看到了"草率判断"的错误，那是小说的主人翁给出的书本上的例子，而这个例子是波利活学活用的例子。"我"在教会波利逻辑谬误后的第五个晚上，觉得应该向她表白。结果，"我"一开口就被波利发现了逻辑谬误，这是作者特别设计的一个转折点。其实"我"这时并非在论证，而是处在修辞层面，也就是根据经验而不是按照逻辑来判断事物。可是，既然"我"教会了波利识别逻辑谬误，波利就采用谬误来回击"我"。

　　这篇小说给我们的启示是逻辑并非枯燥乏味、晦涩难懂的知识，它渗透在我们的生活中，让我们变得更聪明、更智慧。

　　总之，在英语写作中，因果关系方面的逻辑错误是最常见的逻辑错误。因果关系是事物联系的主要方式，没有弄清楚事物之间的因果关系，就不可能拿出合理的解决方案。因果方面的逻辑错误包括"轻断因果""倒因为果""混淆因果"等。

4. 常见逻辑谬误总揽

　　鉴于我们无法用更多的版面来讨论逻辑知识，我们把常见逻辑谬误简单罗列出来，它们包括五个相关性谬误、五个歧义性谬误和十个证据不足方面的谬误。

　　常见谬误产生的根源在于论证目的的二重性：一是论证的逻辑性和真理性；二是自然语言表达多样性的干扰（谷振诣，2007）。

也就是说，论证时要始终遵守逻辑规则，不能出现逻辑谬误。但是，论证必须借助语言，而语言具有多样性，它会干扰论证，或者干扰对论证的判断，谬误由此产生。

我们在对逻辑谬误进行分类时，会从形式逻辑和语言两个层面上进行划分。我们通常把与论证相关的谬误分为形式谬误（formal fallacy）和非形式谬误（informal fallacy）两种。非形式谬误又可以分为相关性的谬误、歧义性的谬误和论据不足的谬误三个方面。

形式谬误属于论证过程的纯逻辑问题。在这里我们只列举非形式谬误。非形式谬误主要有以下几种（谷振诣，2007）。

（1）相关性的谬误

相关性的谬误是指论证诉诸感情、情绪、态度和信念等心理因素而导致的思维错误，它主要包括人身攻击、诉诸无知、诉诸权威、诉诸怜悯和诉诸众人五种错误。

- 人身攻击（illegitimate ad hominem），也叫井里投毒（poisoning the well）。在论证中，以理论者或反驳者的人格或处境为根据，而不是以理论者或反驳者所提出的观点和理由为根据进行辩护或反驳的逻辑错误。
- 诉诸无知（illegitimate ad ignorantiam）是指在论证中，由于没有证明一个命题为假的证据，就断定这个命题是真的，或者由于没有证明一个命题为真的证据，就断定这个命题是假的，这时就产生诉诸无知的谬误。这种论证在超越人类理性能够确认的认识领域中被经常使用。
- 诉诸权威（illegitimate ad verecundiam），是指在论证中用权威的证言代替对论题进行逻辑论证的思想错误。
- 诉诸怜悯（illegitimate ad misericordiam），又称乞求同情，是指借助于打动人们的同情心，以诱使人相信其论题的逻辑错误。

- 诉诸众人（illegitimate ad populum）是指援引众人的意见、见解、信念或常识进行论证的逻辑错误。

论证应当重视情感因素的作用，但不能以感情来替代逻辑合理性，这一点特别要注意。在日常争辩中，我们会发现，一些人道理不足的时候就东拉西扯，用情感因素来影响原有的轨迹。但是写作和日常争辩不同，它是纯理性的行为，不能出现任何逻辑谬误。

（2）歧义性的谬误

歧义性的谬误是指借助语言的多样性有意或者无意犯的一些错误，它主要包括偷换概念、合成谬误、分解的谬误、强调的谬误和诘问的谬误五种错误。

- 偷换概念（play tricks with concepts）是指有意把不同概念当成同一概念来使用的逻辑错误。与之相关的谬误是混淆概念（confused with concepts）和含混笼统的谬误（fallacy of ambiguity）。
- 合成谬误（fallacy of composition）是指在论证中，由部分元素所具有的性质推断整体、集合也具有同样的性质。
- 分解的谬误（fallacy of division）与合成谬误正好相反。在论证中，由整体、集合的性质来推断其部分、元素的性质时产生的谬误。
- 强调的谬误（fallacy of emphasis）：语言表达意义，有显示意义和暗示意义两种。对特定语句的强调具有局部放大作用，它是使语句具有较强暗示意义的重要手段。
- 诘问的谬误（fallacy of interrogation）又称复杂问句，是指把两个以上的问题合并成一个问题，诱使对方做出简单回答的谬误。

（3）论据不足的谬误

论据不足的谬误主要是指论证过程中概念或论题方面的错误，

比喻不当和缺乏因果及样本不足之类的错误，主要包括以下十种。

- 绝对判断（dicto simpliciter）是指把一般原则或普遍命题绝对化时的谬误。绝对判断是导致矛盾的根源。

- 自相矛盾（self-contradiction）是指在论证中断定两个互相反对或相互矛盾的命题同时为真时产生的谬误。

- 假二择一（false alternative），即"非黑即白的谬误"（fallacy of black-or-white thinking）。

- 轻率概括（hasty generalization），有时也称"以偏概全"（taking a part for whole），是以特例或非典型事例为根据而概括出关于一类对象的一般结论的谬误。它是使用简单枚举法进行论证时常见的错误类型。

- 轻断因果（post hoc），也叫假因果（false cause）。日常思维的论证大都与探求事物的因果联系相关。如果只根据时间上的前后顺序就断定两个事物之间有因果关系，就容易产生轻断因果的谬误。

- 统计的谬误（statistical fallacy）是指在使用统计数据作论据时产生的谬误。样本太少的谬误、平均数的谬误、数据不可比的谬误、数据不相关的谬误和赌徒谬误等都属于这类。

- 假类比（false analogy），也称"缪比"。如果把对象的偶然相似作为根据，或者在实质上不同的两类对象之间进行类比，就会产生这种谬误。

- 虚假理由（false reason），又称虚假论据（false grounds of argument），是指违反充足理由律要求的逻辑错误。

- 窃取论题（begging the question），又称循环论证（circular argument），是指把论题本身作为论据，预先假定结论为真，再推知前提之一为真的错误论证。

- 转移论题（shifting judgment），又称转移举证责任（shifting

the burden of proof）。论题是什么就必须是什么，不能歪曲或篡改，否则就会犯转移论题的错误。

5. 避免逻辑错误的有效方法

熟悉逻辑规则是学习的一个方面，活学活用是学习的另一方面，其中最有效的方法之一就是进行批判性阅读和批判性写作，即通过阅读文本指出里面的逻辑错误，最后用文字表述的过程。这个过程不仅可以强化我们的思维，提高我们的动手能力，还可以帮助我们养成有条理的好习惯。

我们来看其中几个例子，它们来自《批判性思维教程》（谷振诣，2007）。

例 1

在最近一次对汽车工厂工人的电话调查中，年纪大的工人较少有人报告说："有管理人员在场会提高他们的工作效率。"在 18 ～ 29 岁的工人中，有 27% 的人说："当他们的顶头上司在场时，他们的工作会更有效率。"相比之下，30 ～ 49 岁的工人中有 12%，50 岁及以上的工人中只有 3% 这样认为。显然，如果我们精品印刷公司主要雇用那些年纪大一些的工人，就会提高我们的劳动效率，而且会节省雇员开支，因为对管理人员的需求会减少。

分层抽样问题

作者基于一项电话调查，做出推论：年纪大的工人工作效率不依赖于他们的管理者是否在场。从而得出结论：如果我们精品印刷公司主要雇用那些年纪大一些的工人，就会提高我们的劳动效率，而且会节省雇员开支，因为对管理人员的需求会减少。该论证在以下几个关键方面是有缺陷的。

其一，文中引用的统计数据的可靠性是不确定的。首先，电话调查是否有可信度，比如是否对全体职工进行了询问。通过电话方式，这显然是不太可能的，因为有些人可能不在家。其次，所设计的问题是否有效度，这些问题作者都没有交代。最重要的是，对于被调查的总体人数，年纪大的和年纪轻的人各占总体人数的多大比例，作者也没有交代。如果个体差异明显，进行抽样调查时，必须采用分层抽样，而不是简单随机抽样，也就是把各种差异所占的不同比例体现出来，这样才符合统计规律。假设该企业有1000人，30岁以下者有500人，30~49岁者有300人，50岁以上者只有200人，那么，在这种情况下，三个百分比之间就没有可比性，也就不能说明什么问题。只有在个体差异不明显的总体样本下所占的比例，才能说明问题。

其二，对于效率问题，作者没有给出具体的交代。它是指工人工作更有劲头呢，还是出的产品更多更合格？而且，更有效率也是比较而言的，效率到底增加了多少，作者也没有交代，如果效率并不是很明显的话，这个调查的意义就不大。再者，管理人员需求减少，也没有实质性的证据。因为，管理者的主要任务原本就不是现场监督，而是从行政到监督的一系列工作，那么，需求减少一说，就无从说起。因此，公司雇佣年纪大一些的工人，会提高劳动效率，且节省雇员开支的结论不能成立。

总之，该论证缺乏调查的可信度，对与调查相关的一些要素没有交代和提供，结论显得很牵强附会，没有说服力。这个调查因此也就没有什么实际意义。

解析：电话调查例子里面的问题不是所有人能够一眼看得出来的。我们阅读了它的分析以后，就会发现该论证非常清晰，作者从逻辑角度详细地分析并指出了调查中存在的错误，让读者了解到这个调查不可信。同时，我们也看到，该文章非常有条理地把问题罗列出来，最后再得出结论。批判性阅读也就是对论证的一个论证。通常它由前提到结论，先概括性地指出它合理与否或者可信与否，然后具体列出论证过程的逻辑错误。阅读这样的分析是非常好的锻炼，建议希望较快地提高批判性思维能力的学生多花点时间阅读。

近年来，越来越多的学生意识到了批判性思维的重要性，鉴于他们的逻辑知识不足，且缺乏锻炼，他们经常很苦恼地问我："老师，怎么可以快速提高批判性思维能力？"

实际上，人的认知分为低级阶段和高级阶段，低级阶段主要依赖记忆，而高级阶段需要综合分析。后者必须依赖前者的信息并对其进行分析，然后才能够进行模仿和进一步加工。

笼统地说，我们必须先补充逻辑知识，并进行适当练习，经常读一些关于有争议性问题的文章，看他人是怎么评论的。下面再给大家看几个例子。

例2

去年初夏建成并开放新的游泳池后，健身中心会员的使用率提高了 12%。因此，为了增加我们的会员数量和收入，应当在今后几年里继续添加新的娱乐设施，诸如添加一个多功能游戏室，一个网球场和一个小型高尔夫球场。作为本区域唯一提供这一系列健身和娱乐设施的场所，我们将会因此而富有竞争优势。

"轻率概括"与"机械类比"

该论证的主要理由是去年初夏建成并开放新的游泳池后，健身中心会员的使用率提高了 12%，因此我们应当在今后几年里继续添加新的娱乐设施，作为本区域唯一提供这一系列健身和娱乐设施的场所，我们将会因此而富有竞争优势。

这一论证存在以下问题：

首先，作者假设开放新的游泳池是会员使用率提高的主要原因。这一假设虽然有一定的合理性，但并不可靠。比如，健身中心使用率的提高，可能还有其他一些原因——去年夏日天气酷热，或经济不景气导致的闲暇时间增加等。文中并没有给出证据排除这些可能性的解释。

其次，即使开放新的游泳池是会员使用率提高的主要原因，并因此而增加了会员数量，仅凭去年的这个样本调查，不能得出未来几年游泳池的开放仍然能保持与去年具有相同效果的结论。比如，其他健身中心也会新建游泳池来吸引会员，在有竞争的情况下，游泳池是否仍会成为吸引会员的亮点？这是令人质疑的。

最后，即使开放新的游泳池在去年并且在未来几年能够增加会员数量，并不能由此类推建设并开放其他娱乐设施也会具有同样的效果。网球和高尔夫与游泳相比，不是大众普及的娱乐项目，靠它们来达到吸引和增加会员数量的目的是不现实的，与专业的多功能游戏厅相比，综合健身中心的多功能游戏室未必有竞争优势。如果这一系列娱乐设施不能充分发挥它的效益，即使它是该健身中心独自具有的，也不能成为其具有竞争力的优势资源。

总之，该论证在分析使用率提高的原因时，未提供排除其他可能解释的证据，犯了"轻断因果"的错误；仅凭去年的一个样本调查就对未来几年的情况作出推断，忽视了时间因素的影响，犯了"轻率概括"的错误；在没有确证开放新的游泳池能增加会员数量的前提下，便匆忙把这一性质推到其他娱乐设施上，而且不考虑其他设施与游泳池的实质差别，这又犯了"机械类比"的错误。

例3

有两个人在山间打猎，遇到一只凶猛的老虎。其中一个人扔下行囊，撒腿就跑，另一人朝着他喊："跑有什么用，你跑得过老虎吗？"头一个边跑边说："我不需要跑赢老虎，我只要跑赢你就够了！"这个故事告诉我们，企业经营首先要考虑的是如何战胜竞争对手，顾客不是选择你，就是选择你的竞争者，所以只要在满足顾客需求方面比竞争者快一点，你就能够脱颖而出，战胜对手。想要跑得比老虎快，是企业战略幼稚的表现，追求过高的竞争目标会白白浪费企业的大量资源。

不恰当的比喻论证

作者引用一则寓言故事来论证企业经营中的道理，这个比喻论证有许多不恰当之处。分析如下：

其一，在寓言故事中，对老虎来说，不是选择你，就是选择我，这可能有一定道理。但是，企业经营中，情况并不是这样。对顾客来说，"不是选择你，就是选择你的竞争者"，这种非此即彼的选择并不成立。如果竞争双方的产品不能满足顾客的需要或者存在其他问题，顾客可以延迟消费，对双方都不选择。

其二，在寓言故事中，只要我跑得快，就可以虎口脱险。可是，这种"优胜劣败"的原则在企业经营中是不适当的。"在满足顾客需求方面比竞争对手快一点"只是"脱颖而出，战胜对手"的必要条件，战胜对手还需要在诸如产品质量、服务和价格等多方面取得领先的优势。另外，企业经营中的竞争一般不是以吃掉一方而使另一方得以幸存的方式进行的，只强调战胜对手，竞争常常会造成两败俱伤的局面，在合作的前提下，追求双赢的竞争才是大家公认的竞争方式。

其三，在老虎面前，两个逃生者之间存在竞争关系，老虎与两个逃生者之间同样存在竞争关系。本土企业之间的竞争，好比逃生者与老虎的竞争。在本土企业竞争中获胜，仍然有可能被"老虎——国外更强大的企业"吃掉。所以，"跑得比老虎快"不是"企业战略幼稚的表现"，而是战略成熟的表现。

总之，作者在引用这则寓言故事进行论证时，缺乏对寓言故事与企业经营这两者之间潜在原则上的相似性和一致性方面的分析，所做出的比喻论证是不恰当的。

例 4

　　20 年前，M 市二中的毕业生只有一半考上大学，现在有 3/4 的毕业生考上了大学。很明显，在过去的 20 年里，市二中提高了教学质量。除去通货膨胀的影响，市政府对二中的财政拨款与 20 年前大致相同，这并没有影响二中教育质量的提高。所以，目前没有必要大幅度地增加对二中的财政拨款。

是否有必要大幅度增加对二中的财政拨款？

　　该论证的结论是：目前没有必要大幅度地增加对二中的财政拨款。得出这一结论所基于的理由是：近 20 年来大致相同的拨款没有影响二中教育质量的提高。论证在几个关键问题上存在逻辑缺陷，分析如下：

　　首先，在没有进行比较的前提下，二中升学率的提高未必意味着教育质量的提高。若使二中升学率的提高成为有说服力的论据，必须将它与同类中学升学率加以比较。没有比较，独立的数据不能说明问题。比如，与 20 年前相比，现在的情况可能是：参加高考的中学生人数相对减少，而高校招生的数量却在大幅度增加。在这种情况下，同一所中学的教育质量没提高甚至下滑，升学率也仍然可能会提高。

　　其次，即使升学率的提高有代表性，它也只是评价教育质量的标准之一。其他诸如学生的道德修养、心理素养、技术专长以及适应社会的能力等，都是评价教育质量的重要标准。只根据升学率提高这个单一的标准得出"教育质量提高"（需要根据多方面的标准来评估）这个综合性的结论，这是"以偏概全"的表现。

　　最后，即使近 20 年来大致相同的拨款计划没有影响教育质量的提高，这一事实并不能证明现在仍然执行大致相同的拨款计划不会影响未来教育质量的提高。现代社会的快速发展对公众受教育水平的要求越来越高，如对中学毕业生的外语、计算机等方面的要求，与 20 年前不可同日而语。教育质量的提高面临更多、更大的挑战，如增加新设备、建造多功能教室、引进或培训新教师等。满足这些基本的教学要求需要大量资金，没有大幅度的资金投入势必会导致未来教育质量的滑坡。忽视当前的一些重大变化，机械地执行与往日大致相同的拨款计划，这是不妥当的。

　　总之，该论证存在诸多的缺陷。作者需要提供与评价教育质量相关的其他信息，还需要对目前教育发展的具体情况作出分析，在此基础上才能判断是否应当大幅度地增加对二中的财政拨款。

综上所述，逻辑学其实是一门非常有趣、实用的科学。每个接受良好教育的人都应该掌握一定的逻辑常识。而逻辑谬误是检验我们逻辑思维的一个重要方面，我们必须对常见逻辑谬误有所了解，避免自己犯这类错误，并指出他人的这类错误。不过，在运用方面，逻辑层面和修辞层面有些不同。修辞层面强调的不是规则，而是为达到某一目的或效果刻意地使用了某一言辞，有时它可以违反逻辑规则；而论证过程中不允许出现任何逻辑谬误，一旦出现逻辑谬误，则该论证无说服力。

三
修辞方面的技巧和方法

　　修辞层面和逻辑层面不同，它的主要目的不是说理，而是为了某一目的刻意选择词汇、句子的顺序安排等，让文章更美。它的英语定义是这样的：the use of some words, phrases, structures or even paragraphs for a particular purpose。

修辞是写作的一大层面，无修辞则无写作，这种说法并不过分，因此，我们也必须好好地把握这方面的技巧和方法。

（一）知道常用写作手法

结构、逻辑和修辞是高级作文的必备要素，但是，很多人只会在结构上做文章，也就是按照结构要求来进行写作，在逻辑和修辞层面却很欠缺。

结构规范是写作的基本要求，我们不是要反对把握作文的结构，可是，仅有结构是不够的，还要在逻辑层面和修辞层面加大学习力度。结构是相对稳定不变的，学会一种固定结构不是很难的事，而逻辑和修辞是让文章变得灵活、巧妙的手法，唯有这三方面有机结合，才可能写出好文章。当然，逻辑思维好的人学习修辞会更容易一些。

我们要强调的是，修辞不仅仅是指修辞手法，它还包括修辞环境。前者是词的选择，后者是段落的安排。

（二）掌握信息的选取

我们首先需要了解的是信息的选取问题。所谓"信息的选取"，是指决定哪些信息要保留下来，哪些信息不要出现在文章里，这样我们写出来的文章才会紧凑，才会主题突出，不会东拉西扯。我们必须了解和牢记的是留下的信息必须是可以突出主题的信息，不能突出主题的信息就不要留下。我们来看下面的例子。

例 1

"Nothing, nothing," I said innocently, and took my suitcase out of the closet.

"Where are you going?" asked Petey.

"Home for the weekend." I threw a few things into the bag.

"Listen," he said, clutching my arm eagerly, "while you're home, you couldn't get some money from your old man, could you, and lend it to me so I can buy a raccoon coat?"

"I may do better than that," I said with a mysterious wink and closed my bag and left.

"Look," I said to Petey when I got back Monday morning. I threw open the suitcase and revealed the huge, hairy, gamy object that my father had worn in his Stutz Bearcat in 1925.

参考译文：

"没事，没事，"我无辜地回答，一边从橱子里拿出箱子。

"你要去哪里啊？"皮悌问。

"回家度周末啊。"我往箱子里面扔了几样东西。

"听着，"他拽着我的手臂，热切地说，"到家后，向你老爸借点钱，然后借给我买浣熊大衣，好吧？"

"有更精彩的，"我神秘地眨眨眼回答，提着箱子离开了。

"瞧啊！"周一回来后，我对皮悌说，并把箱子一扔。打开后，一件巨大的、毛茸茸的、带点腥味的东西露了出来。我老爸在1925 年，驾驶着贝尔凯特车，穿的就是这件大衣。

评析：这是《爱情是谬误》里面的例子。周末时，"我"收拾东西回家了，回家后问老爸借钱的信息没有提供，因为它们和主题无关，起不到突出主题的作用。于是，下一句就是回到了宿舍，这就是合理选取信息的手法，一切与主题无关的信息都不要保留。

例 2

I rose from my chair. "Is it a deal?" I asked, extending my hand.

He swallowed. "It's a deal," he said and shook my hand.

I had my first date with Polly the following evening.

参考译文：

我从椅子上站起身来，伸出手问，"那就成交喽？"

他咽了一口口水，说，"成交。"然后握了握我的手。

第二天晚上，我跟波利第一次约会。

评析：这也是《爱情是谬误》里面的例子。皮悌终于经不起诱惑，答应把女友波利让给"我"了，双方握了手。作者并没有在成交之后表述"我"的快乐之情或者激动情绪，而是直接和波利进行第一次约会了。

例 3

He was a tall, thin man, sad-eyed and serious. Quite unexpectedly, the strange emotion which had overwhelmed me at the station returned, and I was again crushed by the thought that I now stood on the site of the first atomic bombardment, where thousands upon thousands of people had been slain in one second, where thousands upon thousands of others had lingered on to die in slow agony.

参考译文：

他高高的，瘦瘦的，一双严肃哀伤的眼睛。出其不意地，在车站袭上心头的那种压抑感再次出现。想到自己站在第一颗原子弹爆炸的现场，当时数以万计的人转眼之间死去，数以万计的人在漫长的痛苦当中苟延残喘，我再一次感到痛苦难当。

评析：这是《广岛——日本"最快乐"的城市》里面的例子。

作者要见的人是广岛市长，而广岛是作者曾经参与投放原子弹的地方，正因为此，作者踏上广岛的土地之后一直内心灼痛。这时，一双严肃哀伤的眼睛是最好突出主题的。

例 4

"You look puzzled," said <u>a small Japanese man with very large eye-glasses</u>.

"Well, I must confess that I did not expect a speech about oysters here. I thought that Hiroshima still felt the impact of the atomic cataclysm."

参考译文：

"你看起来很困惑，"一个戴着大眼镜的小个子日本人说。

"哦，我得承认，我没想到发言是关于这儿的牡蛎，我以为广岛依然受到原子弹事件的影响。"

评析：这也是《广岛——日本"最快乐"的城市》里面的例子。为什么作者要选取large eye-glasses这个信息？不告诉读者他戴眼镜不行吗？而且还是大大的眼镜。在修辞上large和前面的small构成对比，使得句子比较美观。另外，作者一定是想透过这个选取的信息让读者揣测到这样的信息："我惴惴不安，自认为罪大恶极，不敢指望日本人的原谅"。然而，什么人更容易原谅他人呢？应该是有知识涵养的人吧？那么，眼镜的意象在这里就可以发挥作用了。

总之，怎样选取可以突出主题的信息是决定文章简练紧凑的关键，我们一定要好好把握这一点，并从各种阅读材料中加以吸收。

（三）明确并列的要求

并列是指几个相同范畴的词或短语连在一起使用，比如There

are some desks, chairs and computers in the classroom. 学习这个知识点对于我们罗列和组织相关信息都很有帮助。

在逻辑上，并列的概念属于相同范畴。因此，论证的时候不允许故意使用下面这种修辞手法：

例 1

Fruit-sellers, potters, silversmiths, blacksmiths, butchers, leather-workers, tailors, water-carriers, beggars, porters—whichever way you look you see nothing but Jews.

参考译文：

在摩洛哥这片土地上，处处是犹太人，你可以看见：水果贩、陶艺工、银器匠、铁匠、屠夫、皮革工、裁缝、送水工、乞丐和脚夫。

评析：这是乔治·奥威尔的《马拉喀什》（Marrakech）里的片断，它是作者在1939年写的一篇随笔，文章揭露殖民统治给第三世界人民带来的灾难。

并列部分除了beggars之外，其他都是职业，这种违反逻辑要求的修辞手法是为了突出这里的贫穷和落后。

例 2

What does Morocco mean to a Frenchman? An orange-grove or a job in government service? Or to an Englishman? Camels, castles, palm-trees, Foreign Legionnaires, brass trays and bandits.

参考译文：

摩洛哥对于一名法国人意味着什么呢？橘园？还是一份在政府的工作？那么，对于一名英国人呢？是否意味着骆驼、城堡、棕榈树、外国军团、铜器和劫匪？

评析：这也是《马拉喀什》里面的句子，除了bandits之外，其他都是当地的特色景观，同例1一样，也是为了突出殖民地的贫穷和落后。

另外，在逻辑上还有个规定，就是概念不能全同或交叉。比如，我们不能说"买点土豆和马铃薯"，因为这两个概念是同一种东西的不同称呼；同样，我们也不能说"一个医生，一个大夫"。

总之，写作涉及不同层面的不同手法，有些手法很常用，但我们要避免犯逻辑错误，因为阐释文体的要求是不能在行文过程中使用与逻辑相违背的修辞手法。并列就是这样一种常用手法，它在强调方面的作用很大，但要注意两点逻辑上的规定：一是要使用相同范畴的概念；二是概念不要全同。

（四）清楚排比及其目的

排比是大家比较熟悉的一种修辞手法，也是很多学生乐于使用的一种写作手法，因为排比可以加强语气，看起来也美观，还可以增加字数。它是我们每个人都可以借鉴的一种好方法。

排比的定义是：repetition of two or more similar words, phrases, structures, etc。我们可以使用肯定排比、否定排比、疑问排比和反问排比，还可以使用句子排比和段落排比。

例 1

But one hundred years later, the Negro still is not free. One hundred years later, the life of the Negro is still sadly crippled by the manacles of segregation and the chains of discrimination.

One hundred years later, the Negro lives on a lonely island of poverty in the midst of a vast ocean of material prosperity.

参考译文：

可是，一百年之后，黑人依然不自由。一百年之后，黑人依然贫困交加，依然为种族隔离政策和种族歧视所桎梏。

一百年之后，黑人依然孤零零地生活在贫困的小岛上，周围是极度繁荣的物质海洋。

例 2

With this faith, we will be able to hew out of the mountain of despair a stone of hope.

With this faith, we will be able to transform the jangling discords of our nation into a beautiful symphony of brotherhood.

With this faith, we will be able to work together, to pray together, to struggle together, to go to jail together, to stand up for freedom together, knowing that we will be free one day.

参考译文：

怀有这一信仰，我们就能够从绝望之山中劈出一块希望之石。

怀有这一信仰，我们就能够把那些侮辱我们的杂音转变成充满兄弟之情的美妙交响乐。

怀有这一信仰，我们就能够一起劳动，一起祈祷，一起斗争，一起坐牢，一起争取自由，我们知道有一天我们终将获得解放。

例 3

Let freedom ring from the heightening Alleghenies of Pennsylvania.

Let freedom ring from the snow-capped Rockies of Colorado.

Let freedom ring from the curvaceous slopes of California.

参考译文：

让自由之声响彻在宾夕法尼亚高耸的阿力根尼山峦；

让自由之声响彻在科罗拉多冰雪覆盖的落基山脉；

让自由之声响彻在加利福尼亚的陡峭山坡。

评析：这三个例子都是马丁·路德·金著名演讲《我有一个梦想》（I Have a Dream）里面的片断，他用了一系列排比和漂亮的比喻。他的演讲之所以受到大家的喜爱，主要原因就在这里。

例 4

Let us learn the lessons already taught by such cruel experience. Let us redouble our exertions, and strike with united strength while life and power remain.

参考译文：

让我们从中吸取血的教训；让我们趁生命未息，力量尚存，加倍努力，团结奋斗。

例 5

I see the Russian soldiers standing on the threshold of their native land, guarding the fields which their fathers have tilled from time immemorial. I see them guarding their homes where mothers and wives pray—ah, yes, for there are times when all pray—for the safety of their loved ones, the return of the bread-winner, of their champion, of their protector. I see the ten thousand villages of Russia where the means of existence is wrung so hardly from the soil, but where there are still primordial human joys, where maidens laugh and children play. I see advancing upon all this in hideous onslaught the Nazi war machine, with its clanking, heel-clicking, dandified Prussian officers, its crafty expert agents fresh from the cowing and tying down of a dozen countries. I see also the dull, drilled, docile, brutish masses of the Hun soldiery plodding on like a swarm of crawling locusts. I see the German bombers and fighters in the sky, still smarting from many a British whipping, delighted to find what they believe is an easier and a safer prey.

参考译文：

此刻我眼前看到的是俄国的士兵昂然挺立于自己的国土，英勇地捍卫着他们祖祖辈辈自古以来一直辛勤耕耘着的土地。我看到他们正在守卫着自己的家园，在那里母亲和妻子正在向上帝祈祷——是啊，任何人都总有祈祷的时候——祈求上帝保佑她们的亲人的平安，并保佑她们的壮劳力、她们的勇士和保护者凯旋。我看见成千上万的俄国村庄，那儿的人们虽然要靠在土地上辛勤耕作才能勉强维持生计，却依然能够享受到天伦之乐，那儿的姑娘在欢笑，儿童在嬉戏。我看到这一切正面临着凶暴的袭击，正杀气腾腾地扑向他们的是纳粹的战争机器和它的那些全副武装、刀剑当当有声、皮靴咚咚作响的普鲁士军官以及一群奸诈无比、刚刚帮它征服并奴役了十多个国家的帮凶爪牙。我还看到那些呆头呆脑、训练有素、既驯服听话又凶残野蛮的德国士兵像一群蝗虫般地向前蠕动着。我看见天空中那些屡遭英军痛击、余悸未消的德国轰炸机和战斗机此时正庆幸终于找到他们以为是无力反抗、可手到即擒的猎物（张鑫友译，2000）。

评析：例4和例5是《关于希特勒攻打苏联的演讲》中的内容。例4是句子排比，例5是段落排比。作为国家元首，如何成功地动员国民去帮助自己的对手？如何动员男儿去为国捐躯？排比的修辞手法为达到这一目的起到了很大的作用。

例 6

Has he been betrayed? Has the dictionary abdicated its responsibility? Should it say that one must speak like the president of Harvard or like the president of Yale, like the thirty-first President of the United States or like the thirty-fourth?

参考译文：

　　这就是背叛吗？词典放弃了职责吗？它要说我们必须像哈佛大学校长那样说话吗？或者像美国第三十一任总统或第三十四任总统那样说话？

评析：这是《词典的作用究竟是什么？》里面的一段反问句排比，这种手法既简单又强劲有力。

综上所述，排比是大家都很熟悉的一种修辞手法，它使用起来简单方便，采用相同的词句或结构即可。它的目的是加强语气，引起读者的注意，同时也是为了句式美，它还可以增加字数，是我们可以借鉴的好方法。

（五）了解其他一些修辞手法

以上重点介绍了并列和排比，对于其他一些常用修辞手法，我们也应当略知一二。

1. 对比

对比也叫对偶，其英语是antithesis。英语和汉语的对比有一些差异，英语的对比要求意思相反，不要求字数相等；而汉语的对比意思可以相反，也可以相近，但通常字数相等。

例 1

　　Enter to grow in wisdom, and depart to serve better thy country and thy kind.

参考译文：

　　为长智慧走进来，为国为民走出去。

评析：这是哈佛大学门口的一个警句，我们可以看出它的字数前后不对等，事实上也不可能对等，因为英语的每个名词前通常都要有限定词。但是，这个警句的前后两个动词是正反义，一个进，一个出，形成了对比。

反观该警句的中文翻译，它不仅把相反的意思翻译出来了，前后字数也对等。正因为字数相等，我们才觉得句子很工整，很优美。很多学生可以轻松读出汉语句子的美，却经常看不出英语句子的美，主要原因就在于他们不了解这个英语警句的结构和它里面使用的修辞手法。

清楚了英汉语对比的差异，我们就更容易欣赏英语句子的美了。值得一提的是，在翻译过程中，当目的语无法表达原语的某种修辞美时，会采用另一种手法来弥补，因为修辞的主要目的是制造美，包括视觉美和听觉美。

例 2

Then there is the spice-market, with its pungent and exotic smells; and the food-market, where you can buy everything you need for the most <u>sumptuous</u> dinner, or sit in a tiny restaurant with porters and apprentices and eat your <u>humble</u> bread and cheese.

参考译文：

然后是充满着异香奇味的香料市场，还有食品市场。在这里，你可以买到豪华酒宴需要的山珍海味，或者同搬运工一起坐在小饭馆里吃廉价的奶油面包。

评析：这是《中东集市》里面的句子，因为使用了 sumptuous 和 humble 这一组对比，尽管句子比较长，但看起来却非常优美。

例 3

From them all Mark Twain gained a keen perception of the human race, of the difference between <u>what people claim to be</u> and <u>what they really are</u>.

参考译文：

通过对他们的描述，马克·吐温深刻地洞察了人的特性，以及他们言行之间的差异。

例 4

They vanish from a world where they were of no consequence; where they achieved nothing; where they were a mistake and a failure and a foolishness; where they have left no sign that they had existed—a world which will <u>lament</u> them <u>a day</u> and <u>forget</u> them <u>forever</u>.

参考译文：

他们从世上消失，在这个世界里，他们无关紧要，一无所获；在这个世界，他们就是一个错误，是一场失败，是一种愚蠢；他们悄然离去，什么痕迹也没有留下；在这个世界，人们对其哀伤一日，继而永久遗忘。

评析：例3和例4是《马克·吐温——美国的镜子》中的两个例子。例3中的what people claim to be和what they really are构成对比，一个说来一个做。例4里面有两组对比，一个是lament和forget，哀伤表示记得，然后就是忘却。另一个是a day和forever，a day是模糊概念，表示短暂，而遗忘是永久的。其效果和其他这类例子一样，句式优美，含义深刻。

例 5

After the evidence was completed, Bryan rose to address the jury. The issue was simple, he declared. "The Christian believes that man came from <u>above</u>. The evolutionist believes that he must have come from <u>below</u>."

参考译文：

传唤证人之后，布莱恩站起来，开始对陪审团发言。他说事情原本很简单，"基督教徒们认为人是上帝创造的，而进化论者则认为人来自丛林。"

评析：这个例子是《震惊世界的审判》里面控方律师布莱恩先生说的话，这里above和below是对比：above是指代修辞法，指上帝；below也是指代，指丛林，因为达尔文认为人是由猿猴进化而来的。句子不仅读起来慷慨激昂，而且极其优美。

例 6

The rather arresting spectacle of little old Japan adrift amid beige concrete skyscrapers is the very symbol of the incessant struggle between <u>the kimono</u> and <u>the miniskirt</u>.

参考译文：

小小日本这一引人注意的水上景色夹在混凝土的摩天大楼之间，甚是迷人，象征着和服和超短裙之间的不断斗争。

例 7

<u>Little girls and elderly ladies in kimonos</u> rubbed shoulders with <u>teenagers and women in western dress</u>.

评析：例6和例7都是《广岛——日本"最快乐"的城市》中的句子。例6中的the kimono是传统的象征，而the miniskirt则是现代的象征，这两个词构成一组对比。而例7则是传统与现代的完美融合，二者各有特色，和谐相处。

例 8

All languages are <u>dynamic</u> rather than <u>static</u>, and hence a "rule" in any language can only be a statement of contemporary practice.

例 9

They doubted that "Lincoln could have modelled his Gettysburg Address" on it—a concept of how things get written that throws very <u>little</u> light on Lincoln but <u>a great deal</u> on *Life*.

参考译文：

他们怀疑"林肯写《葛底斯堡演讲》时，是否会参考这本词典。"这一观点并没有让我们知晓林肯是怎么写东西的，倒是清楚了《生活杂志》是怎么写东西的。

例 10

The second brief statement is that there has been even more progress in the making of dictionaries in the past thirty years than there has been in the making of automobiles. The difference, for example, between the <u>much-touted</u> Second International (1934) and the <u>much-clouted</u> Third International (1961) is not like the difference between yearly models but like the difference between <u>the horse and buggy</u> and <u>the automobile</u>.

参考译文：

第二个主要观点是在过去的三十年当中，词典编撰方面取得的进步要比汽车制造发生的变化更大。比如，倍受好评的第二版国际词典（1934 年）和饱受批评的第三版国际词典（1961年）的差异，不是每年变化外观的车型的差异，而是形同马车与机动车辆之间的差异。

评析：例8至例10都是《词典的作用究竟是什么？》里面的内容。例8里面的dynamic和static构成一组对比，一个是"动态的"，一个是"静态的"。例9是两个表示程度的词的对比。例10的much-touted和much-clouted不仅是对比，而且还押头尾韵，最后两个画线部分是"人力车"和"机动车"的代名词。

总之，能读出他人写作中的对偶并且自己学会运用是一件很了不起的事情，因为对偶是最体现形式美的一种修辞手法，它使得文章句式非常优美。

2. 成对词

成对词是词汇学里面的一个概念，它原本是指now and then，here and there这种固定的二字结构，其特点是结构优美，但不能随意改动。

鉴于成对词在结构上很优美，善于修辞者会刻意把两个词放到一起使用，但它们在这种情况下不是真正意义上的成对词，可以根据需要进行改动。有时，写作者还经常让它们押韵。

例1

The Russian danger is therefore our danger, and the danger of the United States, just as the cause of any Russian fighting for his hearth and home is the cause of free men and free peoples in every quarter of the globe.

参考译文：

因此，苏联的危险也是我们的危险，也是美国的危险，正如苏联的保家卫国事业也是全世界追求自由的人们及民族的事业一样。

评析：这是丘吉尔演讲时说的一句话，hearth原来是"壁炉及其周边"的意思，这里它就是home的意思。两个词比一个词更加优美，配上头韵之后，就同时产生了视觉美和听觉美。

例2

In each shop sit the apprentices—boys and youths, some of them incredibly young—hammering away at copper vessels of all shapes and sizes.

参考译文：

  每个商店里面都坐着一些学徒——都是男孩和年轻人，有些年轻得令人难以置信，他们不停地敲打着形状各异、大小不一的铜器。

例 3

  Here you can find beautiful pots and bowls engraved with <u>delicate and intricate</u> traditional designs, or the simple, everyday kitchenware used in this country, pleasing in form, but undecorated and strictly functional.

参考译文：

  在这里，你可以看到各种美观漂亮的锅碗瓢盆，上面雕刻着精细复杂的传统图案；还可以看到当地使用的简单朴素的日常厨具，虽无花纹图案，却造型美观，经济实用。

  评析：例2和例3都是《中东集市》中的句子，画线部分都是成对词，例2押头韵，例3押尾韵，同时产生了视觉美和听觉美。

  值得一提的是，英语的成对词和汉语的四字结构很像，都是为了产生视觉美，但英语中没有四字结构，因此，成对词翻译成汉语的时候，我们会首先考虑四字结构。

例 4

  The style of Dryden is <u>capricious and varied</u>, that of Popo is <u>cautious and uniform</u>; Dryden obeys the motions of his own mind, Popo constrains his mind to his own rules of composition. Dryden is sometimes <u>vehement and rapid</u>; Popo is always smooth, uniform, and gentle.

参考译文：

  就文风而论，德莱顿变化多端，不拘一格；蒲柏则小心谨慎，格调统一。德莱顿信马由缰；蒲柏中规中矩。德莱顿热情如火，行动似风；蒲柏则前后流畅，始终温情。

例5

Dryden's page is a natural field, rising into <u>inequalities, and diversified</u>, by the varied exuberance of abundant vegetation; Popo's is a velvet lawn, shaven by the scythe, and leveled by the roller.

参考译文：

> 观德莱顿之一页，犹如田野一方，高低错落，自然天成，其花草树木，郁郁葱葱，更使其姿态万千；蒲柏之诗文则似碧草一坪，柔如鹅绒，其平整有序，刀割碾压。

评析：例4和例5是英国文学大家Samuel Johnson（塞缪尔·约翰逊）关于Pope（蒲柏）的评论。喜爱英美文学的人都知道，约翰逊先生开创了一代夸饰之风，他非常注意刻意选词，以营造结构上的美感。虽然不少后来的文人批评这种刻意的文风，但并没有因此降低约翰逊在英国文学史上的显赫地位。

在这两段评论中，约翰逊先生拿蒲柏跟桂冠诗人德莱顿进行对比，他用词极其考究，多处使用成对词。

3. 比喻

英语的比喻可以分为很多种，比如暗喻（metaphor）、明喻（simile）、借代（metonymy）、提喻（synecdoche）等。我们通常说的比喻多指暗喻和明喻。

（1）暗喻

关于暗喻，《牛津高阶英汉双解词典》提供的解释是"用一个词或短语的想象的方式来描述另外一个人或一样东西，目的是为了显示二者之间有共同的特点，从而使得描述更生动"。（A metaphor is a word or phrase used in an imaginative way to describe somebody or something else, in order to show the two things have the same qualities to make the description more powerful.）

例 1

Behind all this <u>glare</u>, behind all this <u>storm</u>, I see that small group of villainous men who plan, organise, and launch this cataract of horrors upon mankind.

参考译文：

在这刀光剑影、腥风血雨的背后，我看见一小撮邪恶之人，他们策划、组织、发动了这场人类历史上的浩劫。

评析：这是丘吉尔的演讲词，两个画线部分都是比喻，它们避免了直白描写杀戮的场景，但又更加形象生动。

例 2

It grows louder and more distinct, until you round a corner and see a <u>fairyland</u> of dancing flashes, as the burnished copper catches the light of innumerable lamps and braziers.

参考译文：

声音越来越清晰，转个弯，只见锃亮的铜器映照着无数的灯和火盆，流光飞舞，犹如仙境。

评析：这是《中东集市》里面的句子，作者交代声音变得越来越清晰，拐个弯就看见一个场景。有些人误认为是看见了一个仙境。实际上，a fairyland只是一个比喻而已。

例 3

The dye-market, the pottery-market and the carpenters' market lie elsewhere in the <u>maze</u> of vaulted streets which honeycomb this bazaar.

参考译文：

带顶棚的街道纵横交错，有如迷宫一般，坐落其间的有染料市场、陶器市场和木器市场。

评析：这也是《中东集市》里面的句子，maze是比喻，它的用法和例2里面的fairyland用法相同。

例 4

Quickly the trickle becomes a <u>flood</u> of glistening oil, as the beam sinks earthwards, taut and protesting, its creaks blending with the squeaking and rumbling of the grinding-wheels and the occasional grunts and signs of the camels.

参考译文：

随着大梁越压越低，绳索越绷越紧，石磙的吱嘎和辘辘声与骆驼不时的叹息声交织在一起，榨出的油很快由涓涓细流变成一股晶莹剔透、奔腾不止的洪流。

评析：这还是《中东集市》里面的句子，和例2、例3一样，flood也是比喻，表示油最后奔腾出来，如洪水一般。

暗喻要注意搭配问题，这是我们要注意的，即喻体与喻词之间存在内在的逻辑关系。

例 5

Gone was the <u>fierce fervour</u> of the days when Bryan had <u>swept</u> the political <u>arena</u> <u>like a prairie fire</u>. The crowd seemed to feel that their <u>champion</u> had not <u>scorched</u> the infidels with the <u>hot breath</u> of his oratory as he should have.

参考译文：

布莱恩先生曾经有如一把草原大火横扫政坛，可是其炽热程度已经一去不复返。他的崇拜者似乎感觉到他们曾经的勇士未能像以往一样，用他的锐利言辞把异教徒烧死。

评析：这是《震惊世界的审判》中的比喻及其搭配关系。作者先是把布莱恩的热情比作草原大火，因此就出现了fierce fervour和swept，以及scorch和hot breath这四个词，它们都和火有关。hot breath指布莱恩先生的演讲或言辞。然后作者又把布莱恩先生比作champion，而勇士战斗的地方叫arena，这之间也存在搭配关系。

例 6

The geographic core, in Twain's early years, was the great valley of the Mississippi River, main <u>artery</u> of transportation in the young nation's <u>heart</u>.

参考译文：

吐温年轻时，美国地理中心在密西西比河大峡谷，它是这个年轻国家心脏的交通大动脉。

评析：这是《马克·吐温——美国的镜子》中的句子，heart本来是"中心"的意思，artery是"交通枢纽"的意思。它们都是人体器官的名称，表示非常重要之意，这两者之间形成了搭配关系。

例 7

For eight months he <u>flirted with</u> the colossal wealth available to the lucky and the persistent, and was <u>rebuffed</u>.

参考译文：

长达八个月，他三心二意地与属于幸运者或是持之以恒者的巨大财富调情，遭到断然拒绝。

评析：这也是《马克·吐温——美国的镜子》中的句子，flirt

with原指与他人调情，所以后面就对应了rebuff，一个向他人求婚遭到拒绝时的用词，因此前后构成了搭配关系。

例8

From the discouragement of his <u>mining</u> failures, Mark Twain began <u>digging his way</u> to regional fame as a newspaper reporter and humorist. The instant riches of a <u>mining strike</u> would not be his in the reporting trade, but for making money, his pen would prove <u>mightier</u> than his <u>pickax</u>.

参考译文：

挖矿暴富未成，马克·吐温沮丧至极，他开始设法在新闻记者和幽默作家方面取得成功。写作当然不可能像挖矿那样迅速变富，但是讲到赚钱，他的笔并不比镐子逊色。

评析：这依然是《马克·吐温——美国的镜子》中的句子，dig his way是try to get successful的意思，因为挖矿的动作是dig，所以作者故意使用这个短语。画线部分的单词都与挖矿构成搭配关系。

（2）明喻

关于明喻，《牛津高阶英汉双解词典》提供的解释是"通过使用like或as把一个词或短语比作另一样东西"。(A simile is a word or phrase that compares something to something else, using the word like or as.)

因为明喻有like或as作为特征，因此，向来被看成是很简单的修辞手法。但事实上，英语中的明喻并非都是那么简单。它不仅仅是为了让事物更浅显易懂，把一个抽象复杂的事物比喻成一个具体形象的事物，它还有让意义变得更加含蓄的作用。

张明冈（1985）在《比喻常识》一书中写道："苏联作家奥丘斯特·列努阿尔说，艺术家要更好地表现自己，他就应该隐藏起来，比喻正好能帮助艺术家隐藏——隐藏自己对世界的看法。但是，隐藏要使他最终能最充分、最有力地表现自己。"

例 1

Not because of the distinction of these particular speakers; lexicography, like God, is no respecter of persons.

参考译文：

并非上述要人的特殊身份，而是因为，词典就如同上帝，对所有人一视同仁。

评析：这是《词典的作用究竟是什么？》里面的一句话，它的比喻形象生动，浅显易懂。

例 2

And really it was almost like watching a flock of cattle to see the long column, a mile or two miles of armed men, flowing peacefully up the road, while the great white birds drifted over them in the opposite direction, glittering like scraps of paper.

参考译文：

确实，看着长达一两英里的队伍慢慢前行，就好像看着一群牛马。高空飞翔的大白鹳此时正朝着相反的方向翱翔，仿佛碎纸片一般，闪闪发光。

评析：这是《马拉喀什》的结尾，这个明喻意义深刻，很不简单，未经提示很少有人看得懂。作者采用比喻是为了不让读者轻易看出他的用意，但熟谙文学欣赏的人一定可以看出，这是在暗示殖民统治终归灭亡的高明手法。armed men象征着殖民统治，大白鹳及其飞行方向是不变的自然规律，谁也无法改变或阻拦，scraps of paper表示答案，也就是谜底很快就会揭晓，殖民统治很快就会灭亡。

（3）借代

关于借代，《牛津高阶英汉双解词典》提供的解释是"用一个东西来指另一个与之有关系的事物"。（Metonymy refers to use one thing to refer to something else that is closely connected with it.）

例 1

The Trial That Rocked <u>the World</u>

参考译文：

震惊世界的审判

评析：the world是指the people in the world。

例 2

the White House

参考译文：

白宫

评析：白宫是一种比喻，经常是指美国政府或总统。

例 3

There has been an enormous proliferation of closing and demarking devices and structure in the past twenty years, and anyone who tries to thread his way through the many meanings now included under door may have to sacrifice brevity to accuracy and even have to employ words that <u>a limited vocabulary</u> may find obscure.

参考译文：

在过去的二十年当中，开关装置品种繁多。但凡试图搞清楚门之含义者，势必牺牲简洁性，而获得准确性，甚至还会使用一些让词汇量有限的人觉得晦涩难懂的词语。

评析：这是《词典的作用究竟是什么？》里面的一句话，a limited vocabulary 这里不是指有限的词汇量，而是指词汇量有限的人。

（4）提喻

《牛津高阶英汉双解词典》对"提喻"的解释是"用整体代替部分，或者用部分代替整体的用法"。（Synecdoche refers to a word or phrase in which a part of something is used to represent a whole, or a whole is used to represent a part of something.）

例 1

But neither his vanity nor his purse is any concern of the dictionary's; it must record the facts.

参考译文：

无论是他的虚荣心，还是他的金钱，都和词典无关，词典只记录事实。

评析：这是《词典的作用究竟是什么？》里面的一句话，它用钱包指代里面的钱。

例 2

The kettle is boiling.

参考译文：

壶开了。

评析："壶开了"其实是指壶里面的水开了，这在汉语里也是一样的。

4. 头韵和尾韵

关于"头韵"和"尾韵"，《牛津高阶英汉双解词典》的解释分别是"一个句子中两个或两个以上的单词的开头相同"和"一个句子中两个或两个以上的单词的结尾相同"。（Alliteration refers to two or more words in a sentence which have the same letters at the very beginning. End rhyme refers to two or more words in a sentence which have the same letters at the end. ）

例 1

hearth and home

参考译文：

家园

评析：这是丘吉尔在他的演讲中使用的一个成对词，其目的是产生视觉美和听觉美。这两个单词不仅凑成了成对词，还押头韵。

例 2

shapes and sizes

参考译文：

形状各异，大小不一

评析：这是《中东集市》里面的一个成对词，其目的也是同时达到视觉美和听觉美。它不仅凑成了成对词，还押头尾韵。

例 3

It was a splendid population—for all the slow, sleepy, sluggish-brained sloths stayed at home.

参考译文：

这里的人很了不起——因为那些笨手笨脚、无精打采、呆头呆脑的懒汉都待在家里。

评析：这是《马克·吐温——美国的镜子》一文中的一句话，吐温先生使用五个s开头的单词，加利福尼亚人的特点就跃然纸上了，方法简单明了。

总之，文体美的主要来源之一是修辞，善用修辞非常重要，学会一些修辞手法可以为我们的写作增色。

（六）学会适当引典

引典和我们前面讨论的引言法有一部分相同，但不一定在开篇使用，更多时候是在分析过程中用引典来充当论据，也就是拿他人的话来支持自己的观点。

我们一起来看下面的例子。

First things first, ambition renders us a sense of mission. No matter what decision you make you have to be responsible for your choice. Your choice procures you a sense of orientation, or more specially a sense of mission. And only a strong mission may enable one to accomplish greatness. Caesar of the ancient Roman Empire was urged by his ambition "I came, I saw, I conquered." and became an unrivaled empire builder in the history of Rome. John Milton, stimulated always by his ambition that aimed at writing some "mighty lines" which England would unwillingly forget, had in due time secured his position as the second Shakespeare in the history of English literature.

评析：这是我们前面引用过的那篇在网上被称为"满分"的作文，作者在整篇文章里引典好几处，先引用了罗马大帝恺撒的经典名言"我亲自前往，我亲眼所见，我准备征服！"还引用了约翰·弥尔顿的例子，说他的抱负是能够写出几篇雄文，成为英国文学史上仅次于莎士比亚的文学家。

引典的目的是增强自己观点的可信度，这几个人都雄心勃勃，其话语很好地支撑了作者的观点。

（七）积累级别较高的词

高级写作有一个不可或缺的要素是使用级别较高的词，而不能全部使用常用词。这有两方面原因：一是语体原因；二是内容深度的原因。

高级写作在思想内容方面要求更高，因此，一些级别更高的词能更好地表达这些思想。比如表示程度时，我们最好不要说That's very strange，因为very一词太口语化，级别太低。

一般来说，我们从词的长短上就可以判断哪些单词级别略低，哪些单词级别更高。通常常用词都比较简单，比如very，use，see，finish等，而级别高的词相对更长，比如extremely，employ，observe，accomplish等。

我们一起来看下面的例子。

例 1

There has been an <u>enormous</u> proliferation of closing and demarking devices and structure in the past twenty years, and anyone who tries to thread his way through the many meanings now included under door may have to <u>sacrifice</u> brevity to accuracy and even have to <u>employ</u> words that a limited vocabulary may find obscure.

评析：这是《中东集市》里面的一个段落，这段文字我们在讨论修辞手法时已经看过，因此，参考译文省略。

在这里，我们强调的是三个画线的词enormous，sacrifice和employ。enormous是表示程度的级别较高的词，用在高级写作中替代very。sacrifice 就是give up to的意思，而employ则等于use，但前者是较高级别的词，后者是常用词。

例 2

New dictionaries are needed because English changed more in the past two generations than at any other time in its history. It has had to adapt to extraordinary cultural and technological changes, two world wars, unparalleled changes in transportation and communication, and unprecedented movements of populations.

参考译文：

我们需要新词典，因为在过去的二十多年中，英语的变化比以往任何时候都大。它必须适应文化和科技方面的巨大变化、两次世界大战、交通运输和交流通信方面的巨大变化，以及人口的极速增长。

评析：extraordinary，unparalleled，unprecedented都是表示程度的级别较高的词。高级写作习惯上用一些级别更高的词，而不用常用词。那些日常用词比较口语化，只适合初级写作，高级写作一定有些特别的词汇，包括更长、更雅致、更复杂的单词等。

例 3

If you bear any visible scars of atomic burns, your children will encounter prejudice on the part of those who do not.

参考译文：

如果原子弹给你留下了外伤，那些外表完好无损的人就会歧视你的孩子。

例 4

Because, thanks to it, I have the <u>opportunity</u> to improve my character.

参考译文：

正因为此，我有机会修身养性。

评析：这是《广岛——日本"最快乐"的城市》中的两句话。在口语里，我们可以用meet表示"遭遇"和"满足"，用chance表示"机会"。而高级写作中，一般会选择级别更高的词，如例子中的encounter和opportunity。

例 5

Then as you <u>penetrate</u> deeper into the bazaar, the noise of the entrance fades away, and you come to the muted cloth-market.

参考译文：

往集市深处走去，嘈杂声随即消失，你来到了寂静的布艺市场。

评析：这是《中东集市》里面的例子，penetrate其实就是go into的意思，可是go into太普通了，而penetrate不仅级别高，而且有走得费力的意思，这个词选得非常好。

例 6

Ambition

Ambition is the decision one makes and the resolution with which he carries out that decision. It provides us with the required driving force to <u>accomplish</u> any undertakings in our life. Just as Joseph Epstein, a famous American writer put it, "And as we decide and choose, so are our lives formed." Indeed, once we make up our minds to choose to do something, then our life becomes meaningful and specifically orientated. This notion of life, as far as I observe, is closest to truth and does apply to almost all aspects of life.

First things first, ambition renders us a sense of mission. No matter what decision you make you have to be responsible for your choice. Your choice procures you a sense of orientation, or more specially a sense of mission. And only a strong mission may enable one to accomplish greatness. Caesar of the ancient Roman Empire was urged by his ambition "I came, I saw, I conquered." and became an unrivaled empire builder in the history of Rome. John Milton, stimulated always by his ambition that aimed at writing some "mighty lines" which England would unwillingly forget, had in due time secured his position as the second Shakespeare in the history of English literature.

In the second place, ambition can bring one's potentials to the full. Ambition may well serve as a catalyst activating one's dormant potentials. Without ambition one's potentials will remain slumbering like a dormant volcano. A case in point is Ms. Zhang Haidi, a Chinese Helen Keller. It was her ambition to be a useful person that has turned the almost paralyzed Zhang Haidi into a well-accomplished figure whose achievements would dwarf those of some normal people.

Influential as it is upon us, however, ambition must be channeled in the right direction. If wrongly directed, one's ambition may bring havoc on him and others. Hitler, whose ambition was to conquer Europe by whatever evil means, finally turned him into a demon. It was this demon that almost cast Europe into an unfathomable abyss of anguish and suffering. Another case is Macbeth whose ambition was to become the king of Scotland.

However, his ambition was materialized by the murder of King Duncan. Consequently, <u>unbearable</u> guilt and psychological <u>agony</u> drove him to his tragic doom.

To sum up, ambition can benefit us <u>tremendously</u> if wisely and correctly channeled, otherwise it may ruin others and ourselves. A poet says: life can be bad; life can be good; life can be dirty; life can be sad; life can even be painful. In my mind, a person can make his life beautiful, meaningful and rewarding and stand out as a respectable personage if he is motivated by a well-orientated ambition.

评析：再次欣赏这篇作文，我们就会更加清楚地意识到，高分作文在方方面面都做得非常出色。从画线部分我们可以看到，作者有些词用得很高级，有的词选得很巧妙。我们可以想一想自己的用词习惯，比如画线部分的前三个词，我们会不会写成finish，see和give？如果是这样，你在选词方面的意识就有待加强。

综上所述，高分要素是方方面面的，其中有些词，尤其是表示程度的词，必须选择级别高一些的。这个问题其实很简单，只要我们在阅读过程中加以注意并养成归类的习惯就可以。

（八）处理相同词义

避免用词重复是英语行文的重要原则，我们非知道不可，它的意思就是说相同的词义必须用不同的词来表达，如果不注意这个问题，作文得高分的可能性很小。

例1

If people mean anything at all by the expression "<u>untimely death</u>", they must believe that some deaths run on a better schedule than others. Death in old age is rarely called untimely—a long life is thought to be a full one. But with <u>the passing of a young person</u>, one assumes that the best years lay ahead and the measure of that life was still to be taken.

History denies this, of course. Among <u>prominent summer deaths</u>, one recalls those of Marilyn Monroe and James Deans, whose lives seemed equally brief and complete. Writers cannot bear the fact that poet John Keats died at 26, and only half playfully judge their own lives as failures when they pass that year. The idea that <u>the life cut short</u> is unfilled is illogical because lives are measured by the impressions they leave on the world and by their intensity and virtue.

参考译文：

　　说起"<u>早逝</u>"，人们或有所指，他们定然相信有<u>些人</u>死得更合天意。年迈而终，不能称作未尽天年——长寿即意味着生命的圆满。但<u>英年早逝</u>的杰出人物则会引发感慨：美好年华未尽，评说尚待时日。

　　然而历史并非如此。提及<u>英年早逝</u>，人们自会忆起玛丽莲·梦露及詹姆士·迪安。两个人的生命虽短，却照样圆满。诗人济慈年仅 26 岁便溘然长逝，作家们对此深感惋惜。过了 26 岁之后，他们便不无戏谑地叹息自己一生无所作为。"<u>生命短暂即不圆满</u>"，此种观点荒谬无理。生命的价值，在其影响，在其绚烂，在其留德于世（张鑫友译）。

评析：这是 2006 年的 TEM-8 翻译题，当年的考点之一就是画线部分的词义问题。作为一篇文章，我们可以看到画线部分其实都是"英年早逝"之意，为了不重复，作者在上下文中采用了其他几种表达方式。

相同的词义使用不同的词语来表达是英语写作的一大习惯。处理相同词义时我们主要可以采用两种方法：一是使用近义词；二是根据上下文的意思。此外，还有一些小技巧，比如借代、省译等。

找近义词比较简单，就是找词义相同或相近的词，阅读时我们做好积累即可。根据上下文的意思略难一点，它是指某个词在当前的语境中是这个意思，脱离了此语境，则未必有这个意思。比如，不少学生把"summer death"翻译成了"夏日之死"，这是经不起推敲的，难道冬日不能死吗？

我们一起来看一下这些方法的运用。

例 2

和平和发展是当今世界的两大主题。维护世界和平，加强友好合作，促进共同发展是各国人民的共同愿望。当今，贫困、失业、难民、犯罪、人口膨胀、环境恶化、毒品泛滥、恐怖主义等问题仍然严峻，影响着全球的稳定和发展。中国与西方国家虽然国情不同，但在一系列重大国际问题上具有广泛一致的利益。我对中国与西方各国关系的改善与发展感到高兴。中国政府和人民在相互尊重和平等互利的基础上，与包括西方国家在内的世界各国政府和人民一道，为和平与发展的崇高事业做出贡献。

参考译文：

There are two topics today in the world: peace and development. The maintainance of the world peace, the friendly cooperation and the common improvement is the good hope of all the nations.

Yet we still suffer some severe problems like poverty, unemployment, refugee, crimes, over-population, deterioration of environment, drugs and terrorism which cause bad effect on our aim of the kind.

China shares the common interest with Western countries in a series of international issues in spite of the different characteristics of the respective. So I feel really satisfied to the good relationship between China and Western countries.

Therefore the Chinese government and Chinese people are willing to make a contribution to the lofty cause together with people in other countries on the basis of respect each other and mutual benefits.

评析：作者显然比较熟悉这个问题，他通过改变词形、使用近义词、根据上下文以及省译等形式，实现了相同词义的不同表达。尤其是our aim和the lofty cause译得非常好，"我们的目标"或"崇高的事业"不就是和平和发展吗？

相信大家对这样的政论体文章非常熟悉，它们的特点之一是重复强调某些重要信息，然而，英语的习惯是相同词义尽可能不重复，我们举几个中文例子，目的是希望大家在写作过程中进行语言转换时，把握好英汉语言的这个差异。

例 3

我喝我的清茶

他饮他的花酒，我喝我的清茶。人生，需要一种境界：自我安定。

面对别人的成功和荣耀，我喝我的清茶。我明白那掌声已有所属，匆匆忙忙赶过去，不会有成功等着你。还是自己再创业绩吧，跟着别人永远只能摸着成功的尾巴。

凡事不逃避，我喝我的清茶，荷花居污泥而不染，若为怕水污而种在旱地上，它早就枯死了。人生也一样，避恶、避丑、避邪，只能说明心灵脆弱，一个自我安定的人，是不怕环境污染自己的，而有力量影响他人。古代孟母三迁是为了怕孩子受影响，要为了自己就没有必要逃避了，后来孟子长大成人后也没听说孟母再搬家。

自我安定可不是找一个安宁的所在，而恰恰是在紊乱的环境中保持安定的心境。"定"是一种境界，是居于多变之中的不动摇。只有达到这一境界，才能掌握自己的方向，才能做到："他饮他的花酒，我喝我的清茶。"

参考译文 1：

Life with Plain Tea

While others indulging in wining and dining, I'm just content the pleasure of drinking plain tea because I know life sometimes is in want of a mentality of calmness.

While others rejoicing their success and glory, I'm simply standing aloof at ease enjoying a cup of plain tea. Since the applause has belonged to others, the slavish imitation could make no success therefore I'd rather carve out a career for myself.

I'm gratified with the life with plain tea and never escape from any adversity. I admire the lotus flower in the mud without being tainted would wither and die if it grew on the land for fear of sewage. The evils, ugliness, and risks, are the mud in our life testing our human fragility not necessary to shirk them because a man with a peaceful interior world fears no nasty environment and dares to improve it and bring benefits to others by his own strength. To shun the bad influence in the neighborhood, Mencius's mother had made three removals in his childhood. History shows no record of any more removals after he grew up.

Serenity doesn't merely mean a quiet residence but keep a serene life in a mussy surrounding. It is a state of mind standing to one's own resolution in such a fickle world so that we can be the master of our destiny, that is "Contenting with a cup of plain tea while others indulging in the best wine." （骆宾王译）

参考译文 2：

Contenting Myself with Plain Tea

Human life, it seems to me, needs a placidity of mind. While others may be wining and dining, I am content with plain tea.

Not dazzled by other people's aura of success and glamour, I'll indulge in my simple pleasure. Clearly aware where the credit goes, I won't join in the rush in the vain hope of accepting the prize to be handed to me on a plate. The best a blind follower can do is trailing after the winners. The only alternative is to create wonders of one's own.

I stick to the pureness of my pleasure, never escaping from reality. The lotus grows in the mud without being tainted. If, to avoid the dirt, one plants it on dry clean ground, it simply won't grow. The same holds true for human beings. Shrinking from what is ugly, vile and evil only proves the frailty of one's character. A person in full possession of mental serenity never stands in fear of being mentally contaminated by the filthy environment. On the contrary, he can exercise positive influence all around. Mencius's mother made three removals during his childhood to keep him away from bad influences, which did not pose any problems for her. History does not record any more of such removals after he grew up.

Enjoying the tranquility of mind does not mean hiding oneself in a haven. What is meant is the maintenance of such a mental state in the midst of chaos, i.e. moral immovability amidst kaleidoscopic changes. Only a person who has attained this plane can be a real master of his destiny, contenting himself with <u>the purest and simplest pleasure</u>.（居祖纯译）

评析：这是王书春的《我喝我的清茶》及其翻译。两篇参考译文都属于比较高级的译文，但二者还是有些差别。译文1是骆宾王翻译的，译文2是居祖纯翻译的。首先，译文1的题目选用了life一词，就显得很笼统，而且由于没有动作，缺少点韵味；相反，译文2的标题由于选用了content...with...，则有品茶的动作，颇有韵味。

译文1在第2、3、4段中，都用的是the plain tea，读起来有些别扭。由此可见，他在相同词义不同表达方面还不是那么注意。另外，在第3段第一句，又是be gratified with，又是life with，显得不够灵活。而译文2的翻译处理得很地道，特别是用simple pleasure来表示喝清茶，很神似。不过译文1在动词选择上还是很不错的，比如"品茶"，他分别用了content，gratify，enjoy，rejoice等。关于"安定"，我们可以看到两位大师各自都用了不同的表达，如peaceful，quiet，serenity，tranquility等。

例 4

The din of the stallholders crying their wares, of donkey-boys and porters clearing a way for themselves by shouting vigorously, and of would-be purchasers <u>arguing and bargaining</u> is continuous and makes you dizzy.

参考译文：

货主的叫卖声、赶毛驴的小伙子和脚夫的借道声，以及顾客的讨价还价声，不绝于耳，令人头晕目眩。

例 5

Bargaining is the order of the day, and veiled women move at a leisurely pace from shop to shop, selecting, <u>pricing</u> and doing a little preliminary bargaining before they narrow down their choice and begin the really serious business of beating the price down.

参考译文:

讨价还价是习以为常的事,头戴面纱的妇女迈着悠闲的步子,从一家店逛到另一家店,挑挑拣拣,砍砍价格,为将来正式购买时探探价。

评析:例4和例5都是《中东集市》里面的句子,从画线部分我们看到四个表示"砍价"的词,其中argue是通过上下文义表达的,其他则都是近义词。

例 6

The din of the stallholders crying their wares, of donkey-boys and porters clearing a way for themselves by shouting vigorously, and of would-be purchasers arguing and bargaining is continuous and makes you dizzy.

例 7

The shopkeepers speak in slow, measured tones, and the buyers, overwhelmed by the sepulchral atmosphere, follow suit.

参考译文:

商家拿捏着嗓门,低声说话,顾客受此阴森的气氛感染,也小声地说话。

例 8

One of the peculiarities of the Eastern bazaar is that shopkeepers dealing in the same kind of goods do not scatter themselves over the bazaar, in order to avoid competition, but collect in the same area, so that purchasers can know where to find them, and so that they can form a closely knit guild against injustice or persecution.

参考译文：

中东集市的特点之一是卖相同货物的商家非但不会为了避免竞争分散开来，相反，聚集在一起，这样顾客就知道到哪里找他们，而且还可以结成协作，共同抵制不公和迫害。

例 9

It is a point of honour with the <u>customer</u> not to let <u>the shopkeeper</u> guess what it is she really likes and wants until the last moment.

参考译文：

对于顾客来说，不到最后不让卖家猜到自己到底喜欢什么或想要什么，是一件很有面子的事。

例 10

<u>The seller</u>, on the other hand, makes a point of protesting that the price he is charging is depriving him of all profit, and that he is sacrificing this because of his personal regard for <u>the customer</u>.

参考译文：

另一方面，卖家极力声称开的价格让他毫无利润可言，他之所以不赚钱，是因为他个人对顾客肃然起敬。

评析：上述五个例子也是《中东集市》里面的句子，我们可以从画线部分看到"顾客"一词作者使用了buyer，purchaser和customer，而"卖家"则使用了stallholder，shopkeeper和the seller。

例 11

Perhaps the most <u>unforgettable</u> thing in the bazaar, apart from its general atmosphere, is the place where they make linseed oil.

参考译文：

也许，除了一般的气氛之外，集市中最令人难以忘怀之处就是榨油的地方。

例 12

In each shop sit the apprentices—boys and youths, some of them <u>incredibly</u> young—hammering away at copper vessels of all shapes and sizes, while the shop-owner instructs, and sometimes takes a hand with a hammer himself.

参考译文：

每个店铺里面都坐着一些学徒——都是男孩和年轻人，有些年轻得令人难以置信，他们不停地敲打着形状各异、大小不一的铜器。店主在一边指点，不时地自己锤上一两锤。

例 13

Elsewhere there is the carpet-market, with its profusion of rich colours, varied textures and regional designs—some bold and simple, others <u>unbelievably</u> detailed and yet harmonious.

参考译文：

再往前走，就是地毯市场，这里的产品色彩斑斓，质地繁多，富有地方特色，有些粗犷简约，有些则精细和谐得令人难以置信。

评析：例11至例13也是《中东集市》里面的句子，作者把"难以置信的"一词替换了多次，由此可见这是多么重要的一个表现手法。

例 14

And if something must be <u>eliminated</u>, it is sensible to <u>throw out</u> these extraneous things and stick to words.

参考译文：

如果有什么需要删除的话，明智的做法是删除这些额外的信息，保住单词。

例 15

There can be linguistic objection to the <u>eradication of</u> proper names. The <u>removal</u> of guides to pronunciation from the foot of every page may not have been worth the valuable space it saved. The new method of defining words of many meanings has disadvantages as well as advantages. And of the half million or more definitions, hundreds, possibly thousands, may seem inadequate or imprecise. To some (of whom I am one) the <u>omission</u> of the label "colloquial" will seem meritorious; to others it will seem a loss.

参考译文：

删除专有名词，从语言学角度，实属不当，从每页的脚注里删除发音指南也可能得不偿失，新方法在定义单词方面，许多意思有利有弊，五十多万的定义当中，可能有几百个，甚至上千个不得当或不准确，对于有些人，其中包括我本人，把"口语体"标识删除是件令人快乐的事，对于其他人则可能是一大损失。

评析：例14和例15是《词典的作用究竟是什么？》里面的句子，这两小段中，"删除"一词作者分别用了eliminate，throw out，eradication，removal和omission五个近义词。

例 16

Personal tragedy haunted his entire life, in the <u>deaths</u> of loved ones: his father, <u>dying</u> of pneumonia when Sam was 12; his brother Henry, <u>killed</u> by a steamboat explosion; the <u>death of</u> his son,

Langdon, at 19 months. His eldest daughter, Susy, <u>died of</u> spinal meningitis, Mrs. Clemens <u>succumbed to</u> a heart attack in Florence, and youngest daughter, Jean, an epileptic, <u>drowned</u> in an upstairs bathtub.

参考译文：

　　吐温一生悲剧缠身，挚爱之人相继离世。其父在他 12 岁时因肺炎而病故；其兄汽船爆炸而亡；儿子朗顿，19 个月大就离开了人世；大女儿苏西死于脊椎炎；夫人在福罗伦斯死于心脏病；小女儿简因癫痫溺死在澡盆里。

评析：这是《马克·吐温——美国的镜子》里的一个句子。在这里，我们可以看见，"死亡"一词作者用了death，dying，kill，die of，succumb to，drown等。这些地道的原文应该成为我们的一个标杆，让我们以它为榜样，从中吸收写作与翻译的高分要素。

最后，让我们看看2006年的TEM-8真题的情景。

例 17

　　Joseph Epstein, a famous American writer, once said, "We <u>decide</u> what is important and what is trivial in life, we <u>decide</u> (so) that what makes us significant is either what we do or what we refuse to do. But no matter how indifferent the universe may be to our <u>choices</u> and <u>decisions</u>, these <u>choices</u> and <u>decisions</u> are ours to make. We <u>decide</u>, we <u>choose</u>. And as we <u>decide</u> and <u>choose</u>, so are our lives formed. In the end forming our own destiny is what <u>ambition</u> is about."

参考译文：

　　爱泼斯坦，美国著名作家，曾经说："生活中，我们来判断哪些事情重要，哪些不重要。我们通过选择来决定要做什么，不做什么。但是，无论他人对此态度多么冷漠，这些都是我们自己的抉择。我们不断做出决定，不断做出选择，这样我们的生活就形成了。最后，决定我们命运的即是我们的抉择。"

评析：当年大部分考生都看不懂这个题，是什么原因导致大家看不懂题呢？除了爱泼斯坦的话比较难懂外，原因之一就在于几个画线的单词。

其实文中的ambition就是choose（choice）和decide（decision），也就是"选择"。这样，这段文字就不难理解了。"选择"这个意思不断出现，而且使用了几个不同的词来表达，造成了学生理解上的困难。

总之，相同词义用不同的词来表达是英语行文的一大特点。我们之所以在这一点上不惜赘言，一方面是因为它太重要；另一方面是要让大家清楚地意识到写作即阅读。

（九）学会巧妙布局

布局原来是指对事物的全面规划和安排。从写作的角度来讲，是指通过某种策略（包括先说什么后说什么、选择哪些信息、举什么例子）来达到最终说服他人目的的方法。通常，布局者很清楚他的这种策略可能会产生什么效果。

好的文章无不布局巧妙，其目的是增加说服力并吸引他人注意，激发他人的阅读兴趣。我们先来看《震惊世界的审判》里面的五个例子。

例1

After the preliminary sparring over legalities, Darrow got up to make his opening statement. "My friend the attorney-general says that John Scopes knows what he is here for," Darrow drawled.

"I know what he is here for, too. He is here because ignorance and bigotry are rampant, and it is a mighty strong combination."

参考译文：

庭审前的例行问答后，达罗站了起来，开始发言。"我的检察长朋友说约翰·斯科普知道自己为什么到这里来，"达罗慢吞吞地说，"我也知道。他之所以会被送上法庭，是因为无知与偏执，而且是这二者的强强联合。"

评析：达罗是为"我"辩护的主辩律师，他老奸巨猾，从一开始就料想到了结局。他使用的每一个策略都能够恰到好处地达到其目的。田纳西一个乡村法庭之所以审判"我"，是因为"我"教孩子生物学时不可避免地要提到达尔文的进化论。由此可见当地宗教多么盛行，当地人又是多么愚昧无知。达罗知道这么说一定会激怒当地的宗教信徒，但他的目的就是要惹他们生气，因为这样他们会认真地听他发言。

例 2

Darrow walked slowly round the baking court. "Today it is the teachers," he continued, "and tomorrow the magazines, the books, the newspapers. After a while, it is the setting of man against man and creed against creed until we are marching backwards to the glorious age of the sixteenth century when bigots lighted faggots to burn the men who dared to bring any intelligence and enlightenment and Culture to the human mind. "

参考译文：

达罗绕着热烘烘的法庭慢慢走着，"今天是教师，"他开始发言，"明天就会轮到杂志、书籍和报纸。用不了多久，就会是人斗人的场景，信条斗信条的场景，直到我们大步流星地倒退到辉煌的十六世纪，当时偏执狂们点燃柴火，把胆敢给人类带来智慧、光明和文化的人烧死。"

　　评析：达罗的动作都是故意的，这样大家会更加注意他。他的言辞激烈刻薄，这也是他希望达到的效果，因为他知道，结局很可能是当地的信徒们被他说服。

例 3

　　Dudley Field Malone popped up to reply. "Mr. Bryan is not the only one who has the right to speak for the Bible," he observed. "There are other people in this country who have given up their whole lives to God and religion. Mr. Bryan, with passionate spirit and enthusiasm, has given most of his life to politics."

　　Bryan sipped from a jug of water as Malone's voice grew in volume.

参考译文：

　　杜德利·菲尔德·马龙"噌"的一声站了起来，回答道："布莱恩先生不是唯一有权为《圣经》说话的人。"他继续发言："这个国家还有其他人，他们把一生都献给了上帝和宗教。布莱恩先生把大部分时间、激情和热忱都献给了政治。"

　　面对马龙越来越激昂的声音，布莱恩先生静静地抿水喝。

　　评析：马龙年轻有为，精通法律，反应灵敏，他的反击既巧妙又铿锵有力。The only非常微妙，听众一听就会明白，后面有更多的人更有发言权，因此布莱恩的可信度就会被削弱。投身宗教和投身政治构成一种反差，进一步削弱了布莱恩的说服力。试想他都把精力投身到政治当中去了，顾不上上帝了，还有发言权吗？这样，一些信徒的内心就会产生疑虑或顾忌。看完整篇文章，我们会十分认同马龙的话，他说真理不需要任何人类的支持，真理是永恒的，是永远的赢家。这不仅说明科学的魅力，更说明布局的巧妙在说服他人时的不可估量的作用。

最后一句很有意思，sip是一个非常轻微的动作，说明布莱恩先生佯装喝水，其实在认真地听。

例 4

Now Darrow sprang his trump card by calling Bryan as a witness for the defence. The judge looked startled. "We are calling him as an expert on the Bible," Darrow said. "His reputation as an authority on Scripture is recognized throughout the world."

参考译文：

此时，达罗打出了他的王牌，他叫布莱恩为辩方作证。这让法官格外吃惊。"我们把他称之为《圣经》专家，"达罗说，"作为《圣经》权威，他可是享誉全世界。"

评析：法官怎么可能会答应让控方主辩律师充当辩方证人呢？还别说法官就是和他们一伙的。可是达罗这时采用了大肆褒奖的手段，把布莱恩吹捧到了天上，再也找不到比他更合适的人了，因为他是享誉全球的《圣经》专家啊！如此这般，法官就不反对了。如果法官反对，后面的结果就不会出现。当然，法官同意让布莱恩先生作证也是达罗预料之中的事。巧妙的布局通常会产生预期的结果。

例 5

Darrow read from Genesis: "And the evening and the morning were the first day." Then he asked Bryan if he believed that the sun was created on the fourth day. Bryan said that he did.

"How could there have been a morning and evening without any sun?" Darrow enquired.

Bryan mopped his bald dome in silence. There were sniggers from the crowd, even among the faithful. Darrow twirled his spectacles as he pursued the questioning. He asked if Bryan believed literally in the story of Eve. Bryan answered in the affirmative.

"And you believe that God punished the serpent by condemning snakes for ever after to crawl upon their bellies?"

"I believe that."

"Well, have you any idea how the snake went before that time?"

The crowd laughed, and Bryan turned livid. His voice rose and the fan in his hand shook in anger.

参考译文：

达罗拿着《圣经》念了起来："晚上，然后白天，这就是第一天。"然后他问布莱恩是否相信太阳是在第四天创造出来的。布莱恩回答他相信。

"没有太阳，哪来的白天黑夜呢？"达罗质疑。

布莱恩默默地擦了擦自己光秃秃的头顶，人群中发出嗤嗤的笑声，其中还有那些忠实的信徒。达罗转动着眼镜，继续提问，他问布莱恩是否相信夏娃的故事。布莱恩果断地做了肯定回答。

"那你相信上帝为了惩罚那条蛇，从此就让它爬行了吗？"

"我相信。"

"可是，你知道蛇在此之前是怎么走的吗？"

人群大笑起来，布莱恩的脸色灰白。他抬高嗓门，手中的扇子愤怒地扇动着。

评析：布莱恩先生年高体衰，受不了这个打击，几天后就死了。我一直认为达罗知道会产生这样的结果，因为他很了解自己的对手，布莱恩先生一辈子都那么要强，怎么可能受得了这样当众出丑呢？而达罗也一定是豁出去了，总要有人为科学做祭奠吧？科学之光已经照亮了人类的今天，居然还有人愚昧固执到这种地步，他不死，谁死？能够揣测出达罗的这种布局者一定会获得极大的精神享受。

接下来我们再看两个其他的例子。

例6

What underlies all this sound and fury? Is the claim of the G. & C. Merriam Company, probably the world's greatest dictionary maker, that the preparation of the work cost $3.5 million, that it required the efforts of three hundred scholars over a period of twenty-seven years, working on the largest collection of citations ever assembled in any language—is all this a fraud, a hoax ?

参考译文：

喧嚣之下究竟意味着什么呢？麦里姆公司，一家可能是全球最大的词典编撰公司，他们声称为了这部词典的出版，花费了三百五拾万美金，动用了三百多名学者，耗费了二十七年的时间，编撰出世界上词汇收录最多的一部词典。难道人家是欺骗？是欺诈？

评析：这是《词典的作用究竟是什么？》中的例子。当一些著名的报纸杂志大肆谴责、甚至谩骂韦氏第三版国际词典之时，该文章的作者仅仅说了这么一小段话就动摇了那些迷信权威的读者的信念。确实，谁会拿相当于今天上千万、甚至上亿的资金，耗费近三十年时间，来欺骗他人呢？作者还巧妙地插入说麦里姆公司可不是什么家庭小作坊，而是世界上规模最大的词典编撰公司。

例 7

First things first, ambition renders us a sense of mission. No matter what decision you make you have to be responsible for your choice. Your choice procures you a sense of orientation, or more specially a sense of mission. And only a strong mission may enable one to accomplish greatness. Caesar of the ancient Roman Empire was urged by his ambition "I came, I saw, I conquered." and became an unrivaled empire builder in the history of Rome. John Milton, stimulated always by his ambition that aimed at writing some "mighty lines" which England would unwillingly forget, had in due time secured his position as the second Shakespeare in the history of English literature.

In the second place, ambition can bring one's potentials to the full. Ambition may well serve as a catalyst activating one's dormant potentials. Without ambition one's potentials will remain slumbering like a dormant volcano. A case in point is Ms. Zhang Haidi, a Chinese Helen Keller. It was her ambition to be a useful person has turned the almost paralyzed Zhang Haidi into a well-accomplished figure whose achievements would dwarf those of some normal people.

Influential as it is upon us, however, ambition must be channeled in the right direction. If wrongly directed, one's ambition may bring havoc on him and others. Hitler, whose ambition was to conquer Europe by whatever evil means, finally turned him into a demon. It was this demon that almost cast Europe into an unfathomable abyss of anguish and suffering. Another case is Macbeth whose ambition was to become the king of Scotland. However, his ambition was materialized by the murder of King Duncan. Consequently, unbearable guilt and psychological agony drove him to his tragic doom.

评析：这是前面我们引用过的2006年TEM-8作文真题，作者在第二部分举了好几个正反例子，从恺撒、弥尔顿、张海迪，到希特勒。

举恺撒大帝为例，并直接引用他的名言"I came, I saw, I conquered."无非是想让我们看到一个野心勃勃想雄霸天下的人。弥尔顿亦然，因为他想成为英国文学史上仅次于莎士比亚的人。至于张海迪，作者在她后面插入说她是中国的海伦·凯勒，大家可以思考一下，直接举海伦·凯勒，难道不会更好吗？因为同为残疾人，海伦·凯勒的知名度远远高于张海迪。

可是，只要大家看看上面的画线部分，就会注意到作者的巧妙布局：其一，作者给人留下一种古今中外无所不知的印象；其二，这几个人的名字押尾韵。

综上所述，高分作文的奥妙之一在于布局巧妙。好的布局可以帮助我们达到我们想要达到的目的，而要布局巧妙，就要认真观察他人是怎么布局的，并加以模仿，把学过的知识点运用到自己的写作中去。

第5章

正确评估的方法及技巧

前面我们主要做了两件大事：第一件是让大家知道高分要素有哪些；第二件是让大家明白阅读加上练习是目前最有效的提高写作水平的途径。

这一章可以看成是一种操练，我们通过分析和评估他人的作文来强化上面两方面的知识要点，并提高我们自身的评估能力，进而扬长避短，写出高水平的英语作文。

学生评估的总体问题

学会正确评估他人的作文是提高自身写作水平的一个重要方面。这方面能力的培养和学习英语写作一样重要，它不仅可以帮助我们提高鉴赏水平，还可以帮助我们养成做事有条理的好习惯。

评估他人的作文事实上是在进行论证的论证。评估者可以因此最直接地面对问题，这些问题可以是他们自己错误的反射，能引起自己的注意并在写作时避免；评估者还可以领略他人写作的精彩之处，并加以模仿和吸收。

实际情况是，很多学生根本不知道什么是评估，不知道怎样评估，普遍缺乏意识，绝大部分不规范。我们通过对一篇作文的不同评价来凸显分析过程中使用的不当方法。

南昌大学有一年的英语研究生入学考试作文给出的情景说20世纪初的美国，工人逐渐赚得更多了，很多工人下班后就去看电影，造成了电影市场的空前繁荣，后来电影市场逐渐萧条。

题目要求考生分析其中的原因。让我们从相关性方面简单分析一下。与情景相关的信息有当时的社会背景，包括人们的经济收入、闲暇时间、娱乐方式等。设想，如果电影不是新生事物，而是快被淘汰的事物，还会有很多人去看吗？想看电影，和收入有关吧？就算有钱消费，但没有很多闲暇时间也不行吧？我们一起来看看下面这篇作文。

Reasons for the Prosperity and Declination of Films

The film market in the United States entered its boom in the early 20th century when workers got more salary and worked less time and it gradually fell into its doom at the end of this era. The prosperity and declination of the films are not with no reason.

First things first, as one of the major capitalist countries that had enjoyed all the bounty of the First Industrial Revolution from 18th to 19th century, the USA embraced the unprecedentedly advanced productivity in the early 20th century which laid a solid economic foundation for the development of technology. As a result, film making had chance to further develop and spread as novelty in the billow of technology, intriguing throngs of people in the United States.

In the second place, the conflict between working-class and capitalists was intensified with the further development of capitalism in the USA. Consequently, labor movements sprung up, demanding for higher salaries and shorter working time. And as workers won their rights, the need for enriching leisure time arose. At that moment, films as one of the few mass media caught the attention of the workers who were not literate enough to read books as middle-class did.

Meanwhile, as the improvement of film techniques and the pursuit of more profound content of films, middle-class, the largest amount of population and the biggest consuming group, who ever despised the new form of entertainment and stuck to the more decent and graceful arts such as opera, musical began to poured in cinemas, pushing it to the climax of its history. However, after reaching the acme of its success, it began to decline due to the appetite of the audience for more profound and varied style predicted by the ancient wise man Laozi that a thing will turn its opposite if pushed too far.

Furthermore, when the world threaded its way into the net period, films experienced the strike of multimedia. Customers were facing more choices than ever before, with computers, smart phones as new favourites which offer almost any kind of arts to see from documentaries to talk shows. Take X-box, Facebook for example. They seem always on the top entertainment list. On the other hand, the change of people's living style is among the factors affecting the waxing to the waning of the film market. Most people nowadays live a more stressed, rapid, time-limited life. Thus, more of them make a preference of healthier recreations or fast information. Instead of sitting hours in a movie theater or spending one and a half hours watching a film at home through other facilities, many people would like to choose more wholesome ways like doing sports to have fun or faster approaches such as searching online to get information or buying and selling on it. It is reported that one of the great task for Zhai Nan and Zhai Nv is to stay in front of a computer enjoying writing net messages about everything they do in a day and sharing them with all their friends day and night.

To sum up, there are many reasons for the waxing and waning of the film making. Among them, time, money, taste, especially media style, are the main factors, which decide people's choice of entertainment. Film market, like anything in the world, will and must turn from the prosperity to the declination sooner or later.

评析：第一段虽然是摆出现状，但作者极尽修辞之能事，用了more和less，boom和doom两组对比，然后又把boom和doom替换成prosperity和declination，最后用双重否定be not with no reason来指出其中的理由。

第一个理由是说美国是18~19世纪工业革命的主要资本主义国家，在20世纪初获得了前所未有的先进生产力，为科技发展奠定了坚实的基础。电影制作技术得以在此波涛之中进一步发展和传播，大大刺激了观影群体。从经济角度着手分析消费的原因是值得借鉴的，因为它很有高度。

第二个理由是劳资双方的较量，其结果导致工作时间的缩短以及工资水平的提高。这个分析也很到位，因为资本家是不会主动给工人加薪的，唯有斗争才能争取到权益。而劳动时间的缩短就意味着休闲时间的增加，这样，获得更多收益的工人就会去消费了。在这个理由中提到工人看电影是因为他们的知识水平不足以像中产阶级那样可以看书读报，这一分析很有深度，因为如果工人可以读书看报，看电影的人数就不会如此众多。人总是要休闲或消遣的，除了经济条件之外，还有欣赏能力问题。

与此同时，电影技术大大提高，促使美国最大的人口及消费群体——中产阶级对电影产生了由不屑到青睐的转变，这样就把电影业推向了历史新高潮。紧接着，作者用however一词把话锋转到了衰败方面，并引用中国古代贤人老子的话“物极必反”，这又是高分要素之一，引用名人名言增加证据的可信度。

网络时代的来临给电影市场带来了进一步的挑战，使得电影业经历了从日出到日落的转变，因为娱乐形式开始多样化，人们的可选择形式日渐增多，而且生活方式改变了，他们不会花几个小时在电影院或在家里看电影，有些人宁愿出去运动或在电脑前检索信息，甚至从事网络买卖交易。宅男和宅女的必备功课之一就是把一日发生的任何事情写成网络信息，然后不分白天黑夜地发送出去，与全体朋友分享。

在这样一番论证之下，结论就顺理成章地出来了，三言两语概括之后，文章画上了完美的句号。

文章的逻辑框架特别漂亮，用了一系列连接词和转折词，比如first things first, as a result, in the second place, consequently, meanwhile, furthermore, thus, however, to sum up等。在选词方面，作者选用了boom和doom，prosperity和declination，wax和wane等一系列的成对词。

总之，这篇作文无论是结构还是修辞及思维，都符合高分要求。原因分析得非常全面，并且主次分明，逻辑性强。因此，这篇作文得分为18分。

作为评估练习，评价结果差异之大令人瞠目结舌。有个别学生做得非常好，他们对于高分要素把握特别到位，能够公正客观、有理有据地进行论证，并较为规范地写出一篇分析短文。有些学生则是非颠倒，无中生有地进行一番所谓的分析，毫无章法。

我们一起来看几个例子，评估的问题便从中凸显出来了。

例1

通读全文，个人觉得可以给满分，分析如下：

整篇文字布局美观、篇幅充足、逻辑严密、用词高端。作者采用一系列连接词，如 first things first, in the second place, meanwhile, however, to sum up，这一下就把逻辑框架确定下来了。

首先，作者从工业革命入手，立足点高；其次，指出了劳资冲突，这不仅有高度，而且有深度。

用 meanwhile 过渡到当前之后，分析了消费形式的改变，以及网络时代的特征，并引用老子的话作为证据，最后得出令人信服的结论。

在选词过程，作者非常娴熟地使用了相同词义不同表达，成对词等一系列修辞手法，以此来增加文章的美感。比如 boom 和 doom，prosperity 和 declination，wax 和 wan 等，可见其遣词造句多么用心。

总之，这篇作文逻辑框架漂亮，分析透彻，有高度也有深度，并且逻辑缜密，因此，我认为评满分是合理的。

评析：显然，这位评论者很清楚写作的高分要素，因此，他在三大层面进行了比较准确的分析。在他眼里，这是一篇完美的作文，所以他给了满分。不仅如此，评论者自己有很强的写作意识，他把评论写成了一篇条理清楚的短文，是典型的论证的论证。

例2

我给 92 分。

全篇观点清晰，条理明确，结构有序，分析透彻，逻辑清楚，选词巧妙，是篇佳作。

开篇作者表明了问题，并引出自己的理由。短短几行字，看似简单，却显现出了作者的不凡写作功底，因为作者的表达很书面，句式很美观，用词不同寻常。

两大理由不仅有高度，还很有深度，细致地从经济繁荣分析到生活方式的改变，同时还分析了工人争取权利的斗争因素。正因为经济状况的改变，以及权益的增加，引起了工人消费形式的改变，因果分明，理由充分。

对于电影业走向衰败的原因分析同样有高度，即科技的进一步发展，以及网络时代的来临。

最后，作者采用全称概念，指出电影业也会像其他任何事物一样，由繁荣走向衰退。到此，作文很好地总结了自己的观点，分析强劲有力，从而使得结论可信度极高。

评析：这位评论者的评论和例1的比较接近，对原作文给予了高度肯定和赞赏，分析得也很到位，就是条理上比例1差一些，因为连接词使用得较少，逻辑框架不是很清楚。此外，他的分析没有例1那么具体。

例3

这篇作文我给55分。主要有这些缺陷。

第一，作文采用六段式，而不是传统的三段式，这一点非常不好；第二，有些句子太长，读起来很费劲；第三，理由分析得有些凌乱，不是浅显易懂。

再就是缺乏相关性，在表明原因时，作者居然提到了工人和老板之间的冲突，这和电影事业有什么关系呢？认为这是电影行业发展的原因之一，是作者的猜测，是思维不成熟的表现。

随后，观点混乱，又说人们不愿意待在家里，又说宅在家里，具体要说什么，模糊不清。最后，说电影业一定会走向衰弱，这个结论太绝对。

评析：这篇评论与例1和例2相差甚大，评论者只给了55分，这是什么原因呢？他指出三点缺陷，第一点居然是要采用三段式，可见评论者根本不知道高级作文的写作特点。第二点说原文句子太长，可是书面语的特征之一就是句子相对更长，可见评论者对于高分要素还不太清楚。第三点说原文理由凌乱，不浅显易懂，不知道怎样的理由才算有条理，怎样的内容才浅显易懂？具有讽刺意义的是，该评论者居然说原作的相关信息有问题，而事实上原作者做得最漂亮的一点就是相关信息分析得很透彻、很到位，这一点我们在对作文的背景进行简单分析时就已经提到。事实上，原作者的分析和我们的几乎相同，也就是该思考到的相关要素，他都思考到了，所以原文很有高度和深度。

由此，我们只能得出这样的结论，例3的评论者才是真正缺乏逻辑思维的人，不仅如此，他在原文的结构和修辞方面只字未提，可见他对高分作文的系统要求毫不了解。他的观点是不公正客观的，他只不过是凭借自己的有限知识对他人的作文作了不恰当的评论而已。

另外，该评论者的语体非常口语化，仿佛是在聊天，而不是写出来的内容，明显缺乏规范和条理意识。

例4

这篇作文我给30分。

首先，文章题目只是一个短语，而不是一个句子，这个不适当，一般都是用句子的呀。第一段只有两句话，这也不适当，句子长了容易给人晦涩难懂的印象。

其次，文章有多处语法错误，比如第二段里面的 had enjoyed，怎么可以使用过去完成时呢？ laid a foundation 也不对，因为 lie 是不及物动词啊。

另外，文章离题，偷换了概念，本来是要他分析原因，他却讨论工人阶级的斗争。看起来写了很多内容，但实际上有用的内容很少，作者一直都在东拉西扯。

评析：一篇如此优秀的作文被该评论者评价成了一堆垃圾，而且仅仅给出30分，这确实让我们意识到提高自身评估能力的重要性。

和例3很像，该评论者指出的问题根本不是问题；相反，这些问题证实了评论者在语法、写作规范及逻辑方面的能力欠缺。

综上所述，目前学生在作文评估方面存在着不少问题，主要问题是缺乏正确评估的能力以及与高分作文相关的知识；其次，大部分学生缺乏规范的意识，在评论时，不能用正确规范的书面表达，而是像口头聊天。因此，我们必须加强这方面意识和能力的培养，并知道一些评估的方法和技巧，以快速帮助我们提高自身的写作能力，并避免犯他人所犯的错误。

掌握正确的评估方法和技巧

正确的评估首先意味着自身具备评估英语作文的知识和能力。快速提高评估能力的技巧之一是有针对性地把审读作文的步骤和高分作文所涉及的要点归纳出来；技巧之二是规范批判性写作的格式，即把评语写成一篇符合逻辑、条理清楚的书面作文。

（一）审读作文的步骤

第一步，看题目是否明确，大小写是否规范。

第二步，看是否使用连接词让作文的逻辑框架更加清晰，各段落之间的比例是否得当。

第三步，看审题是否清楚，有没有保持观点的同一性。

第四步，看第一段是否直接规范，即是否提出问题、表明观点。

第五步，看采用的是什么开篇方法，若是定义法，看定义是否准确。

第六步，看作文有没有高度和深度，是否有一定意义。

第七步，看文章的脉络是否清楚，条理是否清晰，主次是否分明。

第八步，看作文是否是书面语，是否使用较高级别的词，相同词义是否用不同词语表达。

第九步，看句式是否漂亮灵活，有没有适当的从句、分词短语等。

第十步，看客观内容多还是主观内容多，证据是假设的还是事实根据。

第十一步，看有没有引用名人名言。

第十二步，看句与句之间的逻辑关系是否密切，结论是否得到充分论证。

（二）规范评语的写作

我们可以把结果写在前面，如上述例3那样，也可以从上至下，按照审读作文的步骤逐一分析。不过较为普遍的方法是从上至下，围绕结构、思维和修辞三个方面来展开证述，最后给出结果。

评估作文本身也要讲究逻辑框架的美观，也要使用适当的连接词来增加其逻辑关系。条理是批判性写作的最显著特征，只有这样，读者才能够清楚地看到点评的要点。首先、其次、总之这类关系词是批判性写作的一个重要标志。

我们相信，把握好这两大方面对于评判他人的作文和改进自己的作文都是大有帮助的。

真题分析及其方法借鉴

在本章的最后一部分，我们提供了若干年的TEM-8真题样文分析，以期为学习者提供更多操练评估技巧的机会，以及优秀与劣质作文的相关信息。

1. 1993年TEM-8真题样文分析

As for a person's essential qualities, some people hold the view that they are inherited at birth, other people hold the opposite point that a person's essential qualities are influenced by environment. What's your opinion?

我们先来审题。

这个题当年考试分数并不理想，因为很多人缺乏背景知识。研究已经表明，人的主要品质是环境影响的，而不是遗传的。有这个背景知识的人，作文会比较好写，因为可以找到很多例子；相反，如果缺乏这个背景知识，选择遗传论，就很难给出让人信服的例子。大家可以看看，得分较低的作文是否有这个原因在里面。

例 1

Inheritance Decides Our Qualities

As for a person's essential qualities, some people hold the view that they are inherited at birth, other people hold the opposite point that a person's essential qualities are influenced by environment. As for me, I agree with the former.

It is known that blood is our strongest bond with our family members, with which we look like our fathers or mothers and we behave the same as them. We can change a lot of things but we cannot change our blood relationship. From films, TV programs, novels and life, we can find many examples in which the son becomes a murderer just because his father was a cruel man. And there are some children who are nice boys at young but become ferocious when growing up just because they inherited the cruel blood of their forefathers. It is recorded in some history books that some ancient noble men, especially members in king's family, all had the killing characteristics. And we can get the information that after marring the relatives of the same family, the decedents become idiots. On the contrary, some children grown up in common families turn out to be great men because their fathers have good qualities and they educate the children well. Yes, education is also a factor that we cannot lack of. Take Obama for an example, whose father graduated from Harford University and he himself also studied there.

So, I believe that the inheritance is the most important factors which decide a person's main qualities. To have a knowledge of this is essential for us, for we can accept our fortune rather than feel frustrated when we do something wrong.

评析：从题目可以看出，作者对性格或品质方面的研究成果并不清楚，这是阅读量少引起的，事实上，这称得上是一个常识，绝大部分人都知道，因此，当年选择写遗传因素的人非常少。

从作者把作文写成三段字数却不是很少、句子结构也不是很简单这方面来推断，他的写作基础不一定很差，可能只是不了解高级写作的要求，其实他完全可以把第二部分分成2~3个小段落。至于他的思维能力，我们分析完第二部分再来判断。

第一段尽管全部复制情景，但还是很规范，而且没有任何语法错误，证明他的写作基础确实不差。

在第二部分第一句，作者说，众所周知，血缘是家庭成员的最强纽带，因此我们长得很像自己的父母亲，言谈举止也和他们一样，我们可以改变很多事情，但改变不了血缘关系。前半句虽然不一定支持他的观点，但至少成立，可后半句就让人困惑。难道有血缘关系就一定长得很像吗？言谈举止就一定一样吗？就算一样，言谈举止就等于性格和品质吗？不确定的要素是不能拿来支持自己的观点的，因为它们起不到支持观点的作用；不相关的信息更不该选取进来，因为它们会大大削弱论证。

那么，作者的主要证据从何而来呢？原来是从电影、电视、小说及生活中来的。在第3章讨论证据的规则时，我们提到两点：一是论据必须是已知为真的命题；二是论据的真实性不能依赖论题证明。小说、电影是虚构的故事，不能作为证据，或者说至少没有说服力。作者说电影、电视里面的一些不错的孩子长大后变得残暴是因为他们遗传了先辈的特性。一些历史书籍也记载了，有些贵族，尤其是王族成员，弑杀成性。还有，作者说近亲通婚生出了很多傻子。

这些证据不仅不靠谱，而且让人啼笑皆非，王族成员可以随意杀人只是体制问题，与性格关系不是很大。就算历史的记载是真实的，也不能排除是其他因素导致的结果。设想，如果这些孩子不是王族后代，他们想杀人就可以杀人吗？而近亲结婚生出傻子已经完全不是性格和品质问题了，而是基因遗传导致的生理缺陷问题。把不相关的问题扯到一起来，不仅起不到支撑观点的作用，反而暴露出作者思维能力的极度欠缺。作者在这里犯了"轻断因果""诉诸远因"的逻辑错误。

第二部分最后关于奥巴马的例子同样不着边际，因为教育已经不是遗传的问题，而是环境因素了，拿论证的对立面充当证据，犯了"自相矛盾"的逻辑错误，而自相矛盾是不堪一击的自我否定。

总之，这篇作文虽然语法方面不错，但是只有三段，而且思维方面非常混乱，完全经不起反驳。因此，该作文得分为8分。

例2

Environment

As for a person's essential qualities, some people hold the view that they are inherited at birth, other people hold the opposite point that a person's essential qualities are influenced by environment. As far as I am concerned, a person's essential qualities are influenced by environment.

First of all, it is obvious that the new born baby is the most innocent person in the world. We can't make the point that which one is better or which one is honest or which one is moral. They are pure just like a white paper which without any words. In this way, we cannot say that a person's essential qualities are inherited at birth.

Second, the family environment <u>influence</u> a person's essential qualities. For most of the babies, the first place where they connect for a long time is the family. As we all know, parents are the main writer who can write in the white paper if the baby is the white paper. In most of <u>case</u>, which kind of parents will create which kind of kids. There is a saying: The parents are their children's first teacher. So the family environment <u>influence</u> a person's essential qualities.

Last but not least, the social environment <u>influence</u> a person's essential qualities. In the history of China, the state between 1966 and 1976 is impressive in Chinese memory. People <u>are think</u> highly about the moral, <u>there</u> are almost no crimes. In that kind of environment, people ruled themselves to be a good citizen. But recently, we can see many crimes in newspapers or magazines, <u>what's</u> more, people think <u>treat</u> others is moral thing, <u>in addition,</u> the food that we eat everyday is not safe. The social environment is bad, so the bad people become more and more.

In a good environment <u>which is</u> moral and kind, people will be friendly, tolerate and so on. All in all, a person's essential qualities are influence by environment. Everyone around you is your teacher who will influence you.

评析：这篇作文的题目过于宽泛，读者可能会以为作者要写环境问题。但作文的整体框架不错，逻辑线条分明，第一段也非常规范。

第二部分的第一段很流畅，句子之间的关系也很密切。但是，从逻辑的角度来说，它不太站得住脚，因为人对世界的认识是基于概念的，脑子里什么也没有，自然很单纯。但是，这无法否定遗传的存在，因为遗传不会在短期内显现出来。虽然证据本身是真实的，但力度不够。第二小段虽然继续谈论婴儿如白纸，但它比较站得住脚了，因为它不是借此来否定对方的论点，而是强调家庭环境对婴儿的影响。后面一小段也可以，讨论社会环境对人的影响。不足的地方是作者写得有点乱，句子之间的关系也不密切。因此，最后的结论就显得有点牵强。有意思的是，不知什么原因，作者还在最后写了一句无关的废话。之所以说它是废话，是因为这句不是从上面推出来的结论，在这里它是完全多余的。假如把它放入第二小段，还可以接受。由此可见，我们一定要先把握规范，规定不允许出现的内容不要出现。

总之，这篇作文结构还比较规范，但题目过大，证据表述过程显得不够清晰，而且语法错误过多，因此，这篇作文得了11分。

例3

A Person's Essential Qualities

When mentioning a person's essential qualities, some people claim that qualities are inherited at birth whereas opponents stand on a different ground and insist that circumstances should take the responsibility for forming one's qualities. As for me, I hold the point that circumstances play a vital role in a person's qualities.

For one thing, a person's qualities form in a long term, it is far from inheriting at birth. As the sayings goes, "Rome was not built in one day." So did the person's qualities, especially the essential qualities. Our human beings are gregarious animals, any circumstance can make inevitable influence in our qualities forming. Meanwhile, the qualities can change in different period, it is not simply inherited at birth.

For another, taking family, school, society into consideration, one's essential qualities, to some degree, depends on the factors. It is no wonder that parents are the best teachers for their children. As for school education, education is a significant factor in one's qualities and we may agree that genius without education is like silver in the mine. What's more, a person's qualities have close relationship with his society. People's core values are based on the social values.

In a word, we can draw a conclusion that circumstance is the main element to form a person's essential qualities, not only in recent characteristics but also in a long term life.

评析：作文的题目属于中性的，即不表明观点的类型，这是可以的。此外，作文的逻辑框架也非常好，让人一目了然，第一部分也很规范。但该部分最后一句不理想，因为从逻辑的角度来说，把一个事实变成自己的观点是不妥当的。

在第二部分，作者用了for one thing，for another，这使得条理非常清晰。但是，尽管作者在第二部分分析得有道理，却称不上很有说服力，因为没有给出具体的例子，只是写出了自己的感受，所以证据比较单薄，不足以令人信服。

总之，尽管文章结构比较规范，但信息有些松散，不够紧凑，画线部分还出现了语法错误。因此，这篇作文得分为12分。

例4

Which Is More Critical to a Person's Essential Quality: Inheritance or Circumstance

When it comes to the factors of influencing people's essential qualities like talents, intelligence, especially characters, there are two main different views. One focuses on the factor of inheritance, the other puts emphasis on the circumstances. I support the latter and my analysis is the following.

The first view is right in explaining why some people can be great scientists, prominent writers, actors, translators, excellent musicians, politicians or top athletes, while most people can not. There are some maxims which indicate the same idea. Take "There is no substitute for talent" for example. But how can we explain why a person who's kind and generous at young became a cruel and wicked man at adult? And how can we explain why a talented person changed into one who went nowhere?

Studies show that the circumstances are critical elements to the form of a person's characters. Studies also show that circumstances take a critical role in creating a real talent. It's not difficult to find those examples in our society. Incorporating the two views, we can draw the conclusion that the qualities inherited are important. But that does not mean less important of the other factors.

Therefore, a person's main qualities are decided by environment rather than inheritance, which is the finding of scientific research and does not need us to argue.

评析：题目是情景规定的，因此没有什么问题。第一段也非常规范，逻辑框架也非常清楚，就是感觉字数少了一些。

在第二部分，作者先指出遗传上的特质，包括一些天赋成分，这能解释为什么有些人能成为科学家、著名作家、演员、音乐家、政治家和运动员，而大部分人不能。他还提供了几个这样的引言作为支撑，比如"天才不可替代"。然后，作者采用反问引入问题的另一面，因为遗传论是无法回答这些问题的。接下来，作者拿出了研究成果来支撑他的观点，可信度因此大大增强，因为科学事实和研究成果是最有说服力的。

作文字数少的原因在这里也有了答案，因为作者从一开始就准备拿科研成果说事，不涉及过多的个人观点，只要围绕科研成果展开来说几句即可，前面提出的问题也足以得到合理的解释。

正因为如此，作者在结尾说，人的主要品质是环境而不是遗传决定的，这是科学研究的发现，无须我们争辩。

总之，这篇作文虽然字数少了点，但整体水平还是比较高的，具有较强的说服力，因此，该作文得分为15分。

2. 1997年TEM-8真题样文分析

Some people hold the view that a student's success in university study follows the same pattern as that of farming, which is characterized by the sowing the seeds, nurturing growth and harvesting the rewards' process. Write an essay of about 300 words on the topic given below to support this view with your own experience as a university student.

Sowing the Seeds, Nurturing Growth and Harvesting the Rewards

我们先来审题。

情景指出大学学习的形式如同农作，其过程的特点是从播种到培育，再到最后收获果实。其实这个问题是个全称概念，天地间，什么事情不是这样一个过程呢？这样就很好写了，一用全称，文章就十分具有说服力，只要在比喻的过程中填充一些例子和细节即可。

例

Sowing the Seeds, Nurturing Growth and Harvesting the Rewards

Success can never be a dated topic. It is one of the most important parts of our life. As for college students, what does a student's success mean for? Some people believe that a student's success in university study is characterized by the sowing the seeds, nurturing growth and harvesting the rewards' process. I can't agree with that anymore. Following reasons will be given to support the view from my own experience.

Firstly, in order to achieve success in universities, students must be aware of that there is no royal road to the summit of success and the first crucial step is to set a goal or lay a social foundation, which resembles the first step to plant a tree—sowing the seeds. It requires massive efforts to start before entering into the next level in students' study, such as a broad range of reading, reciting texts and endless practising. Besides, a sheer desire to accomplish the goal is one of the greatest drives to urge one forward until he or she achieve greatness.

Secondly, once you have well prepared and have laid firm foundation, perseverant spirits and unfailing minds are necessary in your continuing study. People always say, "No pains, no gains." It is because that only constant efforts exerted in studies, can you see the goal to the ultimate success. Reading, for example, is a time-consuming process, which a student has to practice again and again and never quit in this process, to improve his reading ability.

In the end, since you have a good beginning and insist in doing your work, it is time to rip the sweet fruit of your harvest. Knowing that the final achievement is the most worthwhile reward of your efforts is an exceptional experience one can never refuse.

All in all, the road to the success is a proper procedure including the sowing the seeds, nurturing growth and harvesting the rewards.

评析：题目还行，但还可以更明确，比如Studying Is Just Like Farming，突出我们要讨论的主题，现在的题目会让人以为作者要讨论农作问题。

浏览全文就可以看出文章的逻辑框架非常漂亮。但是第一段的第一句话和第二句话的重心有点偏移，让人以为要讨论的是成功，而事实上我们侧重讨论的是学习形同农作问题。因此，我们在突出主要信息的时候一定要仔细。

第二部分一开头，作者强调学生首先要有意识，这种手法不仅有高度，而且很有序，因为意识是改进的前提。作者说，"学习无轻松道路可走，第一步是打下基础，好比树在长成参天大树之前必须先播种"。逻辑关系十分密切，句式非常优美。在下一小段，作者强调坚忍不拔方能实现目标，句式灵活漂亮。最后顺理成章得出"收获甜美的果实"这一结论。

总之，这篇作文不仅逻辑框架好，句式也很漂亮，并且有一定的高度，行文流畅，有说服力。因此，这篇作文得分为16分。

3. 1998年TEM-8真题样文分析

Nowadays with the development of economy, existing cities are growing bigger and new cities are appearing. What do you think is ONE of the major problems that may result from this process of urbanization? Write an essay of about 300 words on the topic given below:

One Major Problem in the Process of Urbanization

我们先来审题。

城市扩建是国家发展的一大策略，因为中国的乡村地域太广，城市容量不足，如果人口不断涌入，则必然要进行城市扩建。当然，扩建过程中会有很多问题，如果从宏观方面着手，就可以谈环境破坏、滥砍滥伐，交通拥挤、道路堵塞等。

例

One Major Problem in the Process of Urbanization

As we all know that existing cities are growing bigger and new cities are increasingly appearing with the development of economy and science, which is the phenomenon of urbanization. Perhaps myriads of people are enjoying the profit brought by urbanization, but urbanization also results in a great number of problems such as social problems, environmental problems and population problems, etc. And I think the environmental <u>problems is</u> one major problem in process of urbanization respectively including the aspects of lands, plants and air.

First of all, urbanization gives rise to the deficiency of land. <u>Because</u> urbanization is the procedure that the existing cities are growing bigger and an increasing number of new cities emerge, which means excessive application of land, so that the land gradually becomes deficient. Secondly, it brings about the exceeded decline of plants coverage, <u>we all know the expropriation of land means chopping the plants down for we can obtain lots of land by this way</u>. With hewing plants, more and more forest will disappear. Last but not least, <u>it's know</u> that plants are the promise of fresh air. With reducing the plants, the metabolism of air becomes tardy. Gradually, the quality of air <u>become</u> worse.

In a word, we should heed the problems caused by the urbanization as we <u>are enjoys</u> the advantages brought by it. Meanwhile, we should try our best to protect the environment.

评析：文章整体上不协调，因为只有三段，而第一段过长，几乎和第二段差不多，结尾却只有三行。通常这种情况，我们会把第二部分拆成两小段，可是如果从secondly这里另起一段，第一段立刻比其他段落都长了，这说明作者没有设计好文章的结构。

这篇作文的第一段很规范，很书面化，还很有高度，因为作者强调的是环境的破坏。不足之处是除了篇幅略长了一些，urbanization还一再重复，这不符合相同词义不同表达的要求，让人觉得作者词汇量不够，如果能够适当替换成expansion等，则会好多了。

第二部分的第一条分析得不错，指出过度开发引起了土地恶化问题。而且在"恶化"和"过度"的表达上，作者替换了deficiency，decline，以及excessive，exceeded等词，"砍伐"也使用了chop和hew。

这部分第二条分析就不如第一条，有点乱，语法错误还不少，"植被被破坏"似乎也说得不清不楚。

总之，这篇文章除了框架不够美之外，说服力也不够；有些词用得也不理想；此外，还有不少语法错误。因此，这篇作文得分为13分。

4. 1999年TEM-8真题样文分析

Some people claim that competition is more important than cooperation in the present-day society. How far do you agree OR disagree with these people? You are to write a composition of about 300 words on the following topic:

Competition or Cooperation

我们先来审题。

这是一个双概念题目，对于双概念题，我们通常要解释它们之间的关系，因为只有理解这两个概念之间的关系，我们才能够把问题阐释清楚。竞争和合作是对立统一关系，竞争总是相对的，没有任何企业是孤军奋战的，否则就无所谓竞争；合作的途径很多，比如并购、特许产品开发等，可举的例子很多。

有些人强调竞争更重要，其实这个角度未必好写，一旦把二者的关系对立起来了，事例可能比较难找。

以苹果手机的利益链为例，苹果公司虽贵为手机行业的第一品牌，却非常愿意和中小微企业分享利益，这和微软公司企图垄断市场独享利益的做法大相径庭。据报道，有一家小公司设计出了一种非常美观的手机套，他们希望获得苹果公司的生产特许。以苹果公司的实力，他们完全可以自己生产这些边缘产品，但苹果公司却给了这家小公司特许权，这就是著名的"苹果皮"。正所谓有饭大家吃，不要吃独食，这对于一个国家和社会的稳定都是大有好处的。今天在中国刮起的"抱团"创业风，也是类似的例子。

例

Competition or Cooperation

Nowadays, competition and cooperation are both significant in the changing world. Some people hold that competition is more important than cooperation in the present-day society, and others deny that. In my view, I'm cling to the latter.

First things first, cooperation helps to the team work. As the team work is more of importance in working, cooperation the key word in the team work, helps us to shoulder with different parts of one whole work. Different kinds of part-working suitable to different kinds of people. Some people are good at leading, but some people are way with doing statistics according to the characters. Then, cooperation helps everyone playing a necessary role in the best suitable steps. That also would improve the working-efficiency at the same time.

In the second place, cooperation helps us increasing the relationship between people. As we communicate with others or working together with others, we share different kind of ideas, thoughts or often opposite views. We acknowledge with others and then familiar with others that helps us to build good relationship with others. If we get along with others, we will be happy and satisfied, in some instance.

Competition is important in the desirable world, but the cooperation is in the same level. We clear the importance of the competition but do not indifferent the significance of cooperation. So we should pay some attentions to them, as there is competition in cooperation, cooperation in competition.

To sum up, I disagree with those people who claim that competition is more important than cooperation. Cooperation is same important with competition and cooperation helps us to the team work and helps us increasing the relationship with others.

评析：第一部分比较规范，作者摆出问题，并指出自己同意第二种观点。第二部分第一段显得有些条理不清，像是在做中文翻译。其实，我们完全可以从更高处着手，说世界是相互联系的，一个行业总是和另一个行业联系在一起。一旦把关系讲清楚了，条理就出来了。反之，如果作者忽略概念之间的联系，孤立论证，就很难有效果。另外，文中有很多语法错误。

第二部分的第二小段，作者谈起了合作的好处，其实这有点偏题，因为题目并不是要谈合作的好处，而是要谈竞争与合作。对双概念题来说，如果二者是对立统一关系，侧重谈论其中一方的优势很容易偏题，这一点大家要注意。而在这一部分的第三小段，作者像是在凑字数。结果，整个中间部分显得很单薄，说服力不强。结尾倒是比较规范，简要复述了第二部分论证的主要观点。

总之，这篇作文由于未能在最开始交代竞争和合作这两个概念之间的关系，因此文章显得条理不清，证据不足，而且画线部分的语法错误较多，选词和句式都不够理想，得分只有11.5分。

5. 2000年TEM-8真题样文分析

Some people simply see education as going to schools or colleges, or as a means to secure good jobs; most people view education as a lifelong process. In your opinion, how important is education to modern man? Write a composition of about 300 words on the following topic:

Education as a Lifelong Process

我们先来审题。

既然题目是讨论怎么看待教育的问题，那么，我们就要把握什么是教育，哪些内容与教育相关，比如教育的重要性和教育的功能等。把框架搭好了，我们写起来就会比较顺手。

例

Education As a Lifelong Process

There is no denying that education plays an essential role in everyone's life. It cannot be simply seen as getting knowledge at schools or colleges, or as a means to obtain a well-paid job. As far as I am concerned, education should be regarded as a lifelong process. Just as a saying says, "It is never too old to learn." Education is important throughout our life.

To begin with, I would like to say that it is education that takes shape of our personal qualities. I do admit that some qualities are inherited, but education is an indispensable element. No matter family education or school education, people learn to be a person conducive to the society. What's more, education helps us mode our character and cultivate our spirituality. Generally speaking, a well-educated person knows how he should behave better. Through education, people know which qualities are good and may try to obtain these qualities. So, education, as a lifelong process, is beneficial for one's personal development.

Secondly, with the rapid development of the modern society, only people keep on receiving education can they adapt to the society. If one quit learning after graduating from universities, then their knowledge and skills can't be comply with the developing world. The 21st century indicates knowledge explosion. Modern technology speeds up the outdated process of knowledge. And with the frequent change of workers and the increasing change of society, no one can learn enough knowledge without learning. Instead, they should live and learn. Education is an important means of one's existence and development. As a result, education should be seen as a lifelong process.

<u>In a short</u>, education is essential not only for one's quality but also for one's development. Therefore, we should receive education throughout our lifetime.

评析：标题的as改成is更好，这样更明确。作文第一段还算规范，如果第一句说成"有人把教育简单地看成是上学"会显得更直接。另外，画线的says改成goes更好。

第二部分的第一段大致是说教育在塑造我们性格方面的作用，第二段作者说的是社会不断发展，我们要继续学习以适应社会。但是，教育的首要功能，即传播知识，却没有写到，这说明作者思考得不是很清楚，也不够深入。因此，作文的主张就没有得到强有力的支持，结论就不是那么有说服力。

总之，这篇作文结构上没有什么大问题，但是一些重要的要素没有提及，以至于作文很平淡，没有什么说服力。因此，它得分并不高，只有12分。

6. 2002年TEM-8真题样文分析

All of us would agree that in order to be successful in the present-day society, we university graduates have to possess certain personal qualities that can enable us to realize our aim. What do you think is the most important personal quality of a university graduate? Write a composition of about 300 words on the following topic:

The Most Important Personal Quality of a University Student

我们先来审题。

其实这个题目学生可以各抒己见，你觉得什么品质更容易成功都可以，这个问题没有什么统一的答案，但是，选择一个好写的角度很重要，这一点我们在前面强调了好几遍。鉴于这里不是讨论道德问题，而是讨论成功，选择具有共性的特点，比如毅力、耐心、诚信等，会更好写。

例1

The Importance on Being Practical

Nowadays, myriads of university graduates flood in our society. Some people points out that university graduates <u>should be endowed</u> certain personal qualities to accomplish that goals. As far as I am observed, the most important personal quality of a university graduate is being practical.

To start with, being practical is the prerequisite to embark on a work. Some university graduates hanker for splendid career but are unwilling <u>to down to earth</u> to accomplish their aims step by step. Some university graduates view themselves as "the first class" of the society and are too proud to keep their feet on the ground. A university graduate should keep being practical in mind before starting a work and avoid such a superficial sight. Only when he or she realizes the importance of this cherish quality can he or she successfully set about a career.

Second, being practical is the guarantee of being a full man. A full man is the perfect embodiment of action and brain certainly, <u>a</u> university graduate has already procured abundant professional knowledge, <u>his</u> brain is equipped with <u>fair</u> rich theories after four <u>years's</u> education. At this time, being practical renders him to employ what he learns to the practical life, leading him to be the giant of both brain and action. Moreover, with this quality, a university graduate understands that only being steeped in every details in the real life can be achieve more knowledge and train his ability, thus being a full man.

Last but not the least, being practical is the catalyst of the success of one's career. Many graduates tend to have great ambitions, but most of them end up with failure, which to a great extent is due to their being practical. Those who succeed in their business know will the importance of being their feets on the ground. Once they determine to a goal, they will make a detailed plan considering their ability and social condition, then implement them step by step until they cultivate in the peak of the success.

In conclusion, being practical is the most important personal quality of a university student. It is not only the prerequisite to embark on his or her career, the guarantee of being a full man, but also the catalyst of the success of life.

评析：这篇作文的题目有两个问题：一是有点儿模糊不清；二是外延比较大。这在正文里面产生了两个结果：一是让人不太能够把握being practical的准确意思；二是作者分析的内容包括工作和生活。

practical主要有两个意思，一个是"实用的"，多指事物；另一个是"实事求是的"，多指人。《牛津高阶英语词典》第七版给出的第二条定义是（of a person）sensible and realistic，即明智的、实事求是的。同时，对realistic的解释是accepting in a sensible way what it is actually possible to do or achieve in a particular situation。

作为主要概念，如果作者先交代practical是指什么，事情就简单多了。把一个概念先交代清楚，并不意味着所有人都不了解这个概念，而是为了达成一个共识，防止某些人不清楚，从而造成误解。如果意思含混不清，甚至要读者去猜测，很明显就不妥当。

在第二部分，作者说了三点，说being practical是"从事工作的前提"，它"让人完满"，是"成功事业的催化剂"。作为主观看法，这当然可以，但是，作者在第一点和第三点上很明显突出的是"脚踏实地"的意思，那么，它和practical的定义就不太相符了。

总之，这篇作文句式比较漂亮，选词也很用心，但是语法错误过多，而且条理不是很清楚。因此，这篇作文得分为12分。

例2

Patience Is Important to Everyone

In order to be successful in a society, we need some personal qualities like smartness, cleverness, honesty, efficiency, or persistence, etc. Good qualities can help us do things better and more quickly. Some work needs intelligence, some needs wisdom, and some efficiency. But it seems that everyone needs patience.

Before we analyze the reasons, it requires us to make clear the definition of patience. Patience refers to the ability to accept delay, annoyance or suffering without complaining. To live and to work in our society, we should know that an individual's abilities like quickness, efficiency are not enough for us to achieve accomplishments or reach our goals because the world we live is a place where things are not isolated but related with each other. When we are required to fulfill some important tasks or missions, we always need help and support from other people. When we want to make success in our professions, we also need support of others. Otherwise we cannot make it. One thing we should recognize is that a person's abilities are different from another's. Now that we need each other, we need to tolerate the differences of different people. To be patient can help us to do it.

However, some people are so efficient themselves that they cannot stand those who are not so quick in doing things. Some people are very smart that they laugh at those who are not so clever. There are also some people who are always impatient with things that they complain everything around them. They do not realize that most of the people are not like them but those people have their own qualities which they may lack of. They do not realize that laughing and complaining often make them isolated. People do not like this and they do not welcome and accept them no matter how clever you are and what gifts you have. On the contrary, people welcome and accept those who are excellent but patient to others. People welcome and accept those who have both an ambitious goal and a down-to-earth style of work. People also welcome and accept those who look plain but do things hard without complaint.

We can also provide some famous people's saying to support this. They say to be successful, talents are not enough, because the world does not lack talents, it needs someone who has good quality. And there were so many talents who turned out to be nothing. And smartness is not enough because there were so many smart people who turned out to be useless. And efficiency is not enough because we had so many efficient people who were also helpless. Only patience is good enough, and it is good for everyone.

With patience, we think carefully before we start doing things so that the possibility of success increases, failure decreases. With patience, individuals can find their disadvantages and at the same time find others' advantages. With patience, difficulties cannot defeat us. Frustration cannot crush us. With patience, not only an individual's abilities but also the collective's can be mixed together to be used to achieve the same goal.

So, as graduates, no matter what job we're going to take, no matter what difficulties we'll meet, no matter how long the road will be to the destination of our goals, and no matter what people we're working together, try to be patient with everything and every person so that we can get help and support we need when we need it, so that we can be accepted as one member in a community, and so that we can finish our tasks better and more quickly with a mixture of hard working and talents and qualities in different aspects of everyone in a team.

评析：这个题目的角度选得很好。我们前面讨论了，在有限的时间内，选择一个好写的角度很重要。一个具有普遍性的特点往往比独特个性更容易找到说服点。作者选择的是持之以恒，所以，他写得很轻松。另外，他从头到尾都使用排比，这样不仅美观，而且字数充足。更巧妙的是，作者多次使用全称概念anyone，这非常有说服力。

鉴于第二部分非常强劲有力，结论就顺理成章了。

总之，作者选择了一个好写的角度，而且修辞手法运用得非常娴熟。从拟题到布局，再到修辞手法，无不体现其高超的写作技巧。因此，这篇作文得分为17分。

7. 2003年TEM-8真题样文分析

An English newspaper is currently running a discussion on whether young people in China today are (not) more self-centered and unsympathetic than the previous generations were. And the paper is inviting contributions from university students. You have been asked to write a short article for the newspaper to air your views.

　　You should supply a title for your article.

我们先来审题。

这是一个典型的主观性命题，需要表明观点：这一代的孩子是否自私和缺乏同情心。当我们觉得某个孩子自私时，可能会不假思索地把这个特点扩大到他们的群体。但事实上他们可能不是自私，只是他们的成长经历和我们的不一样。我们经常用自己的人生观或价值观来衡量他们，而不考虑他们的生长环境。所以我们强调，主观性命题也要尽可能公正客观，不要从自身的感受来判断他人，更不要把个人的特点随便放大，这在逻辑上容易犯"以偏概全"的错误。

例

A New Generation

　　It is said that young people today are not what they used to be. They are more self-centered and unsympathetic than the previous generations were. But is this new generation of teenagers and young adults really so different from their parents or grandparents? I don't think so.

　　About twenty years ago when China started to open the door to the outside world, people entered into universities without any money while went out of universities with permanent jobs waiting for them so that they did not suffer any pressure from the society and they did not need to worry too much. All they should do were to try to focus their energy on their jobs. Words like contribution and dedication were commonly used ones, which showed that people at that time cared about their jobs more, about the society more and other people more.

However, the new generation, commonly referred to as "single child" generation, had a quite different growing environment. In most cases they stayed at home with their mothers and fathers working all day long outside, during which they watched TV programs, read books or did homework without much time playing with companies. In this way, they formed their own way of thinking, a freer and simpler way to look at people and look at themselves. That was something the previous generations could not imagine. And it made them less dependent on others. For them, going outside and facing the world is something everybody should do. If nobody can help you do that, you have to do it yourself. Accepting some of the Western ideas made then even more realistic: care about themselves more while pay less attention to others. Thus an expression that this new generation is more self-centered and unsympathetic was left.

So, today's young people may not be what they used to be, but this generation has a freedom-minded and individualistic nature because of the facts mentioned above. They like to be left alone to solve problems. They have evolved in dramatically different ways than previous generations. If we listen, there is a lot we can learn from them. The future will be a better place if we do.

评析：题目很明确，一看就知道作者支持和理解年轻一代。整体框架也很清晰，用了不同的连接词和转折词来凸显逻辑框架。

第一段很规范，作者提出了问题，还表明了自己的观点，并且用了问句来引起大家的注意。

在第二部分，作者采用了对比法，对两种经济体制下的两代人作了介绍。计划经济时代的人不用找工作，压力小，一心扑在工作和照料家人上，他们更关心他人，关心社会。而新的一代大部分是独生子女，他们习惯独自待在家里，没有玩伴，学会了独立，不在意他人，他们认为自己就应该依靠自己。

能够从时代的角度来分析对比，表明文章非常有高度，得出的结论也就非常有说服力。无论看到什么问题，我们都应该全面、动态地分析，而不应该是片面地以自我为标准进行分析。拿过去的标准或自己的标准来衡量现在的年轻人就显得很不合时宜。

鉴于第二部分分析得非常到位，结论就很顺理成章。作者在结尾处加了一句非常美的建议，说"如果我们学会聆听，会发现很多值得学习的东西"。

总之，这篇作文分析到位，理由充分，结构合理，逻辑性也比较强，因此，这篇作文得分为17分。

8. 2004年TEM-8真题样文分析

It was reported in the press some time ago that a few second- and third-year students in a provincial university decided to try their hands at business in order to get prepared for the future. They opened six small shops near their university. Their teachers and classmates had different opinions about this phenomenon. Some thought that the students' business experience would help them adapt better to society after graduation, while others held a negative view, saying that running shops might occupy too much of the students' time and energy which should otherwise be devoted to their academic study. What do you think? Write a composition of about 300 words on the following topic:

Should University Students Go in for Business?

这个例子我们在前面的章节分析过，这里的分析侧重点不同，我们再来审一下题目：

作为主观题，虽然我们可以任选一方，但是在选择的时候，我们要注意哪边的证据更多、更好写。审题时把这些问题基本想好，就不至于毫无头绪地东拼西凑了。

审题扣住题目的主要概念即可，这里主要概念显然是go in for business，而与经商相关的要素并不只有时间和精力。

经商是一种必须往里面投钱，而且很可能会失败的商业行为，如果你选择赞同经商，那么这些问题你就必须考虑到。此外，失败产生的后果也应该考虑到，比如介入商业的学生是否能够承受得起失败导致的不良后果？

所给情景里面，支持者打出的是实践和经验牌，他们对风险只字不提；而反对者强调时间和精力，也没有考虑到经商的风险。可是写作者必须尽可能全面，这样的分析才具有说服力。

例

Should University Students Go in for Business?

Some time ago, a few second- and third-year students in a provincial university decided to try their hands at business in order to get prepared for the future, which caused heat discussion among the teachers and students. Some thought that the students' business experience would help them adapt better to society after graduation, while others held a negative view, saying that it would occupy too much of the students' time and energy which should otherwise be devoted to their academic study. I accept the later and I don't think it's just a matter of time and energy.

First, doing business is against the rule of Chinese Ministry of Education which regulates that the task of college students is to study carefully in four years' time. And at what period of time to study is a science which every country in the world follows. China is no exception. In the long run of our life, we have a lot of time to choose doing business or not. However, to be successful or not mainly depends on how well our education is. That is why many people continue their learning after owning a career. As a result, most colleges, home or abroad, don't encourage students to go in for business.

Second, making a choice in business is not the same as social practice arranged by colleges, the latter of which, everybody knows, does not have any risk and is not just a matter of time and energy. Doing business means high cost and high danger and it needs more time and energy than you can spare. You have to inject money which might be lost and never come back. No wonder people say that the business field is like a battle field, which indicates there's much uncertainty under it. Can young men take the risk of that? Can they undertake the pressure of the lost? And can they pay the debt if they lose?

Someone might take the glorious winning of Bill Gates as a classic example who achieved great commitment as a student when studying in Harvard University. Yet, this example is not persuasive because it was due to his job that he had to quit from the campus for the inability of doing business and studying academically at the same time.

All in all, to do business needs something more than you can suffer, including time, energy and money. And it requires the partners to have the ability to take the risk and pressure, which is proved inadequate for students during their four years' study.

评析：第一段很规范，也非常巧妙，而且在该部分最后一句指出这不仅仅是时间和精力的问题。不过，情景复制得过多，这一点不太好。

在第二部分第一小段，作者先说大学生经商违反了教育部的规定；按照规定，学生在校期间的主要任务就是专心读书。这不仅使文章具有一定的高度，而且特别有说服力，因为这些不是作者说的，而是教育部的规定。接着作者又说在校期间一心学习是各个国家学生的通常做法，并且，在什么时间段学习是一门科学。

　　在这部分的第二小段，作者指出经商和实习不是一个概念。后者没有风险，前者则有风险，而且它不仅仅是时间和精力的问题，它意味着高成本和高风险，它需要的远远不止时间和精力，需要的还有资金，而且可能会亏本，甚至血本无归。难怪人们说"商场如战场"，这正说明经商背后有太多的不确定性。大学生能够承担得起这份风险吗？他们能够承受得起巨大的压力吗？能够负担得起损失吗？一组排比用得非常强劲有力。

　　最后，作者用比尔·盖茨的例子来作为反驳，指出他恰巧是因为时间和精力不够才从哈佛大学退学的。

　　在结尾，作者说：总而言之，经商远远不是时间和精力的问题，它还需要参与者具有承受风险和压力的能力。事实证明，大学生在校期间经商不合适。

　　一篇作文，有了第二部分这样的论证，那么，其结论就一定是顺理成章的。

　　总之，这篇作文条理清晰、论据充分、逻辑性强，句式和修辞也相当不错，因此，这篇作文得分为17分。

9. 2010年TEM-8真题样文分析

　　Recently newspapers have reported that officials in a little-known mountainous area near Guiyang, Guizhou Province wanted to turn the area into a "central business district" for Guiyang and invited a foreign design company to give it an entirely new look.

The design company came up with a blueprint for unconventional, super-futuristic buildings. This triggered off different responses. Some appreciated the bold innovation of the design, but others held that it failed to reflect regional characteristics or local cultural heritage. What is your view on this? Write an essay of about 400 words. You should supply an appropriate title for your essay.

我们在前面讨论逻辑方法时引用了这个例子，但是我们没有侧重审题和篇章分析。我们先来审题。

审题始终要把握主要概念及概念的相关要素。城市改建始终是一个有争议的话题，地方政府这样做的目的通常是提高经济效益，而反对声通常来自地方保护主义者。

大家对经济效益都比较熟悉，搞经济就看你有没有让大家富裕起来，如果折腾了半天，人们非但没有变得更富有，做项目的资金反而成了大家的经济负担，这样，大家就会对项目进行质疑。另外，要搞经济，有没有足够的资源，包括人力资源和自然资源？如果有，怎么利用这些资源？如果没有，仅仅是外表改变，就没有实质性意义。

革新也是一样的，革新不会凭空从天上掉下来，它同样是基于当地的资源，包括自然资源、人力资源、管理资源和资金来源等，没有这一切，很可能是空话。制订和实施计划关键不是计划本身的好坏问题，而是看它有没有实施的可行性，如果连这一点都不知道，空喊创新，就没有意义。

让我们一起来看看下面的作文是如何提供证据的。

例 1

The Mountainous Area Needs Innovation

A little-known mountainous area near Guiyang is reported to

turn into a "central business district", which triggered off different responses. Some people hold the view that it will damage the local cultural heritage, while others think it is a good opportunity to carry out innovation. However, I <u>pretty</u> appreciate the bold innovation and firmly believe the mountainous area will develop better after the innovation. Here are my reasons.

First of all, innovation is the soul of the nation's development. Every country needs new blood in the process of moving forward. This principle is also suitable for the little-known mountainous area. China is a country with wide scale, every place has its own characteristics, but if we want to show our culture to the world, we need some changes which will be accepted by other countries. So I think the mountainous area in Guiyang should grasp this opportunity to take some changes. During this time, the local government can learn some experiences from this design, analyze the reasons why we cannot put forward this kind of ideas. Also, it's a chance for local people to realize that it's not good to just keep the heritage, and it's time to innovate. Only in that way <u>the new "central business district" will</u> develop better in the future.

Secondly, it will be a good chance to advertise the new "central business district". The foreign design company <u>have</u> brought an unconventional, super-futuristic blueprint for this area. We all know, foreigner's culture is almost different with <u>us, once</u> the "central business district" successfully <u>finished</u> as the blueprint, it will definitely arise the concern not only throughout China, but also the other countries. So, it's a free and wonderful advertisement for the new born district. What's more, it will attract <u>many many</u> visitors and promote the development of this area, even the Guizhou Province. Finally, the original little-known mountainous area may be well-known throughout the world.

Thirdly, it will promote the culture exchange. The new "central business district" will be a good example of the combination of different cultures. It's a win-win choice for both China and the foreign country.

Above all, innovation is important in the process of culture protecting. So I believe if the local government <u>will build</u> the new "central business district" as the foreign company's blueprint, it's absolutely a wonderful choice.

评析：这篇作文的题目很明确，框架也非常好，尤其是第一段。不过第一段的however纯属多此一举，去掉更好，而且pretty的用法有误。

从第二部分第一段的第一句话我们就可以看出作文的高度，因为作者是从国家的角度来讨论问题的，他说一个国家的发展核心就在于创新，发展过程需要新鲜血液，小地方也不例外。任何一个地方都有它自己的特色，如果要向世界展示其文化，就要有变化。因此，该地方要抓住机遇，顺应变化，我认为这说得很有道理。

但是，作者说地方政府可以从中吸取教训，思考自己为什么做不出这样的设计来，还可以就此开始创新，这样才会有好的未来。这一说法不太站得住脚，因为这是作者个人的猜测或意愿，而不是基于对某个事实的分析。

在第二部分第二小段和第三小段，作者则谈起了宣传商业中心的机遇，他认为这可以促进国际文化交流，一次性把商业中心、广告设计、文化交流等概念糅合在一起，反而主次不分明了，似乎和创新没有很大关系，而且作者还用了may be这种表示猜测的单词，因此，证据比较单薄，没有说服力。

总之，虽然这篇作文逻辑框架比较漂亮，但分析过程的信息比较散，没有突出"创新"这一要点，结论是不可靠的。另外，语法错误过多，口语化问题比较严重，因此，这篇作文得分只有12分。

例2

Bold Innovation with Limit

Guiyang, known for its countless mountains, has a lot of areas remaining underdeveloped with little fame. In order to alter this situation, Guiyang government intends to start with an innovation of a little-known mountainous area near Guiyang, inviting a foreign design company to renew it who raises up a plan with unconventional, super-futuristic buildings, which draws heated debates among the whole society. Is such an action reasonable? Yes, I quite appreciate the practice of such bold innovation of the design with a certain limit.

First things first, it contributes to the development of this area, even the whole Guiyang, economically, with the purpose of turning the area into a "central business district" so that it helps exploit the area in Guiyang and develops its economy. Modern infrastructure and facilities are of great necessity, yet among which, more than a few are inevitably away from tradition and even in super-futuristic style.

In the second place, a bold innovation of the design draws more attention from home and abroad, bringing more opportunities for the area and Guiyang. As we all know, a comprehensive renewal of an area creates plenty of jobs, projects, programs, etc. that will offer a great condition for visits and investment. As a result, large amount of fund and thousands of visitors will flood into this area, together with opportunities for Guiyang to have a prosperous future. This could be illustrated by the example of Shenzhen, a little fishery village before the reform and opening up. Yet, it has been transformed into one of the most developed areas in China today after decades of utter bold innovation. Another case in point is Huaxi Village, a little remote and bleak place in the past. Now, it stands out as a new rich industrial village thanks to the bold integrated innovation in its economic pattern and the stark different design of its inner distribution.

Wise as it is to give this area a new look. I firmly hold that the innovation should be practiced with limit. On the one hand, the original incentive is to develop, not to destroy. That is to say, the project is suggested to be carried out on the condition that some measures such as the establishment of reserve zones will be taken to protect those valuable resources here like some relics and other cultural heritage that will never be rehabilitated once destroyed. On the other hand, the renewal does not need to go contradictory to reflect regional characteristics. Instead, the best way is to take in both modern, fashionable factors and traditional elements. Beijing is a role model in this aspect. It is not only a modern typical international city but also the symbol of Chinese tradition no matter in architecture or living style, an excellent example of perfect blending.

To sum up, I do suggest that a bold innovation of the design be on the list for it provides the area with significant developmental opportunities and a wide range of attention. But, the practice should be taken with limit. By doing this, it is believed that the area will present itself in a newer and better way.

评析：这篇作文的题目处理得比较巧妙，表明既要大胆革新，又要把握适度。

第一段开头也不错，比较符合英语作文规范，而且很直接地提出了问题，还使用了插入语。不过，第二部分的第一小段字数比前后段落都少，这样就不那么美观了。此外，yet这个词选得不是很妥当，有inevitably就足够了，使用yet很容易让人钻空子，这样会削弱论证的强度。既然知道有不好的结果，为什么还要去改造呢？使用两个表示转折的词过于醒目，yet放在前面则更加引人注意。

作文的深度还差一点，因为作者没有充分突出贫穷落后的现状导致的严重后果。城市改建首要目的是让人民脱贫致富，如果只是为了怕破坏传统，而置贫困于不顾，那么这种传统有多大意义呢？科学已经表明，经济是社会发展的基础。

作者到第二部分的第二小段才谈经济问题，主次上有些不当。如果把它放在第一小段就好多了，因为最重要的内容要放在前面，笔墨要多一些。凡是思考问题，都要找准最重要的因素。如果在这篇作文中，作者找准了经济发展这个主要因素，其他的次要因素就必须为它让道。保护传统也不能成为阻碍经济发展的借口或障碍，这样也为后面的limit做好了铺垫。在开发过程中，势必要考虑到不能过度开发，因为有些遗产一经破坏，就永远不能修复。

另外，作文里面有个别例子不太经得起推敲，比如深圳，它是因战略意义由国家扶持并通过大量资金投入创造出来的奇迹，一般的小城镇与它是没有可比性的。

总之，虽然作文有一些不足，但它选词比较高端，句式始终很优美，逻辑性强，行文很流畅。因此，这篇作文得分为16分。

例3

The Benefits of Bold Innovation

It is reported that officials in a remote mountainous area near Guiyang, Guizhou Province intended to transform the area into a "central business district" for Guiyang and invited a foreign design company to carry out a plan for unconventional buildings with an entirely new look. This news aroused a heated discussion, with some speaking highly of the bold innovation of the design while others suggesting that this practice brought a dark side to the local cultural heritage. On considering the case in an all-round way, personally, I am more in favor of the former.

The first reason to support my standing is the abundant merits brought by the bold innovation to the local residents. In the first place, the building of "central business district" in that area can promote the process of urbanization advanced in China to some extent. So, local people have an opportunity to get access to the lifestyle of urban people, which broadens their horizon and enjoys the convenience of urban life. In the second place, the bold innovation of the design is capable of attracting investment from home and abroad, which, in turn, boosts the working situation in the area. Local people have no need to go out for making a living. They can manage a job at home, so that they can take care of family, especially their children. If managed and guided under a feasible plan, the remote mountainous area is able to develop into a prosperous area like Shenzhen which is originally a small village.

The second reason that leads to my opinion lies in the possibility of the bold innovation of the design being the forerunner of a brand-new looking toward Chinese architecture. Innovation is the core of development in all kinds of things, and architecture is no exception. Through having a blueprint for unconventional, super-futuristic buildings, we may have a different look toward modern architecture, which, in turn, triggers a new understanding toward the designs of buildings. We are living in the times of

高级英语写作突破：思维和策略

advocating reform and opening up, we are bound to find some new nourishment from the outside. However, when we are emphasizing drawing the innovative essence from other countries, it does not mean that we forsake our local cultural heritage. Local cultural heritage and some regional characteristics should be definitely preserved by Chinese people. And I think we can strike a balance between modern development and the protection of our tradition.

In conclusion, the bold innovation of the little-known mountainous area brings a multitude of benefits, no matter from the perspective of local people or the development of architecture. Innovation brings us new changes and new changes provide us a better future with more opportunity.

评析：看一眼这篇作文就知道，整体很规范，各段落之间也很协调。在第一部分，作者用不同的风格表明了问题和立场，句式非常漂亮，该部分最后一句用了more in favor of 这种一般人不敢使用的结构，我们由此可以判断本文作者写作能力很强。

在第二部分，作者第一句说的是革新对当地人的好处，这是最主要的问题，非常有深度，因为衡量地方经济好坏的一个评估标准就是看当地人能够得到什么好处。作者在这里采用的是总分结构，这对文章的字数、逻辑性和条理性都大有好处。第一个好处是城镇化，当地人因此可以加入到城市的生活方式之中，那样既可以扩大视野，又可以生活得更加便利。第二个好处是可以吸引国内外投资，从而改变当地的就业状况。当地居民因此无须外出营生，在家工作即可，还可以照顾家庭和孩子，说不定，一个类似深圳般繁荣的城市会出现。

第二大理由是关于创新的建筑风格，作者指出创新是任何事情的核心，建筑也不例外，该地区的设计有可能引领中国建筑行业。

320

表示有"可能"时作者使用的词是抽象名词the possibility，这进一步说明作者英语水平较高，因为抽象名词具有"不仅达意，而且更地道"的特点（蔡基刚，2001）。

在用词方面，一个"能够"，作者都分别用了can，capable of，be able to，其他如broadens their horizon and enjoys the convenience，unconventional，super-futuristic buildings，forsake，balance等高级漂亮的选词，无不体现作者的高分意识。

总之，该作文有深度，并且结构整齐规范、句式漂亮、选词高端、逻辑性强、证据有力，几乎包含了所有的高分要素，因此，这篇作文得分为18分。

例4

Why Don't I Support the Rebuilding?

Recently, a little-known mountainous area near Guiyang, Guizhou Province, is reported to want to turn the area into a "central business district" and invite a foreign design company to give it an entirely new look. Although some people really appreciate the bold innovation of the design, I strongly object to this plan.

The first reason why I am against the changing of the local government lies in that the face project of any poor district, including the little mountainous area, in a large scale, is not sensible in such a special period of time when economy is in recession. My objection does not mean that I oppose innovation. On the contrary, innovation is something I can't praise more. New ideas are the soul of development and they are so important for those who are still lagging behind. However, changing is not the same as innovation. For a small town, the heart of an innovation lies in how many resources, natural resource and human resources, history and culture, politics and geography can be employed, which will lead to the subsequent progress of this area and lies in what good results can be brought to the local economy, which will return to the improvement of the local people, lifting the standard of their life and enriching the style of their life. If not, disasters might be on the way before the huge debt for designing and building the city is paid off.

My second reason for objecting to the scheme is based on the following questions: Is there enough ability for the local managers to repay the great amount of money? Are there enough resources that can be dug out so that the poor residents will be got out of poverty instead of falling into deeper difficulties? Some people might take Shenzhen for an example in which a small and old village turned into a world famous metropolitan. I'm afraid the comparison is not proper. Economists point out that a country's economical development depends on its time, geography and people. Shenzhen, whose geographic significance is obvious, is different from the small mountainous area. Thus, numerous funds were poured into it and a miracle city was erected in a short time. Without the opportunity of the return of Hong Kong, Beijing would not offer so many resources to it. And without the resources, there would not be Shenzhen. Any desire for quick moving forward which is not congruous with the regulation is unrealistic. Furthermore, so many lessons and experience can be obtained from the areas where gigantic buildings similar to some famous houses, such as the FuYang White House, were built and turned out to be gimmick.

Therefore, to improve the economical situation first and make good use of the local resources is more critical for small areas than to make some surface changes at high cost. The raise of the economy will win more applause from all aspects.

评析：这是唯一一篇持反对意见的作文。题目非常明确，而且很吸引人。作文逻辑框架非常清晰，中间部分只有两大原因。

作文第一部分很规范，提出问题，表明观点，而且立场非常坚定。

作者在第二部分第一段提出的第一个反对的理由是：任何一个贫穷的地区，包括这个山区，在当前经济不景气的情况下大规模搞面子工程都是不理智的。作文从经济入手，非常有高度，逻辑也非常严密，显得无懈可击，为了不让人产生误会，作者交代，"我反对面子工程不等于我反对创新。相反，创新是我再欣赏不过的东西，创新是发展的灵魂，对于那些落后者尤为重要。然而，变化不等于创新"。

接下来，作者分析了当地的资源，指出有资源则可以给当地经济带来好处，否则"必须清偿巨大债务带来的灾难就为时不远了"。其笔锋锐利，论证强劲有力，句句相扣，异常紧凑。

作者提出的第二个反对理由则基于一系列问句：当地政府有能力偿还债务吗？有足够的资源能够帮助当地居民摆脱贫困而不是陷入更深的困境吗？问题直接，有深度。

对于深圳的例子，作者进行了反驳，他以为这二者无可比性，并指出不可比的原因："深圳的地理优势，是这个小山区所不能比的，大批资金注入深圳，使它变成了一个神话般的城市。如果没有香港回归的机遇，北京就不会投入如此多的资源，如果没有这些资源，就不会有深圳"。此分析透彻，体现了作者良好的逻辑思维。

另外，作者还拿出经济学家的观点来作为证据，经济学家指出，国家经济的发展依赖天时地利人和，进一步增强了其说服力，因为经济学家是经济规律的代言人，而城市改建也是经济的一部分。

通篇多处使用了全称概念，特别是用来指出任何违反规律的大跃进式的发展都是不现实的，并引出一些事实为例，说已经有很多教训可以借鉴，那些盖类似白宫一样高楼的地方最终只是成为了别人的笑柄而已。

总之，在逻辑层面，该作文从观点到结论都提供了充分的证据，其证据强劲有力，很有说服力，因此其结论非常可靠。在语法和修辞层面，作者用心布局，精心组织，刻意修辞。因此，这篇作文的得分为18分。

10. 2014年TEM-8真题样文分析

Nowadays, some companies have work-from-home or remote working policies, which means that their employees do not have to commute to work every day. Some people think that this can save a lot of time travelling to and from work, thus raising employees' productivity. However, others argue that in the workplace, people can communicate face to face, which vastly increases the efficiency of coordination and cooperation. What is your opinion?

Write an essay of about 400 words on the following topic:

My Views on Working from Home

写作前先审题，看题目及其提供的信息要求我们做什么。题目只问我们的意见如何，并没有要求我们选择说支持或不支持。你当然可以做一个简单的支持与否的选择。但是，逻辑思维良好的人可能会发现，它不是一个简单的是否问题，比如大部分人认为在家工作主意不错，可是想在家里工作就能在家里工作吗？事实上，并非所有的工作都可以在家里做，比如秘书，他们的任务就是随时为老板提供信息或处理信息，还包括外出办公等，他们可能也想在家工作，可是，目前这可能吗？但是，有些工作确实可以在家里做，比如艺术类或设计类的工作，而且在家做的效果可能会更好。

那么，我们来看看不同视角和不同层次的作文及其论证过程。

例 1

Home Alone, Friend Away

In nowadays, with the developing of economy and the widely using of Internet, work-from-home is not a dream. Some companies even try to use the work-from-home instead of working in the company. What I want to say is that work-from-home is not a proper way in the financial society.

Firstly, the relationships among people is far away. As we all know, the Microsoft Office was born in America. So in nowadays, work-from-home is a common way in America. Each coin has two sides. While the Internet working style is convenient to people, relationships have been far away. It's obvious that one American just has a few friends in the whole life. The result is that the guilty and illness can not be easily found in a short time in USA. People feels alone and mental pressure at home. The rate of crime in America is most of the world.

Secondly, harmonious society is focusing attention on human nature, not the high degree of using machines and Internet. Many "Zhai Nan" and "Zhai Nv" are appeared in our society in nowadays. People don't need to go to the store or supermarket to buy books and clothes because they have "Tao Bao" and Amazon. They don't need to go out, the transport is so convenient to let all the things come true. Some people has worked in the company for several years, he even seldom meet all the workers face to face. Society is not a society now, society has been divided into billions of cells. The connection between cells is not friendships and love. Harmonious society disappeared.

So, in my point of view, that is not suitable for the people using the work-from-home way to instead the working in the company. Just like our President Zhu said, human nature is always important in each time. That is home alone, friendship away.

评析：作者重新拟了题目，这是允许的，但这个题目显然不清楚。读者很可能会感到疑惑，哪个地方要讨论到朋友呢？况且friend的使用显然有语法错误。文中的语法错误，我们通过画线标示出来，大家注意即可。

既然给出了题目，为了保险起见，最好不要自己另外拟题。第一部分结尾的financial society也很奇怪，为什么要画蛇添足呢？

虽然作文用with...开头，给人绕弯的感觉，这篇作文的第一段还算规范，作者先指出现象，即有些公司采用了在家工作的模式，然后提出了自己的看法。

第二部分第一句让人大致搞清楚了题目的意思，因为作者的第一点理由是人与人之间的关系会因此变得疏远。人与人之间的关系是否会因工作场所的变更而疏远我们暂且不论，有意思的是下一句居然说"众所周知，微软诞生在美国。因此，在美国，在家工作就很普遍"。逻辑关系突然断裂，让人感到一头雾水。微软人都是在家里工作吗？这个信息从何而来？

另外，在家工作方便，人与人之间的关系就会疏远吗？作者还毫无证据地得出了这样的结论："显然，一个美国人在生活中没什么朋友"，结果"犯罪和生病都无人知晓"。可是，这些结论怎么来的呢？这些都让人感到莫名其妙。

如果第二部分第一段让人觉得迷惑不解，那么，其第二段则让人彻底晕了。和谐社会要讲人性，这是当然的，可是和我们的论题有什么关系呢？"宅男""宅女"与前面和后面又有什么关系？可以说，在第二部分我们几乎很难找到两个关系密切的句子。

在第二部分，作者的主张没有得到充分论证，因此不能支撑结尾的结论。最后一句引言也有些荒诞，"正如朱总所言，'人性总是很重要'"。朱总是谁，我们不知道，他有没有说这句话，也不重要，重要的是，这句话在这里起什么作用？

总之，这篇文章除了逻辑框架还算漂亮外，整个分析部分缺乏基本逻辑，思路混乱，而且语法错误较多，因此得分只有8分。

我们强调一下，阐释文体是讲究前因后果的文体，前后句子一定要相关，不能随便把逻辑线索扯断，意思上不能出现跳跃。凡是缺乏逻辑关系的作文读起来都特别拗口，反之，逻辑关系密切的文章则读起来非常流畅。

例 2

My Views on Working from Home

Nowadays, working-from-home has been put forward by some companies and, at the same time, drawn the attention of a large number of office workers. As far as I am concerned, I believe that working-from-home, which possesses bunches of advantages, is totally feasible and promising, and will be a trend in the future.

First and foremost, it is a wonderful method for cost saving. For some multi-national corporations, whose staff may spend most of the days in a week on business trips to clients around the world, office provides its only function as the right place for the Monday routine meeting. And the two-thirds of the office just stay vacant in the rest of the week. These MNCs can simply deduct their office volume from several storeys to several single units, only to maintain basic receptional functions and back services. For those small-scaled companies, the news is a total blessing, which means that they don't have to stay at their office in the city center and afford incredibly high rental. For individuals, they not only save the fees of commuting to work every day, but also don't need to find an unpleasant living place by calculating carefully the distance between home and office.

Secondly, it coordinates the balance between life and work. One can just stay at home for work, and taking care of little kids at the same time. Family hours will never be occupied by the long office hours alone.

Last but not least, the development of technology allows the future of work from home. One can deal with business via e-mail system, hold other-national meetings with colleagues via video meeting software and communicate with supervisors via instant messages.

All in all, working from home is now plausible with various advantages, and will possess a bright future with information technology.

评析：这篇作文的第一段我们在前面也举例了，它非常简单，但很规范，很流畅，显示出作者良好的基本功。当时我们分析的是它的开篇，鉴于它开篇比较好，整体分数却较低，我们看看它第二部分的分析情况。

在第二部分一开始，作者指出，在家工作可以节省成本，跨国公司的员工大部分都在外面旅行，办公场所的功能只是周一碰头，三分之二的房间在一周剩余的时间都空闲着。第二段基本上是谈论成本问题，确切地说是谈论租金和上班的时间，条理很清楚，可是，理由算不上很有说服力，而且无高度可言，因为这些理由虽然不错，但经不起推敲。任何一家公司的员工在什么地方办公取决于公司性质，而不是为了节省空间和成本。

第二部分的第二段说员工可以一边工作一边带孩子，这让人感觉是自己开店，不像经营公司。最后一句也站不住脚，这些都是从个人角度来看的，而不是从公司经营的角度来看的，因此，缺乏高度，也过于理想化。是不是采取在家办公的方式取决于公司，而不是个人。

第二部分后面两小段的字数也少了点，因为它们明显比第一段要短。另外，最后一点理由谈的是未来，现实和未来一旦混为一谈，事情就很难说了，它会大大削弱当前的论证，既然未来都可以实现，那为什么还要费这么多口舌说现在呢？分析的重点应该是拿出当前的证据，而不是用未来的构想或者理想化的前景作为依据。

总之，这篇作文虽简单规范，但是部分理由不是很理想，而且有些语法上的不妥，由此，得到13.5分也就差不多了。

例3

My Views on Working from Home

As the technology developing very rapidly, it seems a trend that working from home is becoming increasingly popular. Some people embrace this idea while others find it unacceptable. Despite what technology has brought us, it's time that we weighed the advantages and disadvantages of working from home. And in my humble opinion, I think it would be better if people stick to the traditional way of working.

First of all, there are a number of job types that may not suit the new way of working from home. Actors and actress should go to a filming place or a theatre to perform; bar tendors cannot serve the customers in their own houses; masse users cannot invite their customers to their houses to do massage. Neither can they manage to do so through the Internet. That is to say, Internet is not always an option. Secondly, even with those jobs which have already been proved to be effective in the way of working from home, it's not necessarily appropriate or efficient. As is known by everyone who has a home, home is a place of comfort and coziness. It is a place for family and friends. People who work at home might be wearing their pajamas all day, which could cause an illusion that they are just being too comfortable and thus reduce the efficiency of work. Even if one has managed to create the exact same working environment at home as in the working place, chances are that s/he could still be easily interfered by a noisy roommate, some party animals or a nagging parent. This can lead us to the third point that a distinct line should be drawn between one's work and personal life. Some may say that working from home saves a lot of time on the way to and from work. They say it because they haven't thought it through. What should also be taken into consideration is what are missed on the way to and from work. People carry different moods when they are at home chilling out and when they are working, and the best thing about the time on the way to work is that one can switch one's mood to another so s/he can be more efficient and focused on work. Also, similar transition happens after a long exhausting day of work. Plus, one would never want to miss the hanging out with colleagues after work, or a boyfriend/girlfriend's picking up at the door of the office building. In contrast, home workers do save a lot of time, but they are also missing so much fun, just because they mix their work and personal life in the same house.

All in all, working from home seems a tempting option due to the high technology today, but something should stay just the way it was, for as human beings, dealing things face to face can never fall out of fashion.

评析：这篇作文的第一段我们在前面已经提到过到，除了画线的词有点不妥外，其他都很规范、流畅，且选词高端。

第二部分的分析显得过长，作者完全可以分成几个小段，但是其分析强劲有力，逻辑关系密切。作者指出有的职业不可能在家工作，如演员、调酒师、按摩师。其次，即便有些行业在家里工作有效，也不等于高效。接下来作者就分析"家"是什么地方。家里非常舒适，适合家人和朋友在一起，但是很难有工作效率，因为它太舒适。为此，作者认为工作和个人生活必须划清界限。对于那些认为家里工作省时的人，作者指出，他们可能没有想清楚。家里冷冷清清，在家里可能会有不同的情绪，等等。再加上公司上班的种种好处，作者所提供的证据可以比较好地支持自己的主张，因此结尾是站得住脚的。

总之，这篇作文写得条理清晰，通篇流畅，不失为一篇好作文。但它的高度不够，没有提及公司的问题，只是重点分析了家里的情况。其次，这篇作文的句式和修辞还不是很好。最后，从画线部分看出，作者笔误或不妥之处有很多，因此，这篇作文仅得15.5分。

例4

My Views on Working from Home

Working from home is a desirable working style for many people due to the saving of time in commuting and the convenience and ease to stay alone. Some companies have truly taken this policy and some people say that it can raise employees' productivity.

However, for me, it is not a matter whether we hope or not.

It is understandable that everyone hopes to have an ease atmosphere for working just like working at home where we don't need to do everything in a hurry. We can take our time in washing, eating breakfast and preparing so that a good mood for job seems ready. Everything will be nice for an individual who likes to do his job without disturbance and clamor. And everything will be nice without being interrupted by someone in the middle of his thinking and creating. Unfortunately, that is not a nice thing for most of the companies whose managers need to disturb his employees at whatever time when they have to. And so they do. Calling, meeting, discussing, reporting and instructing employees are the routine of most companies, big or small. Working from home of course hinders the regularity of the system, which benefits the managers or the whole enterprise more than the employees.

On the other hand, to work at home cannot be necessarily productive because not all of us can be self-controlled without being supervised. Just like a good saying, "Restraint does not mean low efficiency. Unconstraint does not mean productivity." What really matters is how we make a more coordinated connection in the whole system.

However, there are some exceptions. When the job of someone focuses on designing, writing or other artistic creation, he has a thousand reasons to work alone without being troubled by anyone who might disturb him or even destroy his inspiration. And there are some other exceptions, too, like marketing on the net where the staff may not be limited by the working office. As for most of the people whose main purpose is to play one part of the whole, working in the office is their sole choice.

Therefore, from the analysis above, working in companies or from home is not a matter of desire or not. It relies on what job we do and who we serve for. Our choice is not ours to make but the selection we have to follow as one part of a company.

评析：题目是拟好的，因此不存在任何问题。这篇作文和其他几篇作文不同，作者谈论的不是在家工作好不好的问题，而是提出这不是自己想要与否的问题。这最值得关注，说明作者有非常好的思维能力，可以看到别人看不到的问题，因此，从写作意义来看，它非常出色。

在第一段，作者说"有的公司已经采用了这一策略，而且有些人说这可以提高生产力"。这是为第二部分作铺垫，因为在第二部分，作者就围绕这两点展开。这是作者的精心布局，值得大家借鉴。

在第二部分的第一段，作者采用全称，指出人人都喜爱轻松舒适的办公环境，这样就无须赶时间。为了强调，作者使用了两个排比。

接下来，作者却话锋一转，说对于管理者随时可能要召唤员工的企业，这可不是件好事。呼叫、商议、讨论、汇报，抑或指导员工等是任何企业的日常公务，在家工作会阻碍这种模式。而这种模式对管理层或整个企业有利，而非对个人有利。我们前面提到，逻辑思维好的人，很会使用全称，因为它非常有说服力。反之亦然，善用全称概念者，逻辑思维一定很好。

在第二部分的第二段，作者开始质疑在家工作的效率，他说在家工作未必一定有效率，因为并非每个人都可以约束自己。为此，作者引用了一句名言，"约束未必低效，自由未必高产"。这就大大增加了文章的可信度。

在第二部分的第三小段，作者谈到一些例外，说这些职业更适合在家工作，也就是说，在什么样的场所工作，决定性因素是职业本身，不是个人的主观愿望。

在结尾，作者简单重申了自己的观点作为总结。由此可见，作者对写作的高分要素十分清楚。

总之，文章不仅结构规范，句式优美，刻意修辞，最关键的是文章提供的证据非常有说服力，行文流畅，逻辑性强，因此，文章得分为18分。

例5

My Views on Working from Home

Small Office Home Office (SOHO) has always been a tempting and avant-garde concept of working style in modern enterprises. Advocates for SOHO champion that the flexible working style will vastly enhance both the quality and efficiency of completing tasks and benefit the society as a whole, which I strongly agree with for the following reasons.

First of all, it is widely accepted that working environment plays a major role in people's performance. No place offers a more soothing and comfortable atmosphere than the home itself. Just imagine you can lie cozily in the sofa with a laptop on your legs and listen to your favorite tune coming from the stereo. There is no worry about punctuality and grid looks. You can no longer be under supervision and susceptible to the disturbances of your colleagues. All the devices and conveniences at home help you focus and concentrate on the task you are dedicated to. According to an experiment conducted by *Nature Magazine*, brains function most efficiently when they are in relaxed state and free of interferences.

Also, a light-hearted mood is likely to tap the potentials and inspirations especially for those designers or architects whose jobs rely on creativity.

In addition, remote working policies are human-oriented for working mothers. In the past, women's careers are more or less jeopardized when they are about to give birth to children. They are usually exhausted as they have both work and family to care for. Some women give up their work in order to fully devote their energies to their children, which gives rise to a great loss in labor and brain drain for society. Others sacrifice care of them in order to become a workaholic, which results in the loose emotional connection between mother and child and may increase the chance of juvenile crimes as some children are not receiving the due amount of love from their parents. However, with the introduction of work-from-home policies, working mothers are becoming capable of taking head of both their work and family without neglecting either of them.

Last but not least, remote working policies can considerably reduce the emission of greenhouse gases and solve the problem of the traffic congestion since employees don't need to commute from workplaces to houses. This is instrumental for both environment and society.

As far as I am concerned, SOHO working style is a valuable invention for both companies and societies. With the advancement of information technology and Internet, people can communicate and interact with each other from homes as smoothly as they do at offices. Increasingly, SOHO is emerging as an inevitable trend and companies and employees will work out new ways of cooperation and coordination in the future.

评析：这篇文章结构规范、开篇直接、条理清楚、逻辑性强，而且选词造句非常高端，比如no more than这个句型的运用，具体见第二段画线部分。还有相同词义不同表达，比如"在家办公"就替换了几个词，如working at home，SOHO，remote working policies等。

在第二部分，为了增强论证的可信度，作者还引用了一项实验结果，这使得论据十分强劲有力。再者，其句式比较漂亮，修辞巧妙，加上成对词的使用，体现了作者比较强的写作意识和写作能力。

总之，该作文结构规范合理，用词高端，修辞娴熟，条理清楚，证据强劲有力，因此，该作文得分为18分。

11. 2015年TEM-8真题样文分析

There has been a new trend in economic activity—the sharing economy. The biggest sector of the sharing economy is travel. You find a potential host through the website. If you both get along and they are available during your planned trip, you stand a chance of getting a place for free. In addition, people also use website or apps to rent out their cars, houses, tools, clothes and services to others. *Time* magazine has included this trend in a list titled "ten ideas that will change the world." It said, in an era when families are scattered and we may not know the people down the street, sharing things— even with strangers we've just met online—allow us to make meaningful connections. What do you think of *Time*'s comment?

我们在讨论背景法的时候，对这个题目的主要概念进行了分析。在此，我们作一点补充。根据互联网发展的势头以及人们生活方式的改变，共享经济确实会成为一种趋势，比如很多网友在网上发布各种分享信息，包括寻找"驴友"的信息，响应者总是很多。

但是，题目要讨论的是《时代周刊》的观点，并不是讨论共享经济产生的原因和发展趋势。《时代周刊》列出了十大改变世界的经济行为，还说分享经济使得我们建立起更有意义的联系。是否会产生有意义的联系是我们需要论证的。

如果选择同意，我们可以说一些类似经济划算、可以结识更多朋友等理由。这个角度让人感觉还算好写，因为生活里面已经有一些真实的例子，但是要从这个角度写出深度则未必可行，因为毕竟这一现象刚出现不久，情况不是很普遍，而不具备普遍现象的例子说服力就不够。因此，选择这个角度很可能会比较空泛，缺乏深度。

那么，不认同的情况可能会是怎样的呢？会更好写吗？能否写得更有深度呢？一方面，网络虽然给我们结识他人提供了方便，但人与人之间的关系并不会因此而变得更加密切，从陌陌等约会软件可以看出，弊端远大于益处。至少，要以这种方式来结成比较牢固的关系还存在很多问题。另一方面，会选择拼车或拼房等行为的人，大部分都是出于经济目的，其中大部分都是经济条件不是很好的人，那么，在这个浮躁的时代，结识与自己经济状况相当的人意义有多大很难说。

批改试卷的老师看重的是考生的证据或论证过程，大家的观点是什么不重要。下面我们一起来分析考生的作文。

例1

My View <u>On</u> the Sharing Economy

There has been a new trend in economic activity—the sharing economy. I tend to think that is very good for people. And we get lots of convenient. It is meaningful for everyone.

Nowadays people <u>have better life</u> and have higher pursue, such as <u>travel, get</u> a chance to travel is an exciting experience. We will change the world. And open our eyes to enjoy the world. It is sharing economy. It is fantastic. People also use websites and apps to rent out our cars, houses, tools and services to one another. It is very convenient. The sharing economy <u>give</u> our life more fantasy and we can enjoy the life more convenient. Economy is open, and our idea is open. So we tend to change the world with our brain and the chance. Sharing things is a really exciting behavior. <u>Sometime</u> we buy clothes, plan a trip, <u>have</u> a dinner. We could use the Internet to get a convenient ticket. It <u>save</u> time for us and <u>save</u> money for us. Sharing economy is the development of the world. We should use it correctly and make our life colorful. No one could refuse the sharing economy. <u>Especially our young people</u>, we are the trend of the world. We have chance and wealth to change the world and change our own life.

The sharing economy is necessary <u>in nowadays</u>, and it could give us more convenient. Each person should use it by the right way and get the better life. Don't refuse any chance to change our life or make our life better. The sharing economy is a development of the social. The websites give us more convenient. We could get more information through Internet and use the sharing economy better. Of course, it allows us to make meaningful connections, it is really a good chance for us.

评析：这篇作文大约只有300词，这远远达不到TEM-8写作的要求，而且它采用的还是三段式写法，最后一段的字数却又特别多。可见作者没有高级写作的意识，还一味地沉浸在初级写作的模式里。

第一段太简单了，这也许是整体字数不足的一个原因。说它过于简单不仅仅是因为字数的问题，主要是它没有提及情景。

第二部分第一小段的第一句也体现出作者没有很强的写作意识，nowadays一般用来开篇，不用在分析部分。such as后面的举例也不太好，难道travel算是高追求吗？这就反映出作者随想随写，简单地把汉语翻译成了英语。另外，还有很多语法方面的错误。

我们会发现，文章的句子几乎都是初级句子，没有句式的变化，而且内容非常空洞。

另外，我们似乎根本搞不清楚作者的意图。什么是"我们要改变世界"？什么又是"张开双眼欣赏世界"？作者这不是在论证，而是在做介绍，好像是用简短的话语来煽情，连逻辑都可以不用。

一个与上面无太大关系的结果很快就出来了，其中两点是没有经过论证就得出来的结论，而且，短短300词出现的语法错误太多。

总之，该作文不规范，字数也达不到要求，使用的基本上是简单句，而且语法错误过多。此外，证据空洞，逻辑关系松散，因此，评分为8分。

在字数上我们强调一下，大型作文字数要求都比较多，这样才能看出写作者的思维水平。TEM-8作文一般要求在400词以上，如果只写了350多词，可能也马马虎虎过得去，但是如果只有300来词，甚至300词以下，问题就很大了。

确实，字数是不少人的心结，但是，为什么我们不单独用一个小节来讨论字数问题呢？因为没有必要。如果我们能够把相关的要素都罗列清楚，注意后一句和前一句之间的关联，在必要的地方使用总分结构，就不再会有字数方面的担忧；相反，可写的内容会很多，只要翻译的时候注意语法和连接词即可。

例 2

My View on the Sharing Economy

There has been a new trend in economic activity—the sharing economy. People can use websites and apps to share their cars, houses, even a place to stay with others. I think it is a good idea for all the people.

There are some opinions I have been thought. Firstly, it's important to be honest and believable. All the sharing is based on honesty. If people believe on you, all the sharing is to be easy. You can find a potential host through a website. If you both get along during your planned trip, you stand a chance of getting a place to stay for free. But it's not safe sometimes. Secondly, though sharing with your things, you can save money and area. You can share with people who need it. People use websites and apps to rent out our cars, houses, books, tools, clothes and services to one another. It's very convenient. Thirdly, it can increase the contact between people and strangers. You can make many friends and cause a friend group. You can also build a good social relationship. *Time Magazine* has included this trend in a list titled "10 ideas that will change the world." It said, "In an era when families are scattered and we may not know the people down the street—sharing thing even with strangers we have just met online—allows us to make meaningful connections."

I think it's a good idea in economic activity. You can help others and get helped from others.

评析：这篇作文字数不足，也是三段，整体框架不美观。

第一段虽然没有提及《时代周刊》的观点，但还算规范，而且非常简单，语法基础不是很好的学生可以借鉴，因为这样不容易出错。问题在于作者使用的单词基本上是初级单词，句子基本上是简单句，这是不妥的。

从第二部分我们就可以发现，文章恰似一篇初级写作，毫无高度可言，也完全没有句式和句型的变化，读者也不知道主题是什么。首先，作者说，"我们要诚实，要可信，因为分享建立在信任之上，如果人们相信你，分享就很简单，你可以通过网站找到一个这样的人，两人相处融洽的话，可以免费，但有时这样很不安全"。

第二点理由越发让人搞不清楚其目的是什么。作者说，"第二，尽管与你分享东西你可以省钱省地方。你可以和需要的人分享。人们通过网站把车、房、书、工具、衣物、服务租出去，非常方便"。它们之间的关系是什么？作用又是什么？显然我们搞不清楚。这些内容给人的感觉是，当作者把已知的一些句型使用完毕后，就再没什么可写的了。

第三点说它可以增加和陌生人之间的联系，可以结识很多朋友，可以建一个朋友圈，也可以建一种社交圈。两个you can非但没有让我们觉得是在使用修辞，反而越发让人觉得作者词穷句尽。在这一段剩余部分，作者把本不该在这里出现的《时代周刊》的观点复制过来后就结尾了。

作文的结尾也很奇怪，第一句的意思不完整，第二句把分享经济说成了助人。无论论证是否强劲有力，论题是不能够改动的。

总之，这篇作文字数不足，证据薄弱，没有说服力，结论和原论题有出入，并且多处用词不当，所以它仅得8分。

例3

My View <u>On</u> the Sharing Economy

The exotic bizarre notion "sharing economy" <u>might seem</u> to us, this unique, chic movement greatly benefit from the nourishment of skyrocketing coverage of the Internet and online social communities such as Facebook or Wechat, and now it's merely an understandment to say it is prevailing. I find myself appeal to such a fashionable breakthrough, mainly for two reasons. Firstly, "sharing economy" optimizes the usage of various resources in our society; secondly, it lubricates different people, mostly strangers, to get to know to one another.

There is no denying that "sharing economy" helps to achieve the zenith of how to use resources efficiently. Just take a look at what happens in the heated US TV series "Two Broke Girls". In one episode, two handsome, wealthy guys were planning a vocation but worried that there would be no one around to feed and walk their dog. Eventually, our two shabby heroines, Max and Caroline, agreed cheerfully to assume the mission as "pet nanny" in exchange for spending several days at young men's deluxe apartments, equipped with portable Saunas and all. In this way, both parties solved their problems and everyone is a winner. This is true that we also have institutions like hotels, pet houses and second-handed stores that serves as alternatives to sharing economy. But, I think I am not the only one who yearns for the hospitality and convenience of a house instead of hotel windows that aren't supposed to be opened for "the concern of a guest's safety".

Also when people are sharing, exchanging or renting out idle tools, there must be a lot of interaction and socializing who would say that you will not accidentally pick up a lifetime friend or even your other half when you are auctioning your fine-decor, Victorian beach house, or your scarcely-used yellow Buick car, or even a collection of Stephen King's thriller. The potential renter or purchaser must share some interest with you and after this transaction <u>or least</u> is finished, <u>you two</u> may find each other so interesting and want to know more about one another

In a nutshell, sharing economy <u>not only means</u> that everyone can gain access to what they need with a reasonable reciprocation it also leads to a new friend, a new relationship, or even life-changing encounters, I fullheartedly pray for its longevity and prosperity.

评析：这篇作文逻辑框架比较美观。不过，第一段没有直接把情景说出来，而是绕了个弯，这就让我们看不明白了，我们强调第一段要直接的原因就在这里。语法基础不是很好的学生更要注意这一点，不要绕弯，不要进行所谓的创新，而要尽可能规范，这样不容易出错。

在第二部分的第一小段，作者用一整段介绍了一个电视剧的情节，以此作为有效利用资源的证据，这显然不妥，因为阐释文体的作文是不允许过多叙述的。

在第二小段，作者使用了must，might，may这样一些表示假设的单词，说我们"可能会遇上自己的终身朋友或另一半，可能会发展成永久的友谊，可能会希望了解更多"。这么多"可能"怎么能够得出可信的结论呢？要使得证据具有可信度，就应该拿出事实依据，使用确定性的词语。

总之，该作文论据单薄，结论是不可靠的，加上画线部分的语法错误，因此，它的得分为10分。

例4

My View on the Sharing Economy

In the age of Internet, the global economy has been redefined by new <u>phenomenons</u> developed by new generations. The sharing economy, as part of the Internet family, has the potential to shape connections between people into a new level. *Time*'s comment on the sharing economy about its meaningfulness, while truthful to its positive influence, is ignorant of its security issues and its impact on people's privacy. In my humble opinion, the positive position of the sharing economy can be threatened by the following aspects.

The first issue that <u>need</u> to be concerned with is people's safety. Although activities provided by the sharing economy offer people opportunities to travel freely with new contacts of people, meeting strangers is always a huge safety concern. There are reports that people using app to find companions getting robbed, deceived, and even <u>more worse</u>, sexually offended. While we are away from our family members, how we deal with strangers online is a problem that cannot be ignored.

Secondly, platforms we use to establish connection with people may leak personal information which would cause trouble to our daily life. Though there are several platforms which are officially authorized, people still may get into unofficial platforms which mean threat to your personal information. Unauthorized platforms may give away your online profile information for a fortune causing you great trouble in your privacy. Policies and actions should be carried out against those illegal firms in order <u>for</u> the sharing economy to grow healthily.

Last but not the least, while widening your relationships with different kinds of people, sharing economy may prove negative in keeping true friends. We are not yet so "scattered" as pointed out by the *Time*'s comment. In the best hope, we should expect the sharing economy would bring families and friends closer, instead of getting people obsessed with the trending phenomenon.

As a conclusion, sharing economy is an interesting trend that may truly change the world if related authorities put more effort into its safety and privacy issues.

评析：这篇作文整体框架比较美观，第二部分放在前面的字数要多一些，后面的略微少一些，显得很协调，这一点不错。

从第一段我们可以看出作文很规范，句式也很优美。作者在给出现象之后，就表明观点，指出《时代周刊》忽略了安全和隐私问题，这是有一定高度的。

遗憾的是，第二部分开头就是语法错误（见画线部分），这是比较糟糕的事，如果第一段中的phenomena写成phenomenons还情有可原（很多人不知道这个词的复数），但是谓语动词单数第三人称漏加s就是很低级的语法错误了。第二句话也不明确，而第三句there be句型使用不当。如果一整段都错误连连，就很难让人搞清楚作者要表达什么意思。

在第三段和第四段，作者大谈安全问题，这有些偏题，因为它和分享经济没有多大关系，仿佛作者讨论的是网络安全问题，而非分享经济问题。

第四段句式很美，但内容比较空洞。空洞的原因是在缺乏足够证据的情况下直接得出来一个结论。

总之，这篇作文框架和句式都比较美，只是论据不够充分，还有些基本的语法错误，因此，这篇作文得分为12分。

例5

My View on the Sharing Economy

There has been a new trend in economic activity—the sharing economy. *Time Magazine* has included this trend in a list titled "10 ideas that will change the world." It said, "In an era when families are scattered and we may not know the people down the street—sharing thing even with strangers we have just met online—allows us to make meaningful connections." However, some people don't think so. In my view, every coin has two sides. I think the sharing economy has more advantages than disadvantages.

Firstly, the sharing economy will help us save money, especially when we travel. People can use websites and apps to rent out our cars, houses, tools and services to one another. Generally speaking, those things will not cost so much like others. So travelers will save more money to do other things. Secondly, the sharing economy will allow us make connections. In this era, computers, tablets and smart-phones have taken the place in our life. We have spent too much time in getting along with them. The sharing economy lets others come to our life and add vigor and vitality for us. The gap among people will be narrower. Last but not the least, the sharing economy will give us more opportunities to make more friends with others. Computers and smart-phones make us to be isolated from the world, however, the sharing economy helps us open a new door and make friends with others from different regions and even different countries by sharing things.

In our country, harmony is most valuated. The sharing economy fully expresses the meaning of harmony and helping with each other. Confucius, a sage in our country, once said, "What a pleasant thing that a friend comes here from far!" The sharing economy is welcoming friends from far. As I said above, the sharing economy has more advantages than disadvantages. As far as I am concerned, I agree with *Time*'s comment. The sharing economy will be one of 10 ideas that will change the world. Sharing things with one another will be more and more popular.

Because the biggest sector of the sharing economy is travel. There will be more and more travelers choose this way.

评析：题目是统一的，没有什么问题。但整篇文章只有三段似乎有点别扭，尤其是结尾，篇幅显然过长。其中前几行应该属于第二部分。另外，最后一段的As far as I am concerned 这几句去掉会比较好，因为观点通常是在第一段表达出来的，在结尾不一定要重申了。况且这部分已经很长了。

第一段很规范，作者提出问题后就表明了自己的观点，不过引用略多，如果能浓缩一些会更好。

第二部分，作者其实可以把Secondly移到下一段，把Last but not the least再另起一段，这样第二部分就变成三个小段，视觉上会感觉更协调，整篇文章的结构就比较理想了。

第二部分的理由一是可以省钱，二是可以建立关系，其实稍微有点偏，因为题目要求重点讨论《时代周刊》的观点。

最后一段太长了，因为作者把第二部分的内容留到结尾来写了，不仅如此，他还又提出了一个"和谐"的概念，这就不妥了，因为规范的结尾只需要简要概括第二部分的内容，不需要提出新内容。至于引用孔子的"有朋自远方来，不亦乐乎"，虽然是高分要素之一，但是在这里用得不是很贴切，如果能放到第二部分，会好得多。

总之，这篇作文虽然说理一般，但是条理还是比较清楚，逻辑关系也比较密切，行文读起来比较流畅。之所以说它说理方面较为一般，是因为作者只是罗列信息，谈不上很有说服力，而且还有几个比较基础的语法错误。因此，这篇作文得分为13分。

例6

My View on the Sharing Economy

The 21st century has witnessed an exponential advancement in technology and an unstable yet on the whole blooming economy, which have brought about higher life quality around the globe. However, there has also been a worrying decline in the amount and quality of interpersonal relations. As it promotes mutual trust, the spirit of sharing and provides greater opportunities for online relations to become offline friends, the newly introduced sharing economy might become one answer to the problem of human relations and indeed prove to be world-changing, as *Time* magazine predicted.

To begin with, the sharing economy is predicted upon the element of mutual trust, a catalyst of friendship. For instance, a backpacker and a stranger, the latter of whom is willing to provide food and lodging on the other side of the world. There is no certified agency or deposit to bind each party. The whole business is conducted online and requires one person to trust a complete stranger. When two people fulfill their promises, it is very likely that the tenant-landlord relation becomes something more like a friendly relationship, because they both have gone through the process of putting trust into each other.

Moreover, when the sharing economy helps to redistribute resources, it also promotes its core spirit: sharing. The person on the receiving end of help and benefit will pass on the generosity and give a helping hand to others when the occasion comes. Thus, active participants in the sharing economy will also share in their personal lives and thereby make closer connections.

Lastly, the sharing economy can help online relations to evolve into offline friendships, because the participants usually share the same interest or life passion. For example, I once lent a few books to a student on the university's online book-exchanging platform. When she returned the books to me, we began a conversation and found out that we have a lot in common. We have become friends ever since and still go out for an afternoon tea to discuss what new books we have read. This friendship is an amazing gift of the sharing economy.

The sharing economy is of course not a fail-safe. It is even possible that people get cheated or hurt. But on the whole, this fresh trend of sharing is one step towards a more trusting, generous and interconnected society.

评析：该篇作文字数足够，整体框架比较美观，内容也比较丰富，只是第一段略显冗长。

此文一开篇就显现出它与前面几篇范例的巨大差异，它非常书面化，用词高端，句式美观。现象和观点在第一段都表现出来了，而且表达观点的方式与他人不同，这是阅卷老师愿意看到的内容。

在第二部分作者谈到分享的前提——互信，并在第二小段分析分享的核心在于"分"字，还指出分享可以从线上扩展到线下。每一点作者都给出了具体内容，这样观点就得到了支撑。美中不足的是作者在这里插入了过长的叙述。

总之，整篇文章读来比较流畅，内容也还算紧凑。因此，这篇作文得分为15分。

例7

My View <u>On</u> the Sharing Economy

Nowadays, a new trend in economic activity called the sharing economy is becoming increasingly prevalent at an amazing rate, which has even been included by *Time Magazine* in a list titled "10 ideas that will change the world." Sharing economy as a new kind of our economic activity plays an important role in providing strong impetus to the development of our economy as well as in changing people's life. Therefore, in my opinion, I ballot for *Time*'s comment and the reasons are twofold.

To begin with, sharing economy plays an important role in changing people's mind as well as their way of life. We know that the biggest sector of the sharing economy is travel, which is a sensible choice for people to go out and enjoy the fantastic nature. If you both get along and they are available during your planned trip, you stand a chance of traveling for free. What a wonderful chance! Fronted with mountainous pressure from work and study, we've already been cooped up and hand-cuffed. So just take this chance to relax yourself and to broaden your horizon. What's more, as a network-based economic activity, the sharing economy link people and even the world together, which create a good way for people to experience, to make friends, to interact and even to know the world. Just as *Time*'s comment showed us, it allows us to make meaningful connections. Therefore, the sharing economy does change people a lot.

Any more, from the perspective of our society, this kind of economy is beneficial to establish the eco-friendly society and can also promote the advancement of our society. Under this circumstances, people use websites and apps to rent out their cars, houses and so on, which is not only a eco-friendly way but also a economic way. It set a good example for others to change their ways of life to be thrifty, eco-friendly and economical. Besides, as a new way of economy, it also <u>promote</u> the development of network, including technology innovation and providing more useful information. As is related to travel, it is also a good way to stimulate the consumption of travel and then propel and development of local economy.

All in all, taking all those factors above mentioned into consideration, we can safely come to the conclusion that the sharing economy is not only a good and sensible choice to change individual's mind and ways of life, it also <u>provide</u> a strong impetus to the advancement of our society. So, <u>let</u> warmly accept this new trend and be prepared to change our own ways of life.

评析：这也是一篇整齐美观的作文，而且它的第二部分第一段的字数比它的第二小段的字数略微多一些。

在第一段中，作者使用的句式很优美，选词很高端，比如increasingly，prevalent，impetus，ballot和twofold。此外，作者在表达上体现了他的新意，比如at an amazing rate和as well as。第一段只有therefore这个单词使用得不好，事实上，这里根本不需要这个词。

在第二部分，作者先指出分享经济改变了人们的思想和生活方式，并举旅行为例；接着指出分享经济把人和世界联系起来了；最后重复了《时代周刊》的观点。

虽然文字很美，但让人感觉说服力不够，其中一个原因就是用《时代周刊》的观点来充当理由，而《时代周刊》的观点是要我们拿出证据来证明的东西，如果我们用它来充当论据，就犯了"循环论证"的逻辑错误，也就起不到证明的作用。

在第二部分的第二小段，作者从社会的角度进行分析，指出分享经济可以建立生态型社会，并且促进社会的发展；还指出它可以作为一个标杆，影响他人的生活方式，并且反过来促进网络科技的发展。这就有点扯远了，作者似乎忘记了题目是要我们证明《时代周刊》的观点，也就是分享经济会使得我们的联系更加有意义。

不过，这两段使用了不少精彩的单词，高级但并不晦涩难懂，它可以说是我见过的使用高级词汇最多的一篇作文，比如cooped up and hand-cuffed，broaden your horizon，stimulate，propel，thrifty，impetus等。这一点真的值得我们很多人学习。

总之，虽然这篇作文说服力不够，并且单数第三人称动词几乎都没有添加s，这一点肯定是要扣分的，但是，作文从头到尾读来都很流畅，选词高端大气，所以得分为15分。

例8

My View on the Sharing Economy

Sharing economy, a new trend in today's Internet world, has caused great attention. *Time Magazine* has included it in a list titled "10 ideas that will change the world." And it said sharing things allows us to make meaningful connections. I admit that it is a good style for us. But as for a good relationship in an unstable world, I have to say that it is not certain. The uncertainty comes from two aspects.

The first one is that, in this changeable era, people's purpose of sharing things is not certain. For some people, they make sharing with others for the purpose of making money or saving money. But for some others, their deep motive is to make friends, especially opposite sex, more than to make money. However, in a place where data can be completely unknown or untrue, can the possibility to meet a desirable friend be big? In my opinion, it is unrealistic to encounter our dreaming lovers through sharing things more than to find Korean film's love in real life. As psychological analysts pointed out, unknown information is the condition of cheating. In fact, good news from sharing with strangers is bleak. On the contrary, bad news that girls were cheated, raped, or even killed during their sharing is often heard. This kind of reports can be read almost every day.

The second one is that the result of the connection is not sure. During the time when most of the people are busy with their living, I believe that the connection among the sharing parties will be and must be the economical profits. Other relations like making friends or becoming lovers have not been decided yet at all. The main reliability can be found in two questions. The chief one is what friends we want to make. Friends who are better than us in knowledge, ability, finance so that we can learn something from them? Or friends who can give us some help so that we can achieve our success? The second question is how many people of this kind will join in the sharing activity. It is no doubt that most of the people who like sharing the holdings with others are not rich enough and not busy enough with a career. Then, what we can get is what we can imagine. It doesn't mean that sharing is not a way through which one can occasionally meet someone he likes. What it really means is that we cannot count on the relations linked by profit beyond our expectation.

All in all, sharing economy is a good thing for those who want to save money. But for making friends or making some meaning relationship with strangers, we can't be so optimistic. So, Time's idea that connections will be meaningful is not supported.

评析：一眼看去，这篇作文整齐美观。其实，它的第一段很简单，不过是把《时代周刊》的观点拿出来，然后再表达自己的立场。但是，作者有两点不同：一是使用了插入语，句式因此就变得更灵活；二是作者的立场与众不同，他指出，"我承认分享经济是一种不错的形式，但讲到'可以产生有意义的联系'，我不得不说这还未确定"。最后一句作者交代不确定性来自两方面。线条简洁清晰，分类数量少，这通常有两种可能的情况：一是作者逻辑思维良好，他知道顶端的分类不能多，通常不超过三个；二是作者逻辑思维不好，想不到更多的内容。鉴于作者在第一段表现出了非常好的写作能力，我们因此可以推断他属于第一种情况。

在第一段最后一句交代不确定性有两大方面显然是作者的精心布局。在第二部分，作者只要围绕这两方面展开即可，这种布局就使得写作相对简单了。

第一个不确定性是分享的目的不确定。有些人是为了赚钱或省钱；有些人则不是，他们的动机是交友，尤其是异性朋友。而在一个信息不透明或完全虚假的地方，交到理想朋友的可能性大吗？接下来，作者提出自己的看法，说"我以为，通过分享来找到知己就像韩剧中的爱在生活中不现实一样"。此比方虽然有些通俗，但还是恰当的。文章逻辑关系非常密切，句子读起来很流畅。

分析过程中，作者间接引用了心理分析家的话来充当证据，心理分析家指出不确定性是欺诈的条件。作者继而给出了报道中的事实作为具体证据，他指出分享经济中的好消息很少；相反，欺骗、强奸，甚至谋杀事件非常频繁，几乎每天都在发生。这一段逻辑性和说服力都很强，因为作者的证据是事实，不是自己的猜测，更不是假设。

第二个不确定性是关于关系的结果的不确定。作者指出，在一个大家都忙于生计的时代，分享关系必须是利益关系，交友关系不能确定。他巧妙地设计了两个问题，其中最重要的问题是"我们想交什么朋友？有文化、有能力、经济条件好、可以向他们学习的朋友？还是能够给予我们帮助，促使我们成功的朋友？"到底有多少这种人会参加分享经济活动呢？

文章是很有深度的，从作者提供的细节就可以看出，他对上述问题的回答不仅说明他有丰富的背景知识，他还把相关问题思考得非常清楚，而且主次分明。作者这样说道，"毫无疑问，大部分会参加分享经济的人，要么经济条件不是很好，要么没有自己的事业可忙，可以从中得到什么是可想而知的"。

更巧妙的是，为了防止他人钻空子，作者在这里解释了一下，他说"不是说分享经济不能偶尔遇见相知，而是不能过度指望一种依赖利益的关系"。

最后，作者简要概括了上面的观点，就此打上了句号。

整篇作文读来一气呵成，异常流畅。修辞非常刻意，如果第二部分的第一段字数多一点会更好。

总之，这篇作文几乎包含了所有的高分要素，并且运用得十分娴熟，因此，这篇作文得分为18分。

小结：以上我们分析了1993年至2015年之间的一些TEM-8样文。作文水平有高有低。无论何者，我们都根据从题目到结构到思维的方法来分析。

好作文不仅结构规范，字数足够，表达也有新意。此外，它们逻辑关系密切，通过论证顺理成章地得出结论。它们的证据都比较强劲有力，可以有说服力地支持自己的观点。为了提高证据的可信度，作者通常都会引用调查报告或名人名言。它们结构优美、选词高端、句式漂亮，而且基本没有语法错误。有的布局比较巧妙、线条简洁、逻辑分明、修辞刻意，甚至很有意义。

稍差一点的作文，结构还可以，但是可能不够优美，主要是语法错误比较多，论据不充分，甚至犯有逻辑错误，结论经常得不到证据的支持。作者缺乏高级写作的意识，选词和用词都比较一般，也不会刻意营造句式美。

极差的作文，基本上使用简单句，字数不足，开篇过于简单，脱离情景，仿佛是在凑字数，而不是在写作。前后句子通常不相关，也没有逻辑可言，更不像是在论证。

我们重新强调一下，写作有自己的规范，不能随想随写，必须要按照规定来设立框架。下笔之前先构思，然后利用语言修辞来组织思想和文字，行文过程必须符合逻辑，不相关的内容不要扯进来。此外，论据要能够支持自己的观点，具有一定的客观性，不能只是主观意愿。

参考文献

蔡基刚. 2001. 英汉汉语段落翻译与实践[M]. 上海：复旦大学出版社.

谷振诣. 2007. 批判性思维教程[M]. 北京：北京大学出版社.

居祖纯. 2009. 高级汉英语篇翻译[M]. 北京：清华大学出版社.

刘莉华. 2008. 2008 TEM-8写作标准范文背诵[M]. 青岛：中国海洋大学出版社.

王向清. 2006. 逻辑趣话[M]. 长沙：湖南大学出版社.

吴中东. 2010. 专八真题样文[M]. 上海：华东理工大学出版社.

张汉熙. 1993. 高级英语[M]. 北京：外语教学与研究出版社.

张明冈. 1985. 比喻常识[M]. 北京：北京出版社.

张培基. 1983. 英汉翻译教程[M]. 上海：上海外语教育出版社.

张培基. 2006. 英译中国现代散文选[M]. 上海：上海外语教育出版社.

张鑫友. 2002. 高级英语学习指南[M]. 武汉：湖北人民出版社.